AOLAB

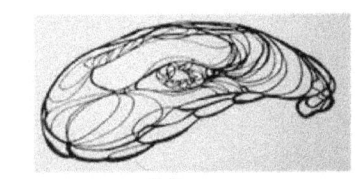

angel brynner.

Agenda.

Seasonal edition

KokoPelliMa Press

OTHER KOKOPELLIMA PRESS BOOKS BY ANGEL BRYNNER

Eutaxis   Ecclesia   Exodus

Erebus   Exist   Esthesis   Epicharis

Elision   Elysum   Empyrean

AOLAB Active Art (therapy) decks BY ANGEL BRYNNER

ZION   HALCYON   DELUGE   BLOOD OF MY BLOOD

FLESH OF MY FLESH   BONE OF MY BONE

BLACKWATER OVERFLOW   EDEN   ZENITH

AOLAB Travelogues BY ANGEL BRYNNER

BOTTOM OF THE NINTH WARD BULLETINS   BLACKWATER RISING

Anthologies BY ANGEL BRYNNER

FIRESTARTER   FIREWALKER

AOLAB Active Art Revisionist books BY ANGEL BRYNNER

(The road to) ZION grievechonic

(The road to) HALCYON grievechronic

(The road to) DELUGE grievechronic

(The road to) BLOOD grievechronic

Globalboho

AOLAB

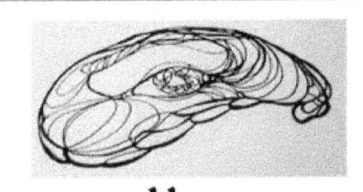
angel brynner.

Agenda.

Seasonal edition

KOKOPELLIMA PRESS

Copyright 2022 by Angel Brynner

All Rights Reserved

Printed in the United States

Kokopellima Press. www.kokopellimapress.com

Catologing-in-Publication Data

Brynner, Angel

Globalboho AOLAB Agenda. Seasonal edition.

Hardcover ISBN: 978-1-950077-85- 4 -

This is a work of non-fiction. No part of This publication may be reproduced or transmitted in any form or by an means, electronic or mechanical, including photocopying, recording, NFT or any other information storage and retrieval system, without written permission of the Publisher.

Cover artwork and book design:

AOLAB/AngelBrynner.

Website: http://www.angelbrynner.com

"Like no planner experience you've ever had. Enjoy the wild ride."
-AB

Let's get into IT.

"...It's good to have a personal agenda."

If found, there is a reward.
Name: Email:

Globalboho Geist.

An explanation of the Globalboho AOLAB agenda protocol to help you get your sea legs.

A perfect place to begin.

INSTRUCTIONS:
IT'S SIMPLE.

SECTION ONE:
the seasonal gear up.
IMAGINE YOUR IDEALS. EXPLORE,
DEFINE & WRITE THEM OUT.

SECTION TWO:
AIM AT WALKING THOSE IDEALS OUT.
DOCUMENT AS YOU GO.

Give yourself the GOLD STAR from jump
& just do what you think it'd take to deserve it.

Yep. Simply do that sh*t. On repeat.
Instead of the sh*t you keep doing that ain't working.

You do not have to use all of the prompts but the more you know as you go, the better you'll flow. &When it comes to figuring out the baseline structure of <u>Your intended life</u>
Have fun with it.

GO HAM [hard as a m*therf*cka]

or~ Aim at laid-back discipline & automation.

Every Day Is An '"In-Process" **Shot**'
At Living Your Best Life.

Oh. & <u>USE it.</u> Write in the margins.
Scrawl all over it lovingly or
beat the f*ck outta this agenda.
Sacrifice it to the pursuit of truly
knowing **you** & Manifesting
your penultimate life, well lived.

Said the Globalboho way?

ENJOY THE RIDE.

IN THIS SEASONAL
GLOBALBOHO AOLAB AGENDA
THERE ARE:

GB GEAR UP SEASONAL LAYOUTS
GB GNOSIS SPRINGBOARD SECTIONS
SAMPLE IDEAL MONTH, WEEK, DAY[FW]/DAY[HC]SPREADS
3MONTHLY GROUPS
5 WEEKLY SPREADS PER MONTH
31+ FREE WRITE DAILY SPREADS
+ GRATITUDE LOGS
WRITERHEAD IDEA ARCHIVES,
& SOME BLANK SPACE TOO.

WHY SO MUCH?

BECAUSE MISTAKES ARE BEAUTIFUL, HILARIOUS,

& ACTUALLY PAR FOR THE **REAL** COURSE.

WE ALL COURSE-CORRECT AS WE GO & AS WHAT WE LEARN ABOUT

OURSELVES EXPANDS.

<u>THIS IS KINDA HARDCORE. If you work it.</u>
<u>PACE YOURSELF.</u>

Peace,
-Angel Brynner.

13

Globalboho

Gear Up

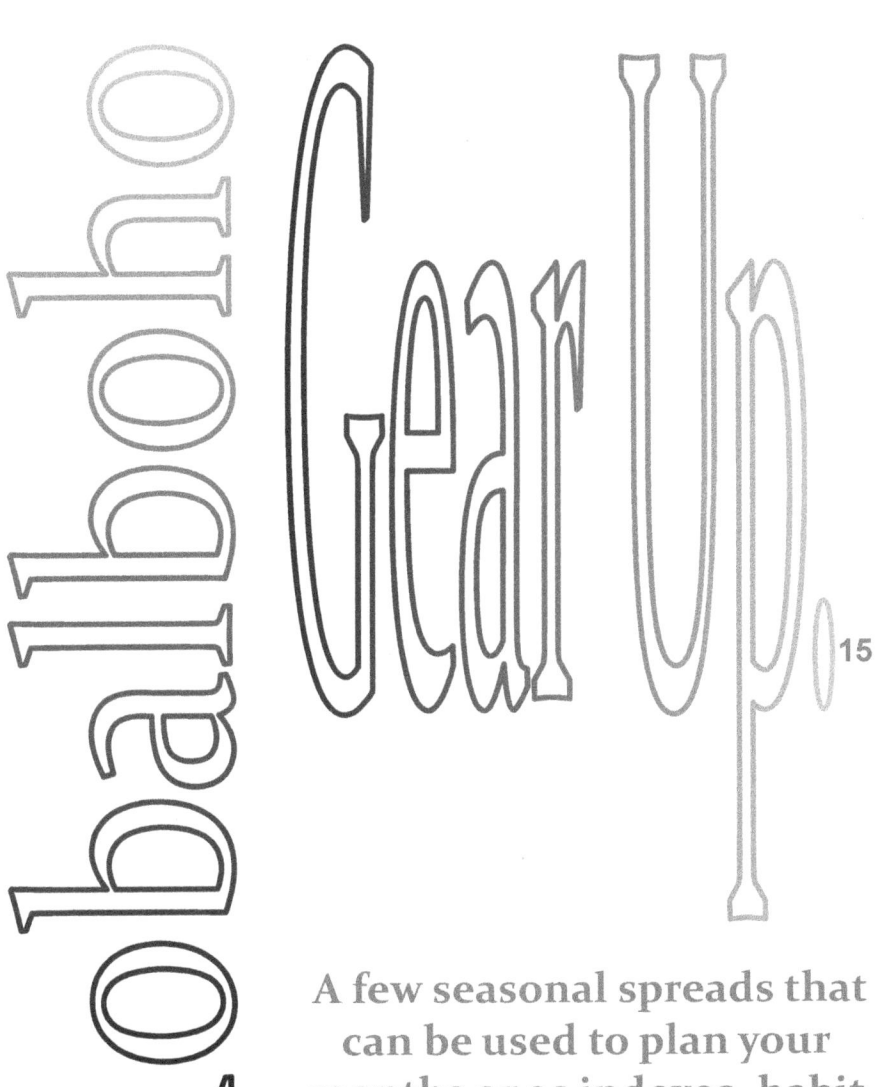

A few seasonal spreads that can be used to plan your months or as indexes, habit trackers & logs.

A perfect place to begin.

date	month	month	month
1			
2			
3			
4			
5			
6			
7			
8			
9			
10			
11			
12			
13			
14			
15			
16			
17			
18			
19			
20			
21			
22			
23			
24			
25			
26			
27			
28			
29			
30			
31			

Seasonal calendar

Work.

Play.

Seasonal Theme:

Ethos:[17]

date	month	month	month
1			
2			
3			
4			
5			
6			
7			
8			
9			
10			
11			
12			
13			
14			
15			
16			
17			
18			
19			
20			
21			
22			
23			
24			
25			
26			
27			
28			
29			
30			
31			

Seasonal calendar

Work.
Play.

Seasonal Theme:

Ethos: [19]

date	month	month	month
1			
2			
3			
4			
5			
6			
7			
8			
9			
10			
11			
12			
13			
14			
15			
16			
17			
18			
19			
20			
21			
22			
23			
24			
25			
26			
27			
28			
29			
30			
31			

Seasonal calendar

Work.
Play.

Seasonal Theme:

Ethos:[21]

date	month	month	month
1			
2			
3			
4			
5			
6			
7			
8			
9			
10			
11			
12			
13			
14			
15			
16			
17			
18			
19			
20			
21			
22			
23			
24			
25			
26			
27			
28			
29			
30			
31			

Seasonal grooming calendar

Seasonal Grooming grid BINGO [what & when?]:

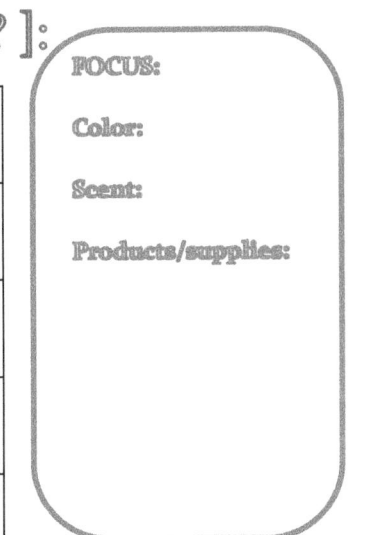

FOCUS:

Color:

Scent:

Products/supplies:

Go.	See.
Do.	Serve.

date	month	month	month
1			
2			
3			
4			
5			
6			
7			
8			
9			
10			
11			
12			
13			
14			
15			
16			
17			
18			
19			
20			
21			
22			
23			
24			
25			
26			
27			
28			
29			
30			
31			

Seasonal grooming calendar

Seasonal Grooming grid
BINGO [what & when?]:

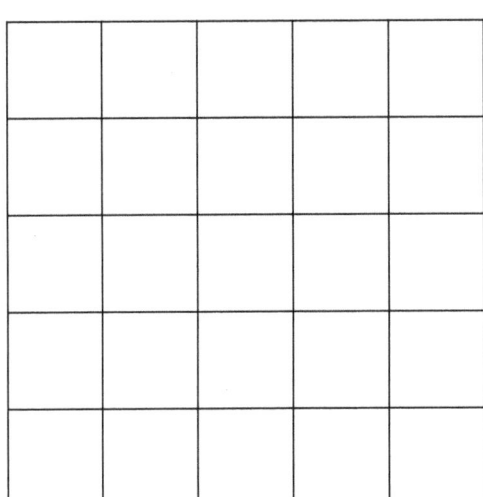

FOCUS:

Color:

Scent:

Products/supplies:

25

Go.	See.
Do.	Serve.

seasonal Travel

Away   Stay-cation   Dream trek

Locale
dates
Url/link
T2dt [thingsa do there]
T2gb4 [thingsnget b4]

Locale
dates
Url/link
T2dt [thingsa do there]
T2gb4 [thingsnget b4]

seasonal Travel

Away   **Stay-cation**   Dream trek

Locale
dates
Url/link
T2dt [things to do there]
T2gb4 [things to get b4]

Locale
dates
Url/link
T2dt [things to do there]
T2gb4 [things to get b4]

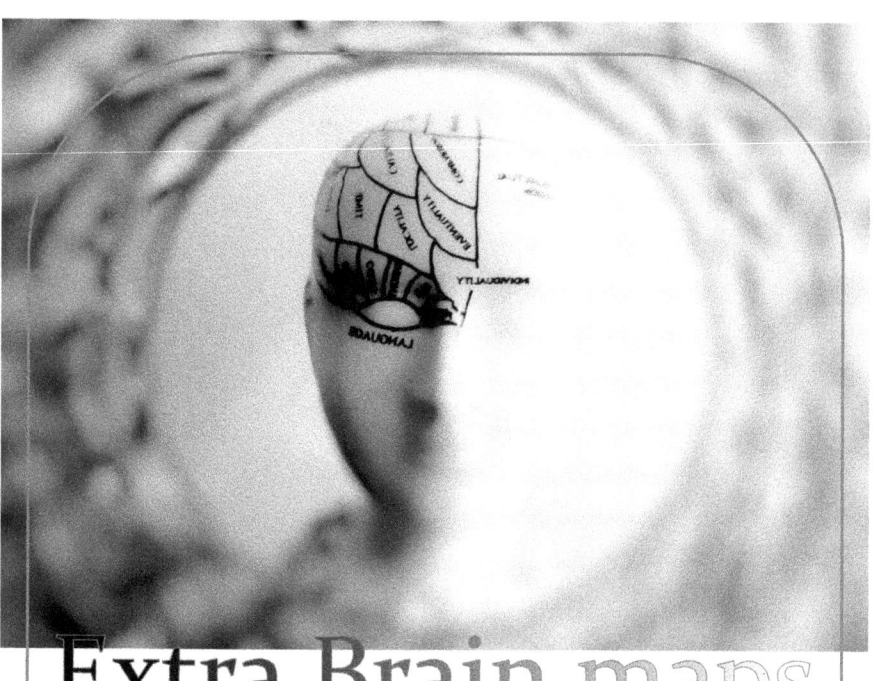

Extra Brain maps

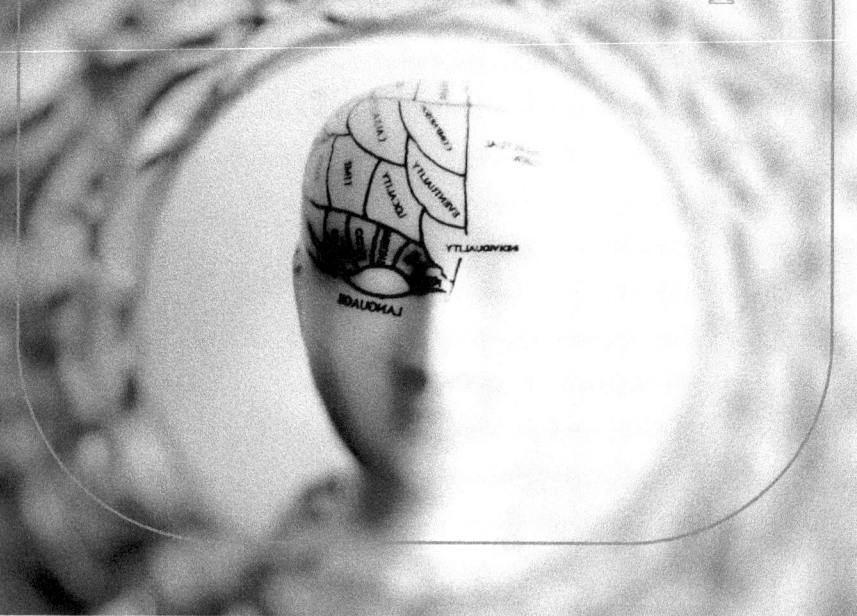

Seasonal workout focus

Seasonal wellness focus[29]

Project codename:	Magii Specialists Masterminds ("Who CAN shoot the dayum dawg?"):	KNOWN [Accessible] INTEL Gnosis needed [people, books, TEDx talks, documentaries, examples]:	Project codename:	Magii Specialists Masterminds ("Who CAN shoot the dayum dawg?"):	KNOWN [Accessible] INTEL Gnosis needed [people, books, TEDx talks, documentaries, examples]:
	1.			1.	
Dawn: D-Day:	2.		Dawn: D-Day:	2.	
Modus Operandi [M.O.]:	3.		Modus Operandi [M.O.]:	3.	
	4.			4.	
How2Skin it Steps: E.g., Make a detailed supplies needed list	Dawn/M/D Day 8/22/23/ 9/13 / 10/1/23	New INTEL: issues & fixes as they arise: e.g., Delivery delays.	How2Skin it Steps: E.g., Make a detailed supplies needed list	Dawn/M/D Day 8/22/23/ 9/13 / 10/1/23	New INTEL: issues & fixes as they arise: e.g., Delivery delays.

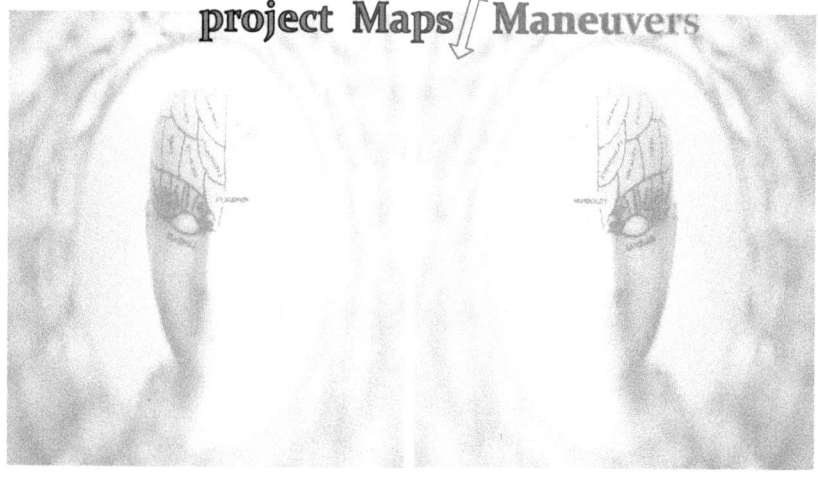

project Maps / Maneuvers

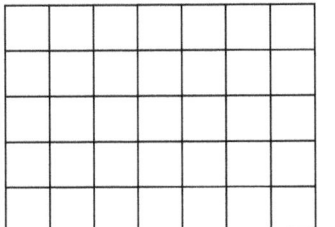
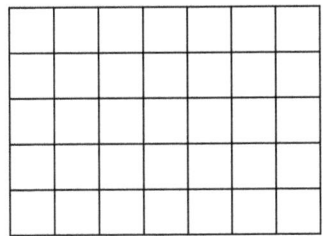

Seasonal habit trackers

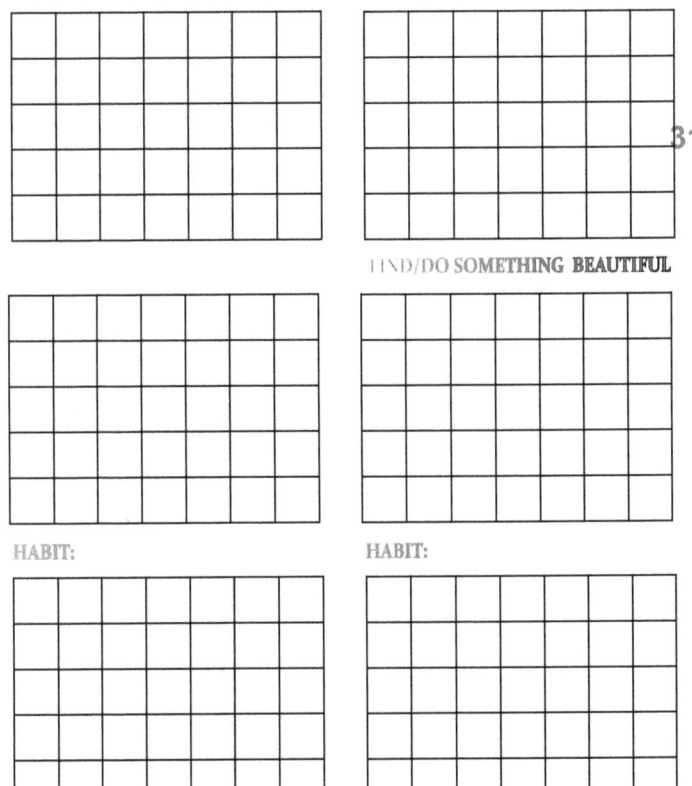

FIND/DO SOMETHING BEAUTIFUL

HABIT: HABIT:

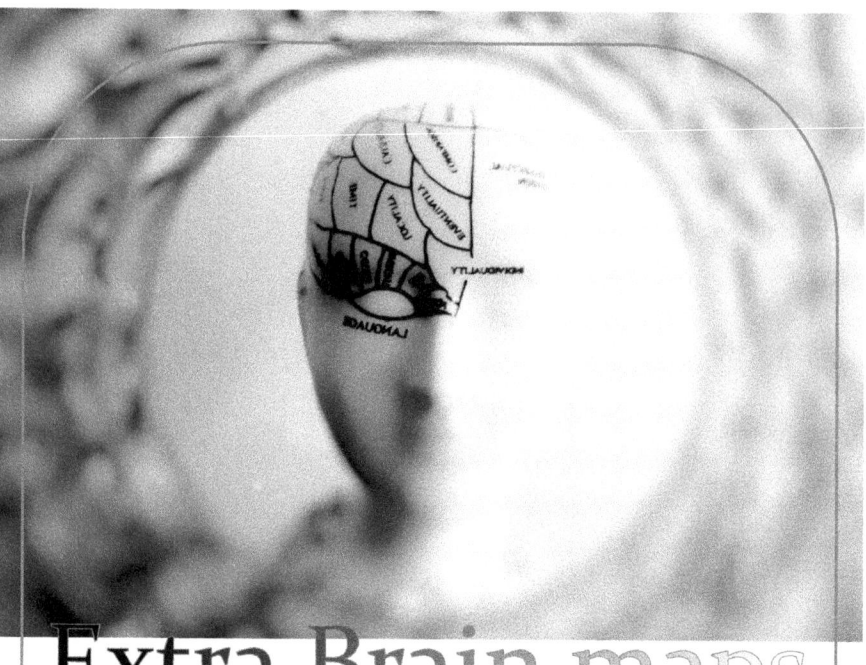

Extra Brain maps

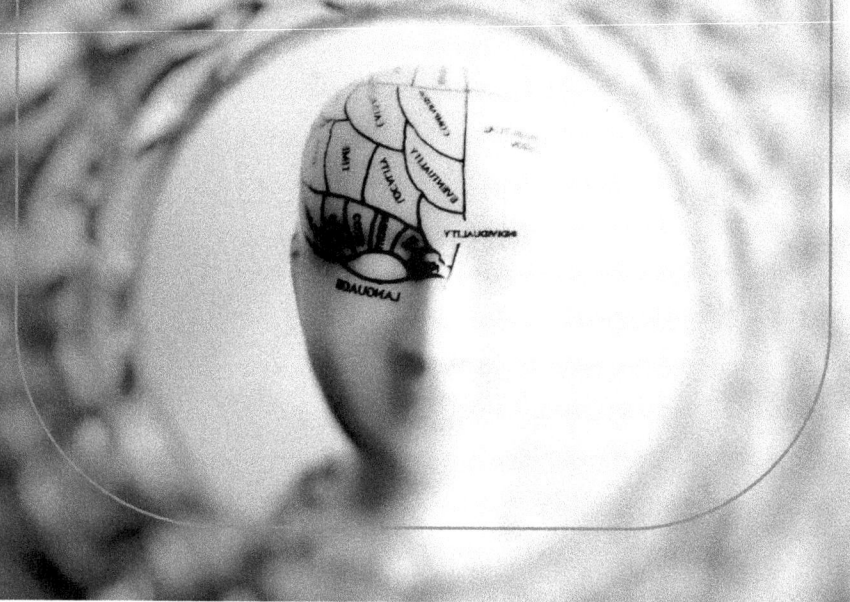

Seasonal dietary focus

Seasonal spiritual focus[33]

project Maps \ Maneuvers

Project codename: Dawn: D-Day: Modus Operandi [M.O.]:	Magii Specialists Masterminds ("Who *CAN* shoot the dayum dawg?"): 1. 2. 3. 4.	KNOWN *[Accessible]* INTEL Gnosis needed [people, books, TEDx talks, documentaries, examples]:	Project codename: Dawn: D-Day: Modus Operandi [M.O.]:	Magii Specialists Masterminds ("Who *CAN* shoot the dayum dawg?"): 1. 2. 3. 4.	KNOWN *[Accessible]* INTEL Gnosis needed [people, books, TEDx talks, documentaries, examples]:
How2Skin it Steps: E.g., Make a detailed supplies needed list	Dawn/M/D Day 8/22/23/ 9/13 / 10/1/23	New INTEL: issues & fixes as they arise: e.g., Delivery delays,	How2Skin it Steps: E.g., Make a detailed supplies needed list	Dawn/M/D Day 8/22/23/ 9/13 / 10/1/23	New INTEL: issues & fixes as they arise: e.g., Delivery delays,

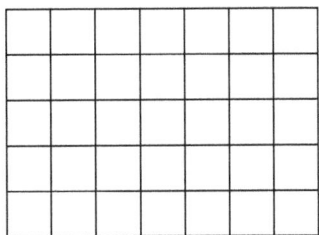

Seasonal habit trackers

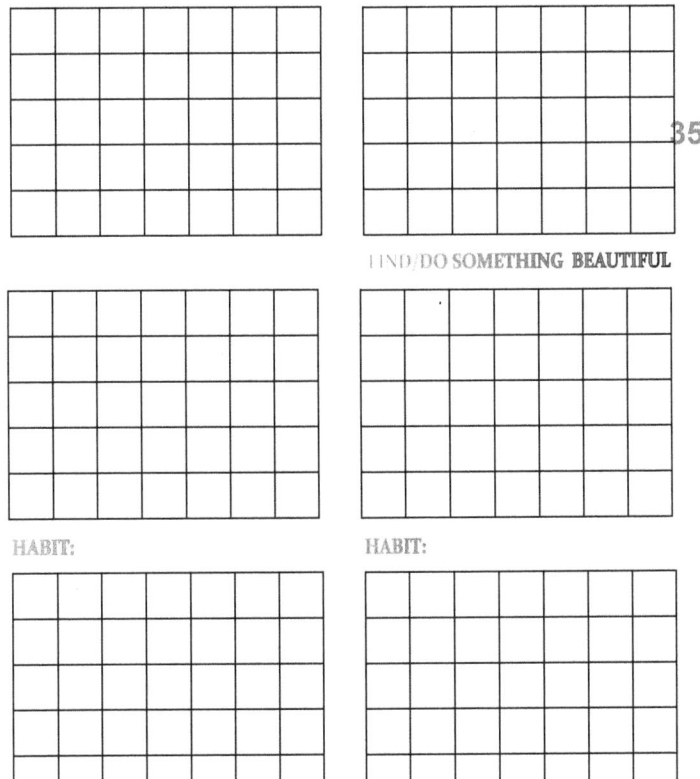

FIND/DO SOMETHING BEAUTIFUL

HABIT: HABIT:

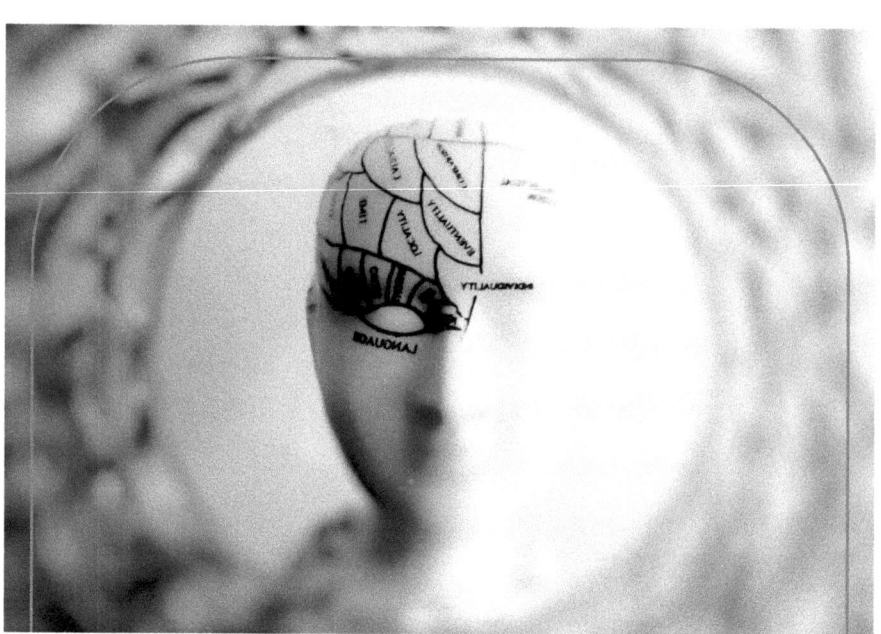

That ONE big goal this season

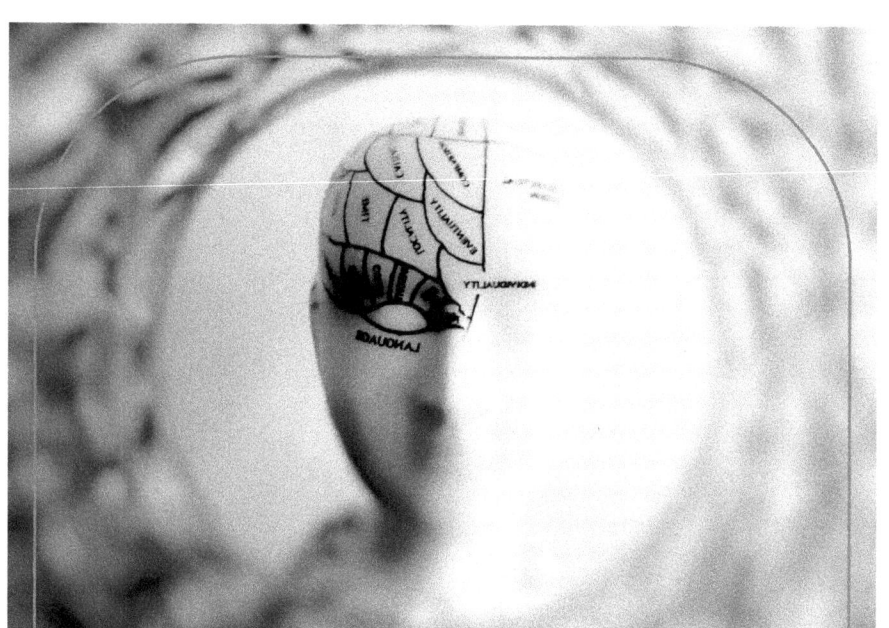

That ONE big goal this season

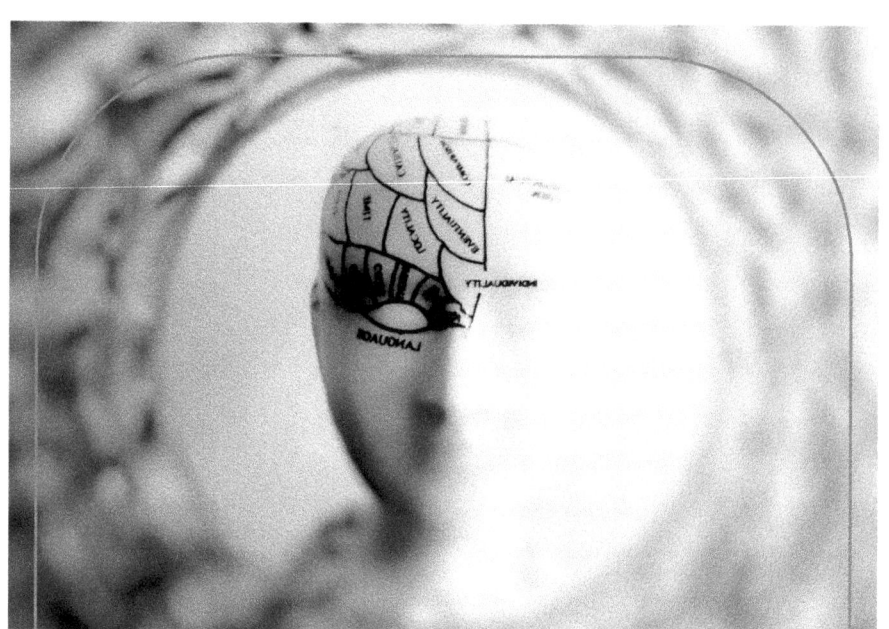

That ONE big goal this season

Globalboho Gnosis

A few info sheets on different holistic roads that may pique your interest on the road to deep diving YOU.

The "good news" is
the world ain't what it used to be.
It's a wilder kind of war out there
Than before...& a little extra
weaponry rocked on the way to
your whathaveyous couldn't hurt.
So...gear up & get out there & win!

Helmet of Salvation/Ephesians 6:17
Breastplate of Righteousness /Ephesians 6:14
Belt of Truth /Ephesians 6:14
Sword of the Spirit /Ephesians 6:17
Shield of Faith/Ephesians 6:16
Feet of Peace/Ephesians 6:15

"& when you've done all you can think To do, stand."
- Ephesians 6:13

[Dive deeper on your own]

ARMOR of GOD

solfeggio frequencies

- 174 hz / removes pain
- 285 hz / influences energy field
- 369 hz / liberation from guilt & fear
- 417 hz / facilitates change
- 528 hz / repairs DNA (love frequency)
- 639 hz / heals relationships
- 741 hz / awaken intuition
- 852 hz / attracts soul tribe
- 963 hz / connect with light & spirit

Vibe Tribe [Hertz]:

174 **285** **369** **417** **528** **639** **741** **852** **963**

extras:
432 hz / miracle tone of nature

Brain waves:

- THETA 4 to 8 hz / meditation & creativity
- BETA 13 to 35 hz / problem solving
- ALPHA 8 to 13 hz / relaxed reflection
- DELTA 0.5 to 4 hz / deep sleep
- GAMMA 35+ hz / heightened awareness

[Dive deeper on your own]

Hertz Vibe Tribe

Five elements theory is a Chinese **philosophy that describes** how **the fundamental elements** in nature **flow into & interact with each** other.

fire
summer

wood
spring

earth
cautantowwit
Indian summer
harvest

water
winter

metal
autumn

[Dive deeper on your own]

The Five Elements

Short & Sweet:

A "Loka"
Is a state of
consciousness
One is interacting
With the world
from, whether
One is aware of
It or not. They sync
With spiritual realms
Above & below ours
In Hinduism.

[Dive deeper on your own]

A "Chakra"
is usually
seen as an
Energy center
That needs to
"be in balance."

The Upper Lokas [Level of Awareness]	location	Deals with / Awareness of:
Satyaloka		illumination
Tapoloka		Divine sight
Janaloka		Divine love
Maharloka		Direct recognition/ Universal unity
Svargaloka		Willpower/Mind over matter
Bhuvarloka		Reason/ Seat of the soul
Bhuloka	earth	Memory/ Time transcendence

The 7 chakras taught in the west:	Location:	Deals with / Awareness of:
Sahasrara	crown	Inspiration & oneness
Vishuddhi	throat	communication
Anahata	heart	Pure love & compassion
Manipura	Solar plexus	Empowerment free will
Svadhisthana	sacral	Sex, power, creativity, desire, intimacy
Muladhara	root	Grounding & survival

The Lower Lokas [animal instincts/ states of darkness/ Levels of fixation]	location	Deals with/ fixated on
Atala	hips	Fear & lust
Vitala	thighs	Anger & resentment
Sutala	knees	Jealousy & envy
Talatala	calves	Confusion & doubt
Rasatala	ankles	Selfishness & pride
Mahatala	feet	consciencelessness
Patala	soles	Hatred & malice

The 21 (actual) chakras

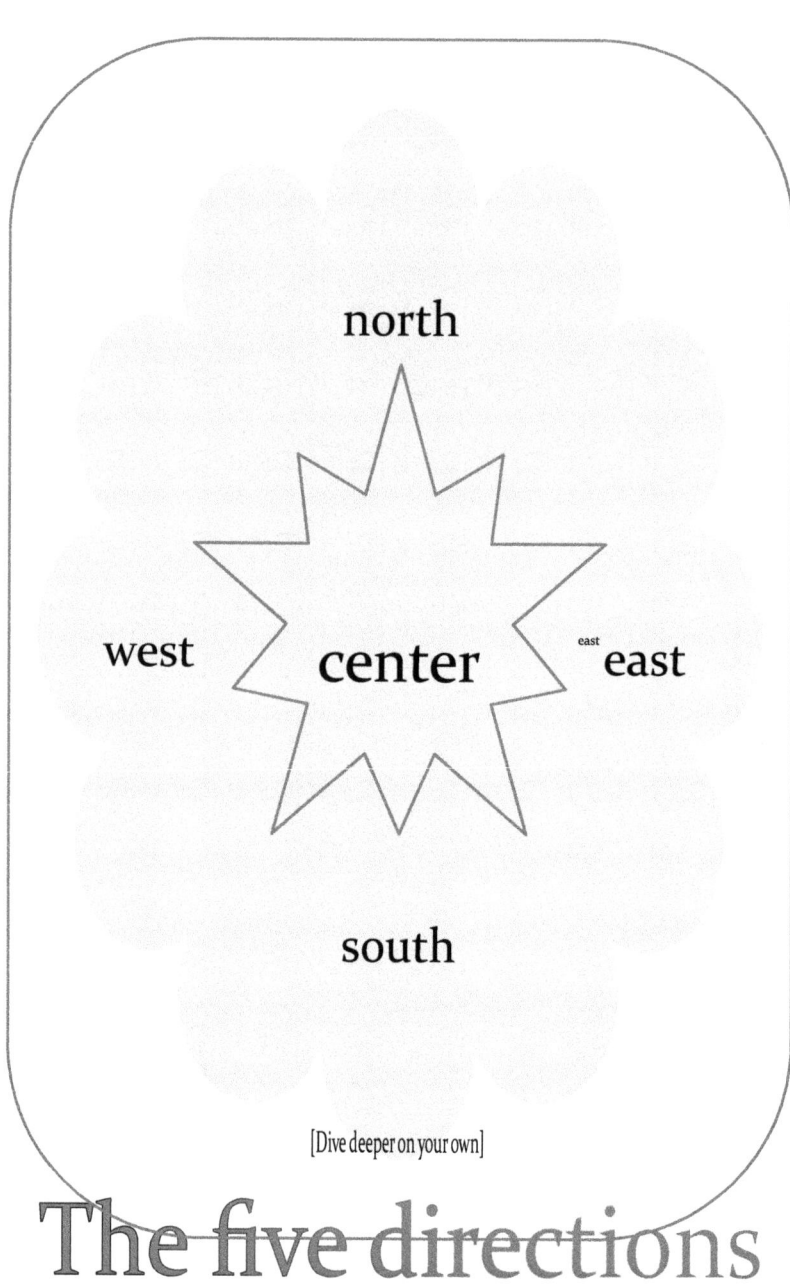

According to Trungpa, we don't
Wait until we die
to enter the
BARDO realm that
Tibetan Buddhists
See as waiting for us
Upon death. We
dance in & out of the
6 states as we live
Our lives. Our
Experience of the
Present is always
Colored by one
Of six psychological
States.

Freedom
From this
Madness is
Possible.

Dive deeper on your own.

The god realm
[bliss]

The jealous god realm
[jealousy & lust for entertainment]

The human realm
[passion & desire]

The animal realm
[ignorance]

The hungry ghost realm
[poverty & possessiveness]

The hell realm
[aggression & hatred]

Chogyam Trungpa's Bardos

NOTES

The Ideals...

JUST4FUN

resuscitate
reframe
reflect
restore
8r
relax
relate
repair
rally

Recalibrate.
Rebrand.
Revamp.
Redo.
Recast.

Revise your reality.

START	174		285
CYCLE	369	Vibe Tribe	417
STOP	528	[Hertz]:	639
	741		852
		963	

START
CYCLE
STOP

SEASON:
HARVEST   AUTUMN
WINTER   SPRING
   SUMMER
Seasonal focus:

NEW MOON:
FULL MOON:

HOLIDAYS:
This month's "I & i" DAY:
This month's "I & i" HOUR:

This month's HIGHEST TIMELINE log-line:

This month's affirmation:

This month's workout focus:

This month's physical challenge:

This month's shower & bathing meditation:

ideal MONTH:
JAN FEB MAR
APR MAY JUN
JUL AUG SEP
OCT NOV DEC

Movie of your life

bigGOAL:
Aim to do's

bigTASK:
Gotta do's

PICK4 Impossible   PICK4 SANCTUARY   PICK4 SELF-CARE
Things 2 try: GETERDONES: GETERDONES:

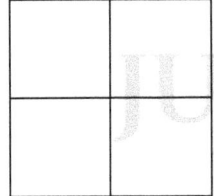
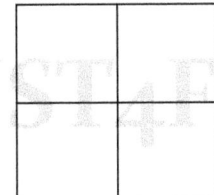
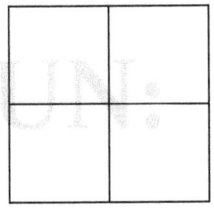

JUST4FUN:

New Moon Resonance

1. Imagine what you aim to Bring into your zone..
2. Set new intentions.
3. Journal & Meditate.
4. Scrub &/or soak your body.
5. Get out in some moonlight.

New/Things 2do.

Things 2do/Full.

1. Cleanse your space [Mental & physical].
2. Crystals! Charge 'em If ya got'em.
3. Celebrate any wins.
4. Release what no longer Serves you.
5. Get out in some moonlight.

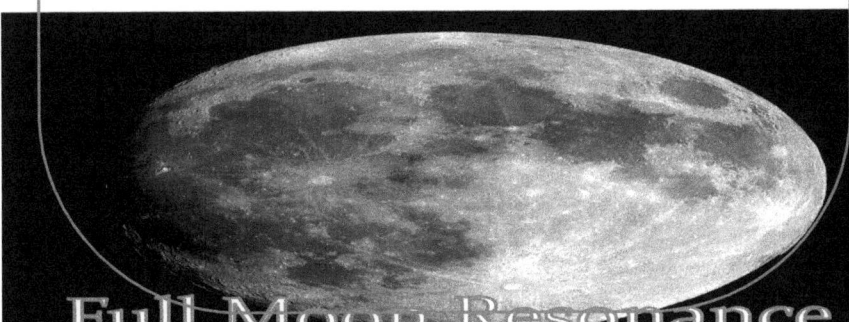

Full Moon Resonance

WHO ARE YOU   HOW DO YOU EXPRESS IT?

ideal
POINT
OF THE
MONTH:

[NECESSARY]
COUNTERPOINT
OF THE MONTH:

(EVERY POINT HAS A COUNTERPOINT)

PICK 4 MOVIES 2 WATCH:

PICK 4 BOOKS 2 READ:

THEME SONG

COLOR

POET

CRYSTAL

FLOWER

HERB

Give yourself ONE day a week. One way or another. For you. Find a way.

BUILD YOU UP BETTER HABIT TO IMPROVE:

GIVE IT UP OR REPLACE ?

WITH WHAT ?   HOW ?:

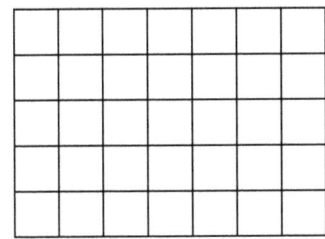

TREAT YOURSELF
Curious about it? LEARN IT

Wish you were able 2 do it? TRY IT

Place you want 2go? GO 2IT

Love to have it outside? TRY IT @HOME

JUST4FUN FOCUS:

THING 2LOVE ABOUT YOU

SPIRIT SUBJECT 2 FOCUS: ON

ODD INTEREST 2DEEP DIVE:

BEAUTY FEATURE/FOCUS:

CLEAN UP NICE FOCUS:

STYLE FOCUS:

SMELL 2 LOVE:

SHAKE THAT ASS!/NOW MOovVE!!

FIND/DO SOMETHING BEAUTIFUL

TRAVEL:
SCHEDULED   STAY-CATION

THINGS2DOTHERE

DREAM TREK:

VISUALS

HABIT:

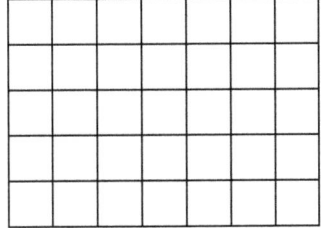

Project codename:	Magii Specialists Masterminds ("Who CAN shoot the dayum dawg?"):	KNOWN [Accessible] INTEL Gnosis needed [people, books, TEDx talks, documentaries, examples]:	Project codename:	Magii Specialists Masterminds ("Who CAN shoot the dayum dawg?"):	KNOWN [Accessible] INTEL Gnosis needed [people, books, TEDx talks, documentaries, examples]:
	1.			1.	
Dawn: D-Day:	2.		Dawn: D-Day:	2.	
Modus Operandi [M.O.]:	3.		Modus Operandi [M.O.]:	3.	
	4.			4.	
How2Skin it Steps: E.g., Make a detailed supplies needed list	Dawn/M/D Day 8/22/23/ 9/13 / 10/1/23	New INTEL: issues & fixes as they arise: e.g., Delivery delays,	How2Skin it Steps: E.g., Make a detailed supplies needed list	Dawn/M/D Day 8/22/23/ 9/13 / 10/1/23	New INTEL: issues & fixes as they arise: e.g., Delivery delays,

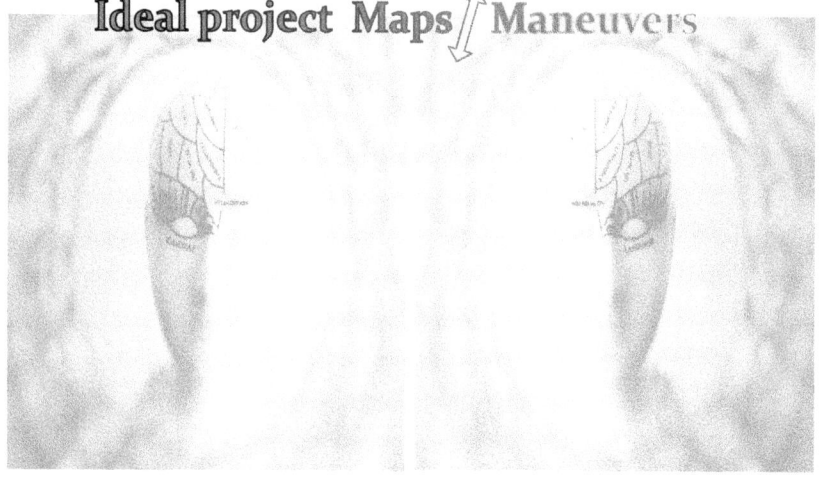

Ideal project Maps / Maneuvers

Ideal project Maps \ Maneuvers

Project codename:	Magii Specialists Masterminds ("Who CAN shoot the dayum dawg?"):	KNOWN [Accessible] INTEL Gnosis needed [people, books, TEDx talks, documentaries, examples]:
	1.	
Dawn: D-Day:	2.	
Modus Operandi [M.O.]:	3.	
	4.	
How2Skin it Steps: *E.g., Make a detailed supplies needed list*	Dawn/M/D Day 8/22/23/ 9/13 / 10/1/23	New INTEL: issues & fixes as they arise: e.g., Delivery delays.

Project codename:	Magii Specialists Masterminds ("Who CAN shoot the dayum dawg?"):	KNOWN [Accessible] INTEL Gnosis needed [people, books, TEDx talks, documentaries, examples]:
	1.	
Dawn: D-Day:	2.	
Modus Operandi [M.O.]:	3.	
	4.	
How2Skin it Steps: *E.g., Make a detailed supplies needed list*	Dawn/M/D Day 8/22/23/ 9/13 / 10/1/23	New INTEL: issues & fixes as they arise: e.g., Delivery delays.

THE Ideal WEEK:

NOTES:

WEEK OF 26

WEEKLY GREEN DRINK LOG

THE vibe AIMED 4:

THE PLAYLIST:
1.
2.
3.

THE DREAM:

THE MAIN GOAL:

THIS WEEK:

SELF CARE FOCUS

STYLE INSPO:

BEAUTY/GROOMING ZONE:

WORKOUT CHALLENGE FOCUS

MEDITATION/ FOCUS

PRAYER REQUEST

DECOMPRESSION TREAT

THIS WEEK'S WHATHAVEYOUS:

1.
2.
3.
4.
5.
6.
7.

7 THINGS YOU LOVE ABOUT YOU: (SELF PEP TALK)

1.
2.
3.
4.
5.
6.
7.

APPOINTMENTS	TIME & DATE	TYPE

WEEKLY DAY UP AFFIRMATION

THIS WEEK'S NIGHTLY AFFIRMATION

"I AM..."
(OF THE WEEK)

SPIRITUAL SHOTGUN:

What aspect of God, icon, archetype, angel, energy or spirit animal is riding out into the world *with* you this week?

LOVE ON OTHER'S LIST [L.O.O.L]

Who can you quietly do a cool thing for?

Aww~! Brain dump:

Sweethearts,
Did cool things,
Who are you FN with this week?

(FILL AS NEEDED)

Target Weekly meal plan:

Whole 30? Keto? Vegan? "All Thai, all week"? Paleo? Vegetarian? Carnivore?
Healthy Decadence?

Fast/ cleanse/ omad/ IF/ Juicing/ FODMAP

Grocery items 2 get 2 hit it:

...the WEEKend RIT[UAL]S:

How can you bless them for for blessing you?

Argh! brain dump:

The jerks, the K*rens,
The nonsense,
Who are you so not FN with this week?

How did you forgive them **to** fully let their energy go?

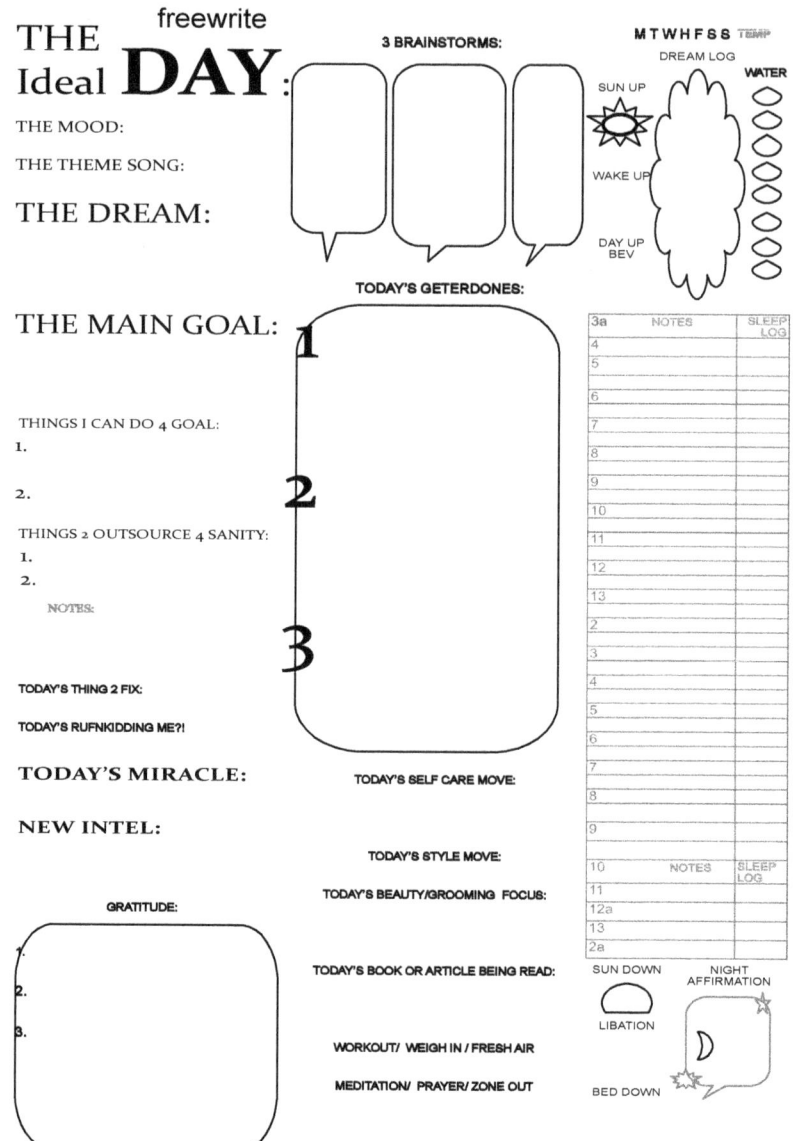

What Days You Doing?

THE pregaming:

THE recap:

date	Gratitude LOG
1	
2	
3	
4	
5	
6	
7	
8	
9	
10	
11	
12	
13	
14	
15	
16	
17	
18	
19	
20	
21	
22	
23	
24	
25	
26	
27	
28	
29	
30	
31	

MONTH ONE.

JUST4FUN

&r

resuscitate
reframe   reflect
restore   relax
relate   repair
          rally

Recalibrate.
Rebrand.
Revamp.
Redo.
Recast.

Revise your reality.

174   285
369   Vibe   417
      Tribe
528 [Hertz]: 639
741   852
    963

START   START
CYCLE   CYCLE
STOP   STOP

SEASON:
HARVEST   AUTUMN
WINTER   SPRING
         SUMMER
Seasonal focus:

MONTH:
JAN FEB MAR
APR MAY JUN
JUL AUG SEP
OCT NOV DEC

NEW MOON:

FULL MOON:

HOLIDAYS:
This month's " I & i " DAY:
This month's "I & i " HOUR:

This month's HIGHEST TIMELINE log-line:

This month's affirmation:

This month's workout focus:

This month's physical challenge:

This month's shower & bathing meditation:

Movie of your life

bigGOAL:
Aim to do's

bigTASK:
Gotta do's

PICK4 Impossible   PICK4 SANCTUARY   PICK4 SELF-CARE
Things 2 try: GETERDONES: GETERDONES:

JUST4FUN:

New Moon Resonance

1. Imagine what you aim to Bring into your zone..
2. Set new intentions.
3. Journal & Meditate.
4. Scrub &/or soak your body.
5. Get out in some moonlight.

New/Things 2do.

Things 2do/Full.

1. Cleanse your space [Mental & physical].
2. Crystals! Charge 'em if ya got'em.
3. Celebrate any wins.
4. Release what no longer serves you.
5. Get out in some moonlight.

Full Moon Resonance

WHO ARE YOU   HOW DO YOU
               EXPRESS IT?

ideal POINT OF THE MONTH:

[NECESSARY] COUNTERPOINT OF THE MONTH:

(EVERY POINT HAS A COUNTERPOINT)

ORDERED IN:

PiCK4MOVIES 2WATCH:

PiCK4 BOOKS 2READ:

| THEME SONG | | | POET | FLOWER |
| COLOR | | | CRYSTAL | HERB |

Give yourself ONE day a week. One way or another. For you. Find a way.

THIS MONTH'S:
(capsule closet)
[Current rotation]

THIS MONTH'S dayUP Geterdone:

THIS MONTH'S b4BED Geterdone:

BUILD YOU UP BETTER HABIT TO IMPROVE:

GIVE IT UP OR REPLACE ?

WITH WHAT ?   HOW ?:

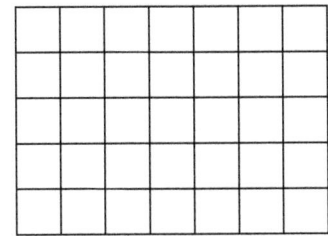

TREAT YOURSELF
Curious about it? <u>LEARN IT</u>

Wish you were able 2 do it? <u>TRY IT</u>

Place you want 2go? <u>GO 2IT</u>

Love to have it outside? <u>TRY IT @HOME</u>

Otha Dailies

JUST4FUN FOCUS:

THING 2LOVE ABOUT YOU

SPIRIT SUBJECT 2 FOCUS: ON

ODD INTEREST 2DEEP DIVE:

BEAUTY FEATURE/FOCUS:

CLEAN UP NICE FOCUS:

STYLE FOCUS:

SMELL 2 LOVE:

SHAKE THAT ASS!/NOW MOovVE!!

81

FIND/DO SOMETHING BEAUTIFUL

TRAVEL:
SCHEDULED   STAY-CATION

THINGS2DOTHERE

DREAM TREK:

VISUALS

HABIT:

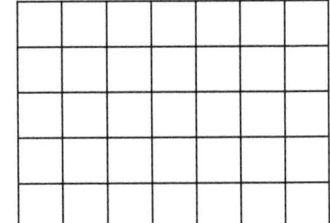

Project codename:	Magii Specialists Masterminds ("Who CAN shoot the dayum dawg?"):	KNOWN [Accessible] INTEL Gnosis needed [people, books, TEDx talks, documentaries, examples]:	Project codename:	Magii Specialists Masterminds ("Who CAN shoot the dayum dawg?"):	KNOWN [Accessible] INTEL Gnosis needed [people, books, TEDx talks, documentaries, examples]:
	1.			1.	
Dawn: D-Day:	2.		Dawn: D-Day:	2.	
Modus Operandi [M.O.]:	3.		Modus Operandi [M.O.]:	3.	
	4.			4.	
How2Skin it Steps: E.g., Make a detailed supplies needed list	Dawn/M/D Day 8/22/23/ 9/13 / 10/1/23	New INTEL: issues & fixes as they arise: e.g., Delivery delays,	How2Skin it Steps: E.g., Make a detailed supplies needed list	Dawn/M/D Day 8/22/23/ 9/13 / 10/1/23	New INTEL: issues & fixes as they arise: e.g., Delivery delays,

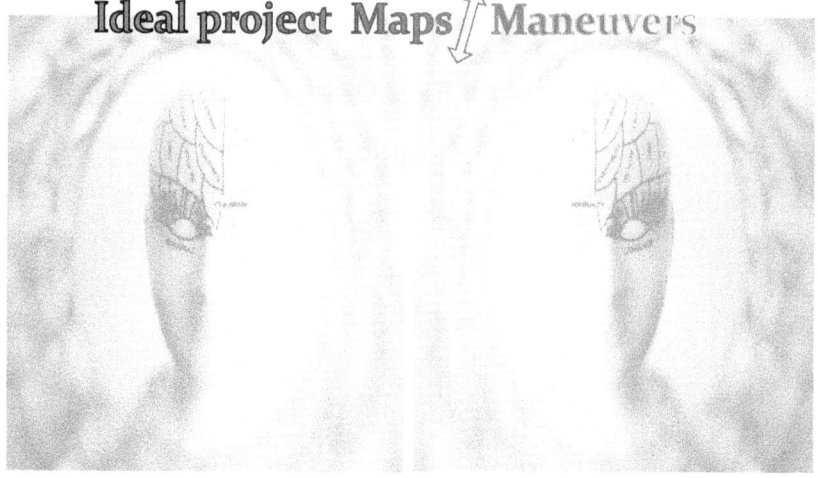

Ideal project Maps / Maneuvers

Ideal project Maps & Maneuvers

Project codename:	Magii Specialists Masterminds ("Who CAN shoot the dayum dawg?"):	KNOWN [Accessible] INTEL Gnosis needed [people, books, TEDx talks, documentaries, examples]:
Dawn: D-Day: Modus Operandi [M.O.]:	1. 2. 3. 4.	

How2Skin it Steps: E.g., Make a detailed supplies needed list	Dawn/M/D Day 8/22/23/ 9/13 / 10/1/23	New INTEL: issues & fixes as they arise: e.g., Delivery delays,

Project codename:	Magii Specialists Masterminds ("Who CAN shoot the dayum dawg?"):	KNOWN [Accessible] INTEL Gnosis needed [people, books, TEDx talks, documentaries, examples]:
Dawn: D-Day: Modus Operandi [M.O.]:	1. 2. 3. 4.	

How2Skin it Steps: E.g., Make a detailed supplies needed list	Dawn/M/D Day 8/22/23/ 9/13 / 10/1/23	New INTEL: issues & fixes as they arise: e.g., Delivery delays,

THE WEEK:

THE vibe AIMED 4:

THE PLAYLIST:
1.
2.
3.

THE DREAM:

THE MAIN GOAL:

NOTES:

WEEK OF 26

WEEKLY GREEN DRINK LOG

THIS WEEK:

SELF CARE FOCUS

STYLE INSPO:

BEAUTY/GROOMING ZONE:

WORKOUT CHALLENGE FOCUS

MEDITATION/ FOCUS

PRAYER REQUEST

DECOMPRESSION TREAT

THIS WEEK'S WHATHAVEYOUS:

1.
2.
3.
4.
5.
6.
7.

7 THINGS YOU LOVE ABOUT YOU: (SELF PEP TALK)

1.
2.
3.
4.
5.
6.
7.

APPOINTMENTS	TIME & DATE	TYPE

WEEKLY DAY UP AFFIRMATION

THIS WEEK'S NIGHTLY AFFIRMATION

(OF THE WEEK)

SPIRITUAL SHOTGUN:

What aspect of God, icon, archetype, angel, energy or spirit animal is riding out into the world *with* you this week?

LOVE ON OTHER'S LIST [L.O.O.L]

Who can you quietly do a cool thing for?

Aww~! Brain dump:

Sweethearts,
Did cool things,
Who are you FN with this week?

(FILL AS NEEDED)

87

Target Weekly meal plan:

Whole 30? Keto? Vegan? "All Thai, all week"? Paleo? Vegetarian? Carnivore? Healthy Decadence?

Fast/ cleanse/ omad/ IF/ Juicing/ FODMAP

Grocery items 2 get 2 hit it:

...the WEEKend RIT[UAL]S:

How can you bless them for for blessing you?

Argh! brain dump:

The jerks, the K*rens,
The nonsense,
Who are you so not FN with this week?

How did you forgive them to fully let their energy go?

THE WEEK:

THE vibe AIMED 4:

THE PLAYLIST:
1.
2.
3.

THE DREAM:

THE MAIN GOAL:

THIS WEEK'S WHATHAVEYOUS:
1.
2.
3.
4.
5.
6.
7.

NOTES:

WEEK OF 26

WEEKLY GREEN DRINK LOG

THIS WEEK:

SELF CARE FOCUS

STYLE INSPO:

BEAUTY/GROOMING ZONE:

WORKOUT CHALLENGE FOCUS

MEDITATION/ FOCUS

PRAYER REQUEST

DECOMPRESSION TREAT

7 THINGS YOU LOVE ABOUT YOU: (SELF PEP TALK)
1.
2.
3.
4.
5.
6.
7.

APPOINTMENTS	TIME & DATE	TYPE

WEEKLY DAY UP AFFIRMATION

THIS WEEK'S NIGHTLY AFFIRMATION

"I AM"...
(OF THE WEEK)

SPIRITUAL SHOTGUN:

What aspect of God, icon, archetype, angel, energy or spirit animal is riding out into the world *with* you this week?

LOVE ON OTHER'S LIST [L.O.O.L]

Who can you quietly do a cool thing for?

Aww~! Brain dump:

Sweethearts,
Did cool things,
Who are you FN with this week?

(FILL AS NEEDED)

Target Weekly meal plan:

Whole 30? Keto? Vegan? "All Thai, all week"? Paleo? Vegetarian? Carnivore?
Healthy Decadence?

Fast/ cleanse/ omad/ IF/ Juicing/ FODMAP

Grocery items 2 get 2 hit it:

...the WEEKend RIT[UAL]S:

How can you bless them for for blessing you?

Argh! brain dump:

The jerks, the K*rens,
The nonsense,
Who are you so not FN with this week?

How did you forgive them **to** fully let their energy go?

THE WEEK:

THE vibe AIMED 4:

THE PLAYLIST:
1.
2.
3.

THE DREAM:

THE MAIN GOAL:

NOTES:

WEEK OF 26

WEEKLY GREEN DRINK LOG

THIS WEEK:

SELF CARE FOCUS

STYLE INSPO:

BEAUTY/GROOMING ZONE:

WORKOUT CHALLENGE FOCUS

MEDITATION/ FOCUS

PRAYER REQUEST

DECOMPRESSION TREAT

THIS WEEK'S WHATHAVEYOUS:

1.
2.
3.
4.
5.
6.
7.

7 THINGS YOU LOVE ABOUT YOU: (SELF PEP TALK)

1.
2.
3.
4.
5.
6.
7.

APPOINTMENTS	TIME & DATE	TYPE

WEEKLY DAY UP AFFIRMATION

THIS WEEK'S NIGHTLY AFFIRMATION

"I AM..."
(OF THE WEEK)

SPIRITUAL SHOTGUN:

What aspect of God, icon, archetype, angel, energy or spirit animal is riding out into the world *with* you this week?

LOVE ON OTHER'S LIST [L.O.O.L]

Who can you quietly do a cool thing for?

Aww~! Brain dump:

Sweethearts,
Did cool things,
Who are you FN with this week?

(FILL AS NEEDED)

How can you bless them for for blessing you?

Argh! brain dump:

The jerks, the K*rens,
The nonsense,
Who are you so not FN with this week?

How did you forgive them **to** fully let their energy go?

Target Weekly meal plan:

Whole 30? Keto? Vegan? "All Thai, all week"? Paleo? Vegetarian? Carnivore?
Healthy Decadence?

Fast/ cleanse/ omad/ IF/ Juicing/ FODMAP

Grocery items 2 get 2 hit it:

...the WEEKend RIT[UAL]S:

THE WEEK:

THE vibe AIMED 4:

THE PLAYLIST:
1.
2.
3.

THE DREAM:

THE MAIN GOAL:

THIS WEEK'S WHATHAVEYOUS:
1.
2.
3.
4.
5.
6.
7.

NOTES:

WEEK OF 26

WEEKLY GREEN DRINK LOG

THIS WEEK:

SELF CARE FOCUS

STYLE INSPO:

BEAUTY/GROOMING ZONE:

WORKOUT CHALLENGE FOCUS

MEDITATION/ FOCUS

PRAYER REQUEST

DECOMPRESSION TREAT

7 THINGS YOU LOVE ABOUT YOU: (SELF PEP TALK)
1.
2.
3.
4.
5.
6.
7.

APPOINTMENTS	TIME & DATE	TYPE

WEEKLY DAY UP AFFIRMATION

THIS WEEK'S NIGHTLY AFFIRMATION

"I AM..."
(OF THE WEEK)

SPIRITUAL SHOTGUN:

What aspect of God, icon, archetype, angel, energy or spirit animal is riding out into the world *with* you this week?

LOVE ON OTHER'S LIST [L.O.O.L]

Who can you quietly do a cool thing for?

Aww~! Brain dump:

Sweethearts,
Did cool things,
Who are you FN with this week?

(FILL AS NEEDED)

Target Weekly meal plan:

Whole 30? Keto? Vegan? "All Thai, all week"? Paleo? Vegetarian? Carnivore?
Healthy Decadence?

Fast/ cleanse/ omad/ IF/ Juicing/ FODMAP

Grocery items 2 get 2 hit it:

...the WEEKend RIT[UAL]S:

How can you bless them for for blessing you?

Argh! brain dump:

The jerks, the K*rens,
The nonsense,
Who are you so not FN with this week?

How did you forgive them **to** fully let their energy go?

THE WEEK:

THE vibe AIMED 4:

THE PLAYLIST:
1.
2.
3.

THE DREAM:

THE MAIN GOAL:

NOTES:

WEEK OF 26

WEEKLY GREEN DRINK LOG

THIS WEEK:

SELF CARE FOCUS

STYLE INSPO:

BEAUTY/GROOMING ZONE:

WORKOUT CHALLENGE FOCUS

MEDITATION/ FOCUS

PRAYER REQUEST

DECOMPRESSION TREAT

THIS WEEK'S WHATHAVEYOUS:

1.
2.
3.
4.
5.
6.
7.

APPOINTMENTS	TIME & DATE	TYPE

7 THINGS YOU LOVE ABOUT YOU: (SELF PEP TALK)

1.
2.
3.
4.
5.
6.
7.

WEEKLY DAY UP AFFIRMATION

THIS WEEK'S NIGHTLY AFFIRMATION

"I AM"...
(OF THE WEEK)

SPIRITUAL SHOTGUN:

What aspect of God, icon, archetype, angel, energy or spirit animal is riding out into the world *with* you this week?

LOVE ON OTHER'S LIST [L.O.O.L]

Who can you quietly do a cool thing for?

Aww~! Brain dump:

Sweethearts,
Did cool things,
Who are you FN with this week?

(FILL AS NEEDED)

How can you bless them for for blessing you?

Target Weekly meal plan:

Whole 30? Keto? Vegan? "All Thai, all week"? Paleo? Vegetarian? Carnivore? Healthy Decadence?

Fast/ cleanse/ omad/ IF/ Juicing/ FODMAP

Argh! brain dump:

The jerks, the K*rens,
The nonsense,
Who are you so not FN with this week?

Grocery items 2 get 2 hit it:

How did you forgive them **to** fully let their energy go?

...the WEEKend RIT[UAL]S:

date	SIX WORD STORY LOG
1	
2	
3	
4	
5	
6	
7	
8	
9	
10	
11	
12	
13	
14	
15	
16	
17	
18	
19	
20	
21	
22	
23	
24	
25	
26	
27	
28	
29	
30	
31	

97

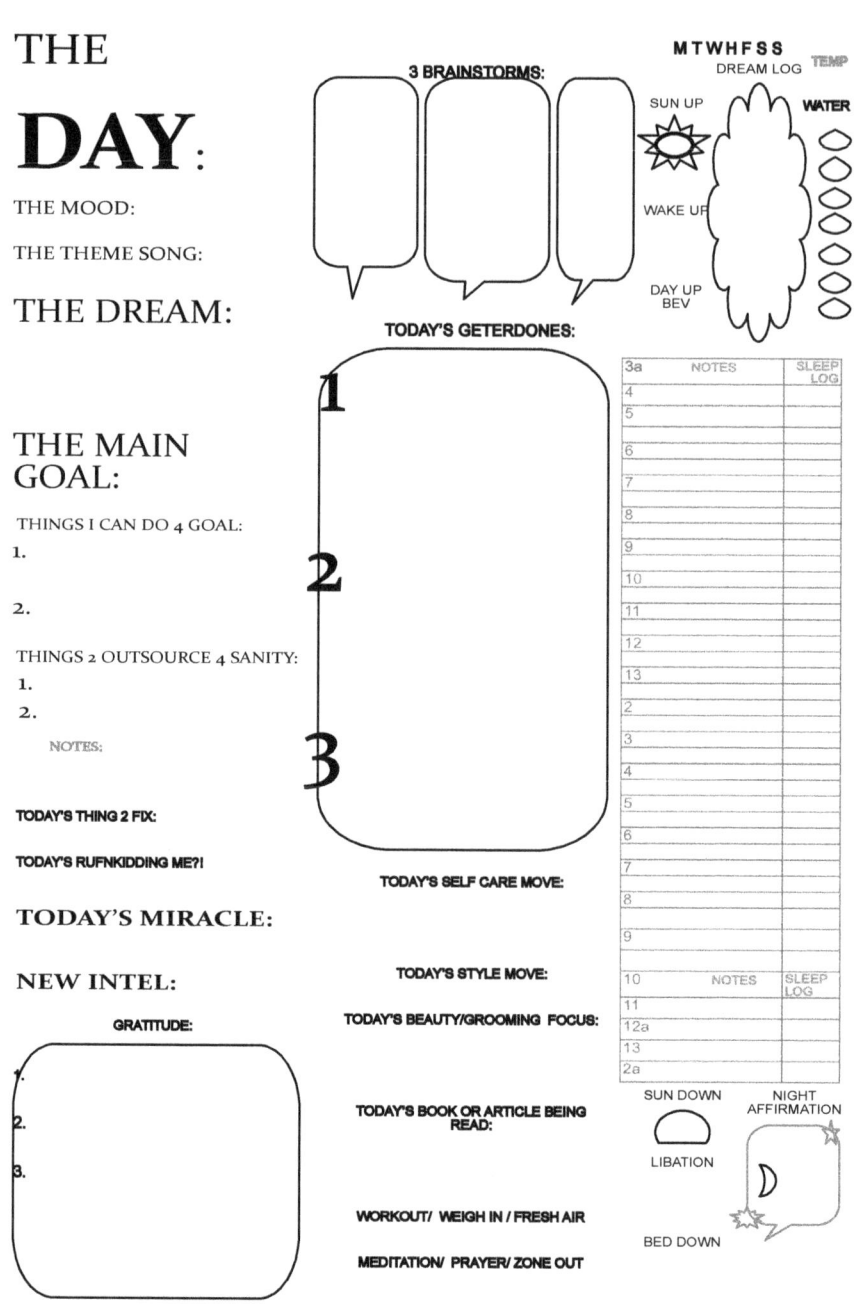

THE pregaming:

THE recap:

THE DAY:

THE MOOD:

THE THEME SONG:

THE DREAM:

THE MAIN GOAL:

THINGS I CAN DO 4 GOAL:
1.
2.

THINGS 2 OUTSOURCE 4 SANITY:
1.
2.

NOTES:

TODAY'S THING 2 FIX:

TODAY'S RUFNKIDDING ME?!

TODAY'S MIRACLE:

NEW INTEL:

GRATITUDE:
1.
2.
3.

3 BRAINSTORMS:

TODAY'S GETERDONES:
1
2
3

TODAY'S SELF CARE MOVE:

TODAY'S STYLE MOVE:

TODAY'S BEAUTY/GROOMING FOCUS:

TODAY'S BOOK OR ARTICLE BEING READ:

WORKOUT/ WEIGH IN / FRESH AIR

MEDITATION/ PRAYER/ ZONE OUT

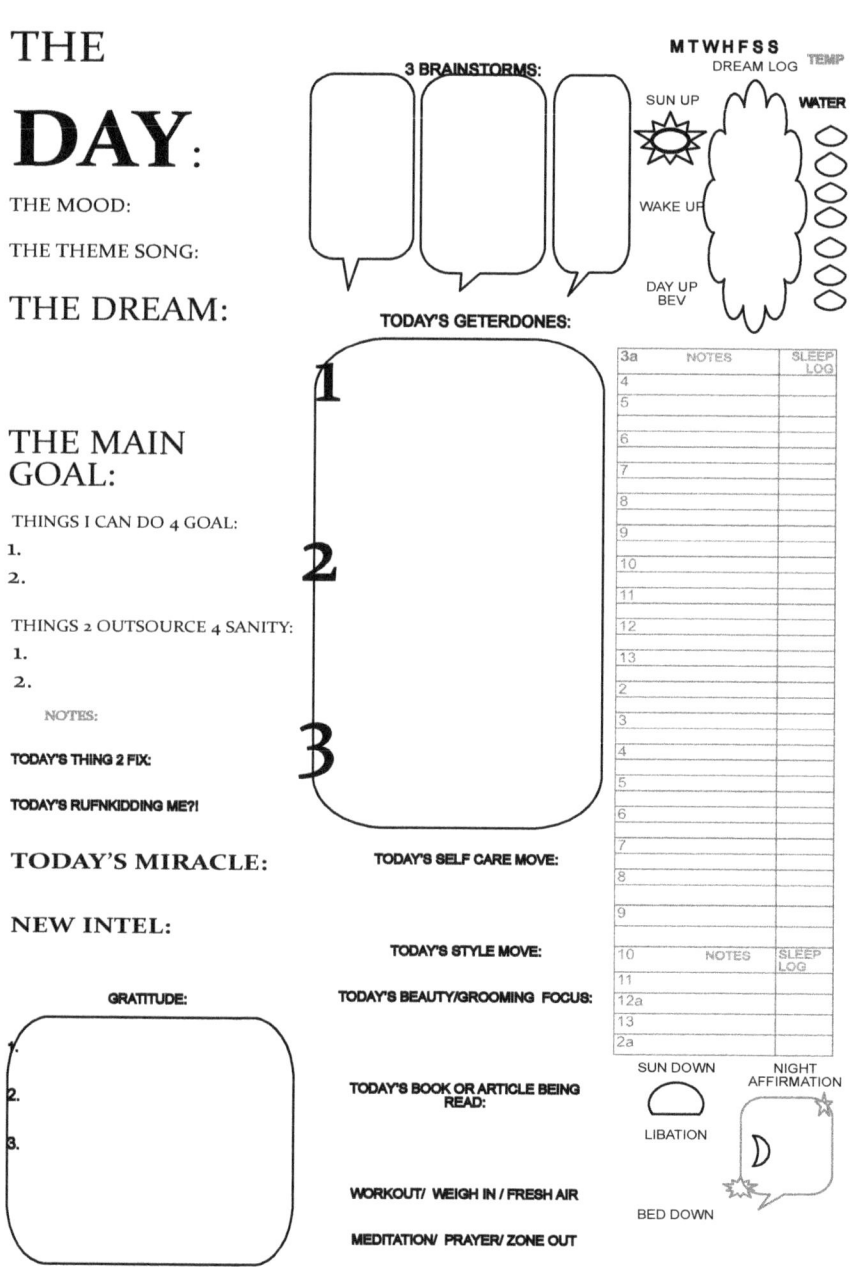

M T W H F S S
DREAM LOG   TEMP
SUN UP   WATER
WAKE UP
DAY UP BEV

3a	NOTES	SLEEP LOG
4		
5		
6		
7		
8		
9		
10		
11		
12		
13		
2		
3		
4		
5		
6		
7		
8		
9		
10	NOTES	SLEEP LOG
11		
12a		
13		
2a		

SUN DOWN   NIGHT AFFIRMATION

LIBATION

BED DOWN

THE pregaming:

THE recap:

THE
DAY:

THE MOOD:

THE THEME SONG:

THE DREAM:

THE MAIN GOAL:

THINGS I CAN DO 4 GOAL:
1.

2.

THINGS 2 OUTSOURCE 4 SANITY:
1.
2.

NOTES:

TODAY'S THING 2 FIX:

TODAY'S RUFNKIDDING ME?!

TODAY'S MIRACLE:

NEW INTEL:

GRATITUDE:

1.

2.

3.

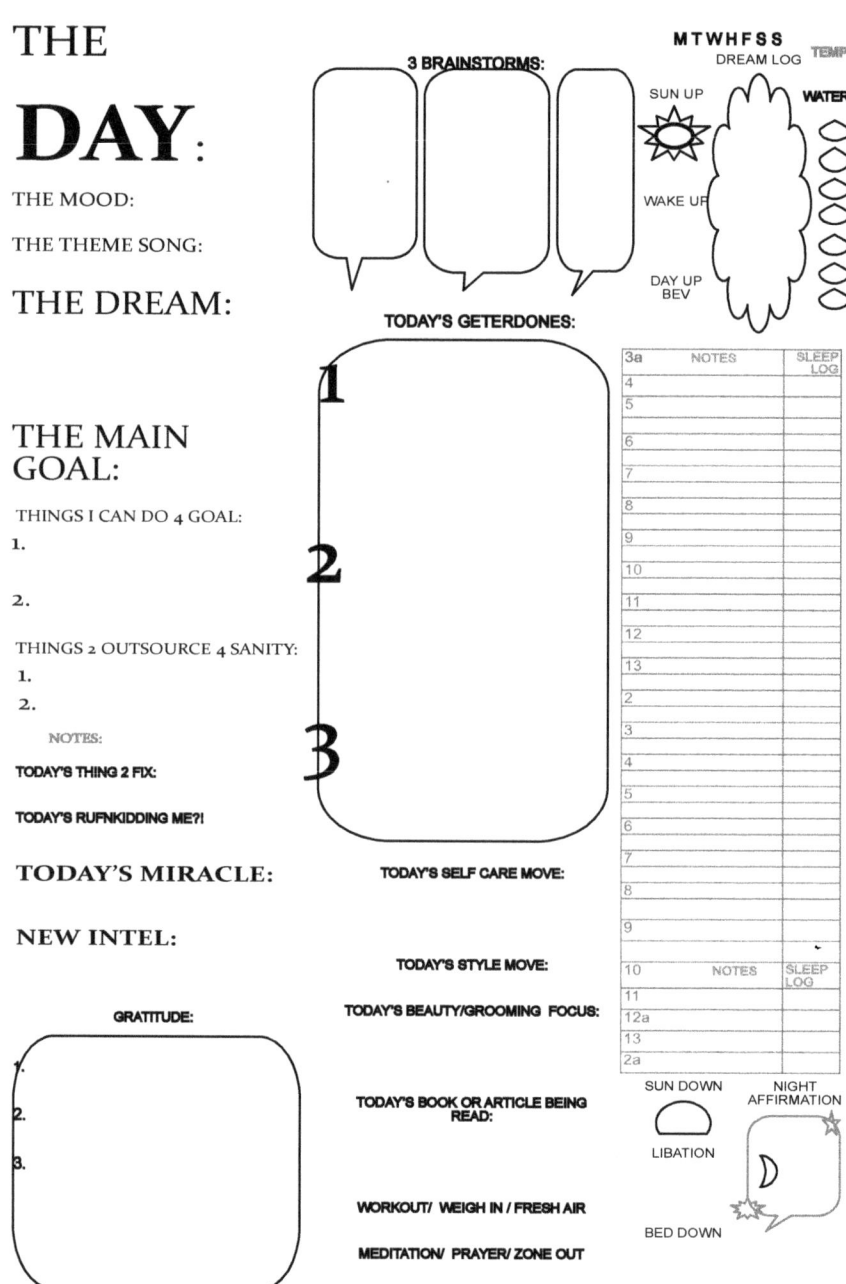

3 BRAINSTORMS:

TODAY'S GETERDONES:

1

2

3

TODAY'S SELF CARE MOVE:

TODAY'S STYLE MOVE:

TODAY'S BEAUTY/GROOMING FOCUS:

TODAY'S BOOK OR ARTICLE BEING READ:

WORKOUT/ WEIGH IN / FRESH AIR

MEDITATION/ PRAYER/ ZONE OUT

M T W H F S S
DREAM LOG   TEMP
SUN UP   WATER
WAKE UP
DAY UP BEV

3a	NOTES	SLEEP LOG
4		
5		
6		
7		
8		
9		
10		
11		
12		
13		
2		
3		
4		
5		
6		
7		
8		
9		
10	NOTES	SLEEP LOG
11		
12a		
13		
2a		

SUN DOWN   NIGHT AFFIRMATION

LIBATION

BED DOWN

THE
pregaming:

THE recap:

THE
DAY:

THE MOOD:

THE THEME SONG:

THE DREAM:

THE MAIN GOAL:

THINGS I CAN DO 4 GOAL:
1.

2.

THINGS 2 OUTSOURCE 4 SANITY:
1.
2.

NOTES:

TODAY'S THING 2 FIX:

TODAY'S RUFNKIDDING ME?!

TODAY'S MIRACLE:

NEW INTEL:

GRATITUDE:
1.
2.
3.

3 BRAINSTORMS:

TODAY'S GETERDONES:
1
2
3

TODAY'S SELF CARE MOVE:

TODAY'S STYLE MOVE:

TODAY'S BEAUTY/ GROOMING FOCUS:

TODAY'S BOOK OR ARTICLE BEING READ:

WORKOUT/ WEIGH IN / FRESH AIR

MEDITATION/ PRAYER/ ZONE OUT

M T W H F S S
DREAM LOG   TEMP
SUN UP
WAKE UP
DAY UP BEV
WATER

NOTES | SLEEP LOG
3a
4
5
6
7
8
9
10
11
12
13
2
3
4
5
6
7
8
9
10 NOTES SLEEP LOG
11
12a
13
2a

SUN DOWN
LIBATION
BED DOWN

NIGHT AFFIRMATION

THE
pregaming:

THE recap:

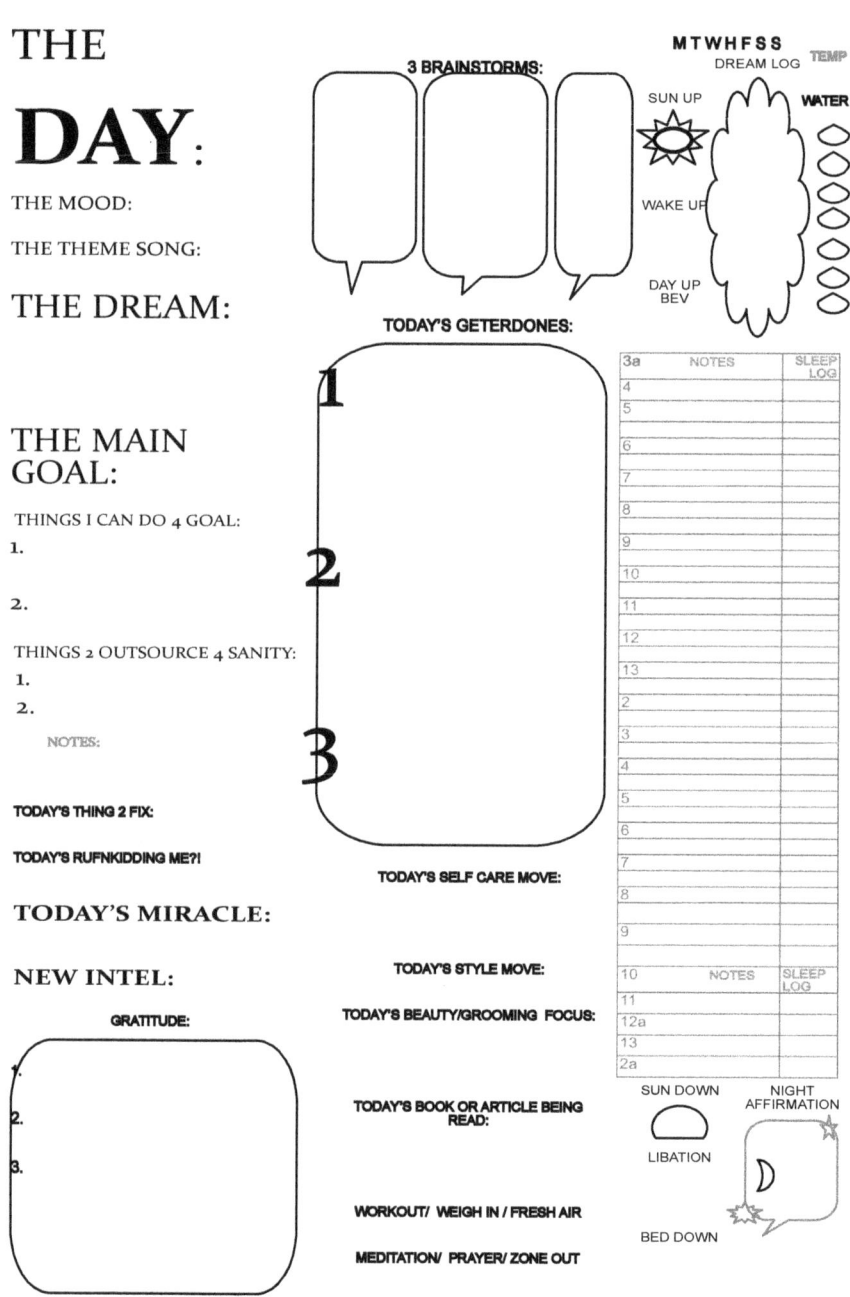

THE
pregaming:

THE recap:

THE
pregaming:

THE recap:

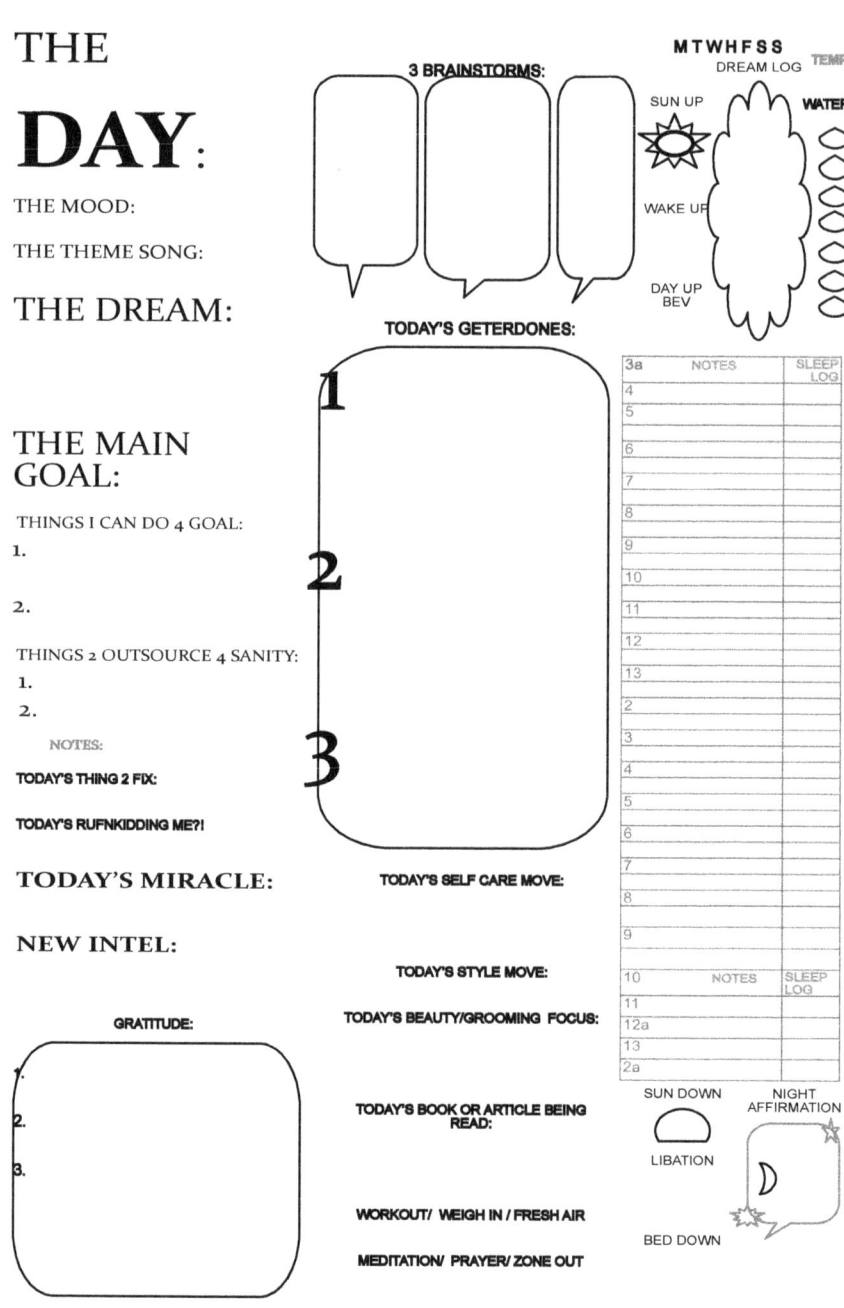

THE
pregaming:

THE recap:

THE
DAY:

THE MOOD:

THE THEME SONG:

THE DREAM:

THE MAIN GOAL:

THINGS I CAN DO 4 GOAL:
1.

2.

THINGS 2 OUTSOURCE 4 SANITY:
1.
2.

NOTES:

TODAY'S THING 2 FIX:

TODAY'S RUFNKIDDING ME?!

TODAY'S MIRACLE:

NEW INTEL:

GRATITUDE:

1.

2.

3.

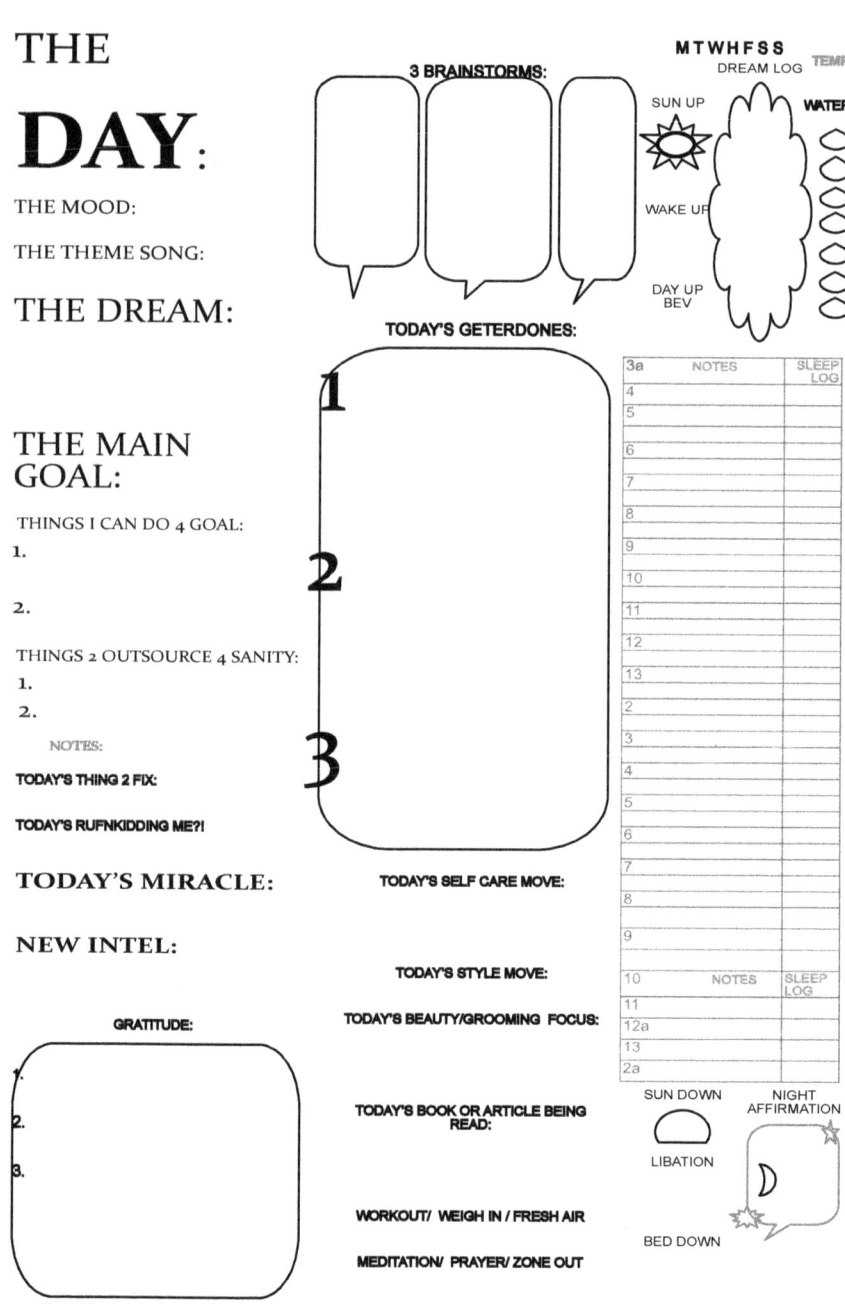

3 BRAINSTORMS:

TODAY'S GETERDONES:

1

2

3

TODAY'S SELF CARE MOVE:

TODAY'S STYLE MOVE:

TODAY'S BEAUTY/GROOMING FOCUS:

TODAY'S BOOK OR ARTICLE BEING READ:

WORKOUT/ WEIGH IN / FRESH AIR

MEDITATION/ PRAYER/ ZONE OUT

M T W H F S S
DREAM LOG   TEMP
SUN UP   WATER

WAKE UP

DAY UP BEV

3a	NOTES	SLEEP LOG
4		
5		
6		
7		
8		
9		
10		
11		
12		
13		
2		
3		
4		
5		
6		
7		
8		
9		
10	NOTES	SLEEP LOG
11		
12a		
13		
2a		

SUN DOWN   NIGHT AFFIRMATION

LIBATION

BED DOWN

THE
pregaming:

THE recap:

THE DAY:

THE MOOD:

THE THEME SONG:

THE DREAM:

THE MAIN GOAL:

THINGS I CAN DO 4 GOAL:
1.
2.

THINGS 2 OUTSOURCE 4 SANITY:
1.
2.

NOTES:

TODAY'S THING 2 FIX:

TODAY'S RUFNKIDDING ME?!

TODAY'S MIRACLE:

NEW INTEL:

GRATITUDE:
1.
2.
3.

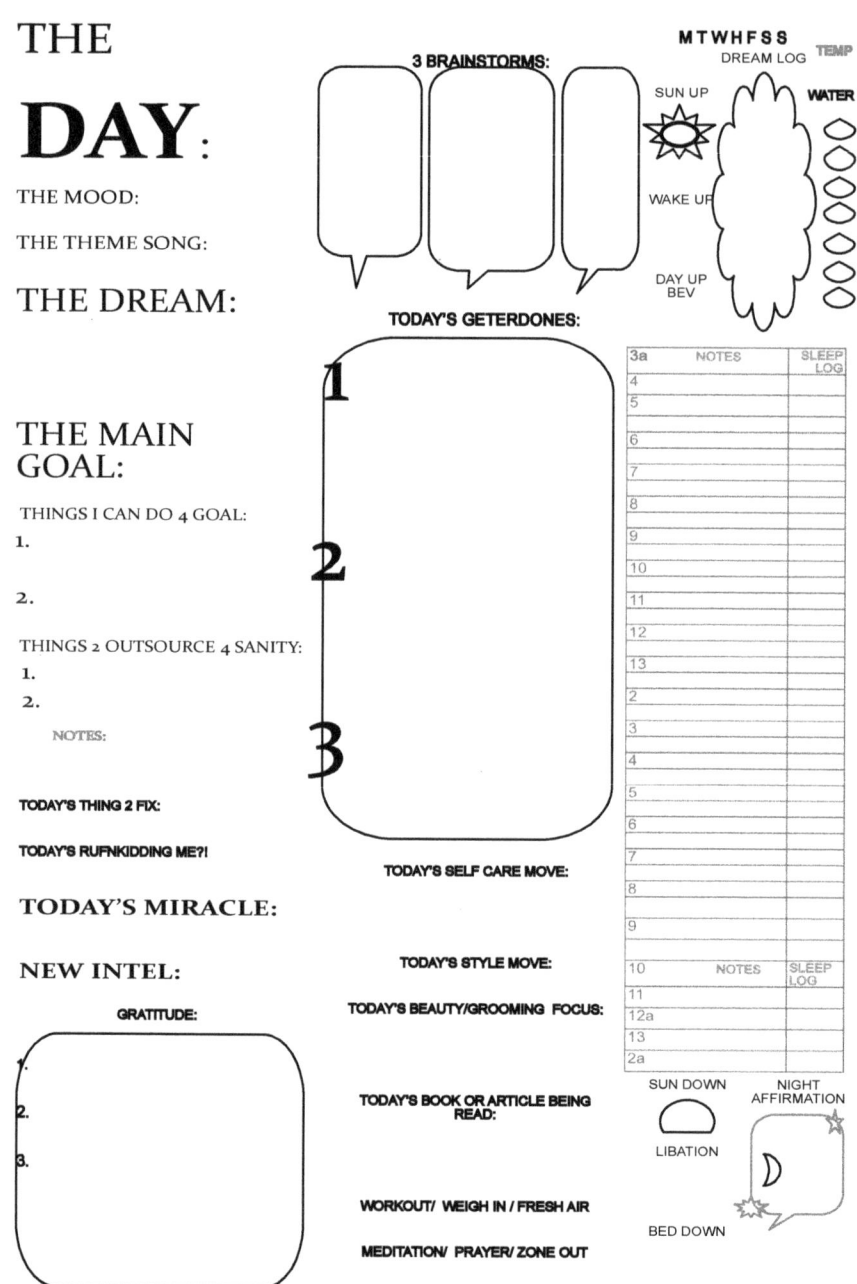

3 BRAINSTORMS:

TODAY'S GETERDONES:
1
2
3

TODAY'S SELF CARE MOVE:

TODAY'S STYLE MOVE:

TODAY'S BEAUTY/GROOMING FOCUS:

TODAY'S BOOK OR ARTICLE BEING READ:

WORKOUT/ WEIGH IN / FRESH AIR

MEDITATION/ PRAYER/ ZONE OUT

M T W H F S S
DREAM LOG   TEMP
SUN UP
WAKE UP
DAY UP
BEV
WATER

SLEEP LOG

NOTES

3a
4
5
6
7
8
9
10
11
12
13
2
3
4
5
6
7
8
9
10 NOTES SLEEP LOG
11
12a
13
2a

SUN DOWN
LIBATION
BED DOWN
NIGHT AFFIRMATION

THE
pregaming:

THE recap:

THE DAY:

THE MOOD:

THE THEME SONG:

THE DREAM:

THE MAIN GOAL:

THINGS I CAN DO 4 GOAL:
1.
2.

THINGS 2 OUTSOURCE 4 SANITY:
1.
2.

   NOTES:

TODAY'S THING 2 FIX:

TODAY'S RUFNKIDDING ME?!

TODAY'S MIRACLE:

NEW INTEL:

GRATITUDE:
1.
2.
3.

3 BRAINSTORMS:

TODAY'S GETERDONES:
1
2
3

TODAY'S SELF CARE MOVE:

TODAY'S STYLE MOVE:

TODAY'S BEAUTY/GROOMING FOCUS:

TODAY'S BOOK OR ARTICLE BEING READ:

WORKOUT/ WEIGH IN / FRESH AIR

MEDITATION/ PRAYER/ ZONE OUT

M T W H F S S TEMP
DREAM LOG

SUN UP
WAKE UP
DAY UP BEV

WATER

3a	NOTES	SLEEP LOG
4		
5		
6		
7		
8		
9		
10		
11		
12		
13		
2		
3		
4		
5		
6		
7		
8		
9		
10	NOTES	SLEEP LOG
11		
12a		
13		
2a		

SUN DOWN
LIBATION
BED DOWN
NIGHT AFFIRMATION

THE
pregaming:

THE recap:

THE
DAY:

THE MOOD:

THE THEME SONG:

THE DREAM:

THE MAIN GOAL:

THINGS I CAN DO 4 GOAL:
1.

2.

THINGS 2 OUTSOURCE 4 SANITY:
1.
2.

NOTES:

TODAY'S THING 2 FIX:

TODAY'S RUFNKIDDING ME?!

TODAY'S MIRACLE:

NEW INTEL:

GRATITUDE:

1.

2.

3.

THE
pregaming:

THE recap:

THE DAY:

THE MOOD:

THE THEME SONG:

THE DREAM:

THE MAIN GOAL:

THINGS I CAN DO 4 GOAL:
1.

2.

THINGS 2 OUTSOURCE 4 SANITY:
1.
2.

NOTES:

TODAY'S THING 2 FIX:

TODAY'S RUFNKIDDING ME?!

TODAY'S MIRACLE:

NEW INTEL:

GRATITUDE:

1.

2.

3.

3 BRAINSTORMS:

TODAY'S GETERDONES:

1

2

3

TODAY'S SELF CARE MOVE:

TODAY'S STYLE MOVE:

TODAY'S BEAUTY/GROOMING FOCUS:

TODAY'S BOOK OR ARTICLE BEING READ:

WORKOUT/ WEIGH IN / FRESH AIR

MEDITATION/ PRAYER/ ZONE OUT

M T W H F S S
DREAM LOG   TEMP

SUN UP

WAKE UP

DAY UP BEV

WATER

3a	NOTES	SLEEP LOG
4		
5		
6		
7		
8		
9		
10		
11		
12		
13		
2		
3		
4		
5		
6		
7		
8		
9		
10	NOTES	SLEEP LOG
11		
12a		
13		
2a		

SUN DOWN

LIBATION

NIGHT AFFIRMATION

BED DOWN

THE
pregaming:

THE recap:

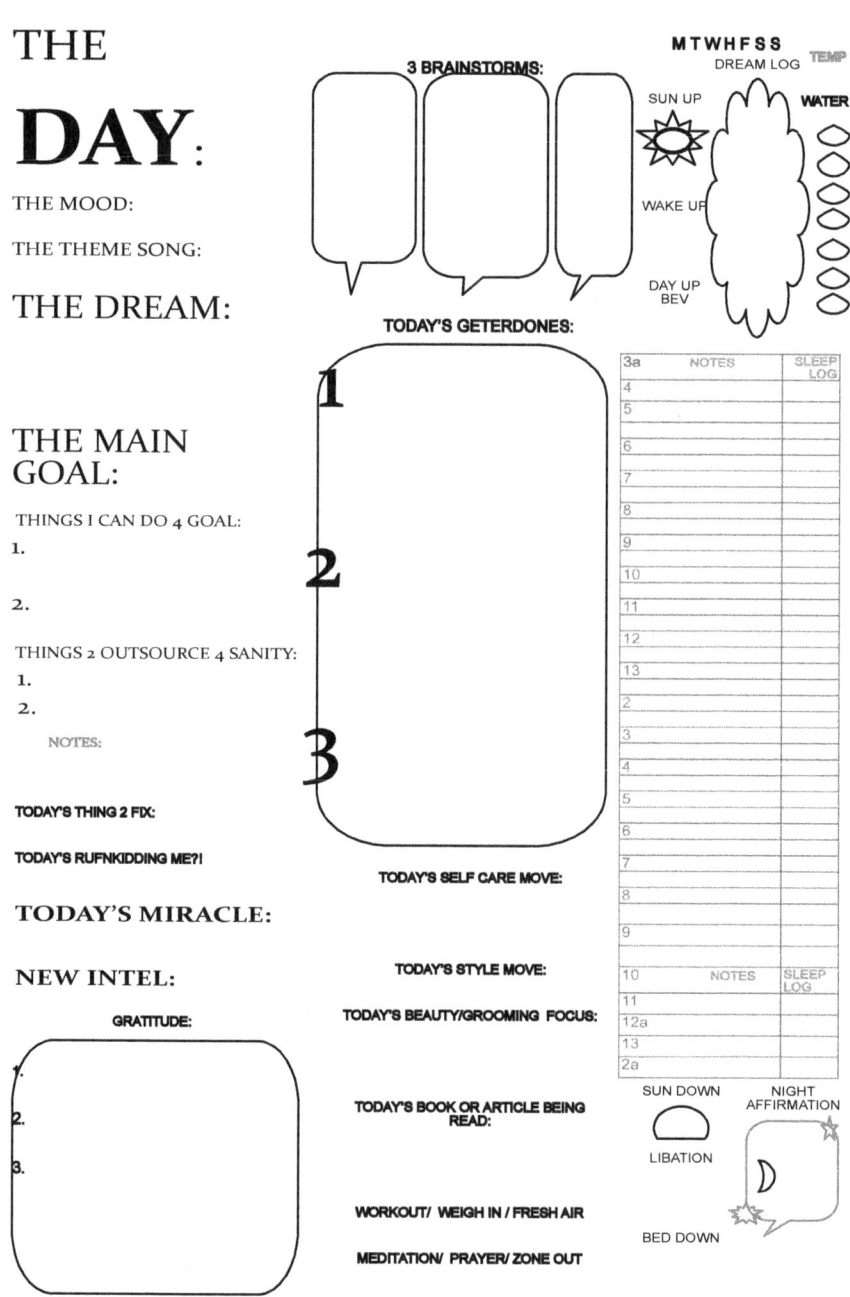

THE
pregaming:

THE recap:

THE
DAY:

THE MOOD:

THE THEME SONG:

THE DREAM:

THE MAIN GOAL:

THINGS I CAN DO 4 GOAL:
1.
2.

THINGS 2 OUTSOURCE 4 SANITY:
1.
2.

  NOTES:

TODAY'S THING 2 FIX:

TODAY'S RUFNKIDDING ME?!

TODAY'S MIRACLE:

NEW INTEL:

GRATITUDE:

1.
2.
3.

3 BRAINSTORMS:

TODAY'S GETERDONES:

1
2
3

TODAY'S SELF CARE MOVE:

TODAY'S STYLE MOVE:

TODAY'S BEAUTY/GROOMING FOCUS:

TODAY'S BOOK OR ARTICLE BEING READ:

WORKOUT/ WEIGH IN / FRESH AIR

MEDITATION/ PRAYER/ ZONE OUT

M T W H F S S
DREAM LOG   TEMP

SUN UP

WAKE UP

DAY UP BEV

WATER

3a	NOTES	SLEEP LOG
4		
5		
6		
7		
8		
9		
10		
11		
12		
13		
2		
3		
4		
5		
6		
7		
8		
9		
10	NOTES	SLEEP LOG
11		
12a		
13		
2a		

SUN DOWN

LIBATION

BED DOWN

NIGHT AFFIRMATION

THE
pregaming:

THE recap:

THE
pregaming:

THE recap:

THE
DAY:

THE MOOD:

THE THEME SONG:

THE DREAM:

THE MAIN GOAL:

THINGS I CAN DO 4 GOAL:
1.

2.

THINGS 2 OUTSOURCE 4 SANITY:
1.
2.

NOTES:

TODAY'S THING 2 FIX:

TODAY'S RUFNKIDDING ME?!

TODAY'S MIRACLE:

NEW INTEL:

GRATITUDE:

1.

2.

3.

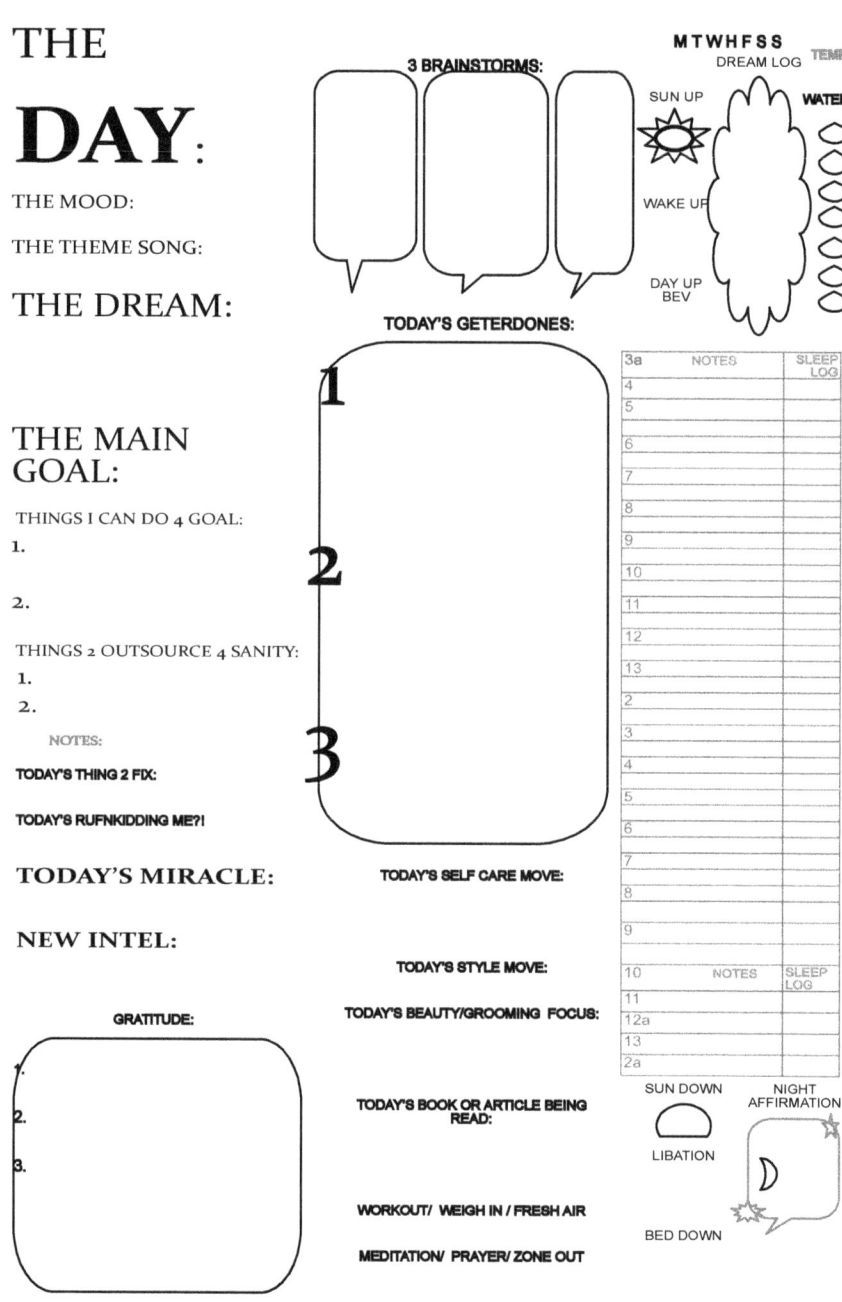

3 BRAINSTORMS:

TODAY'S GETERDONES:

1

2

3

TODAY'S SELF CARE MOVE:

TODAY'S STYLE MOVE:

TODAY'S BEAUTY/GROOMING FOCUS:

TODAY'S BOOK OR ARTICLE BEING READ:

WORKOUT/ WEIGH IN / FRESH AIR

MEDITATION/ PRAYER/ ZONE OUT

M T W H F S S
DREAM LOG   TEMP
SUN UP
WATER
WAKE UP
DAY UP BEV

3a	NOTES	SLEEP LOG
4		
5		
6		
7		
8		
9		
10		
11		
12		
13		
2		
3		
4		
5		
6		
7		
8		
9		
10	NOTES	SLEEP LOG
11		
12a		
13		
2a		

SUN DOWN   NIGHT AFFIRMATION

LIBATION

BED DOWN

THE
pregaming:

THE recap:

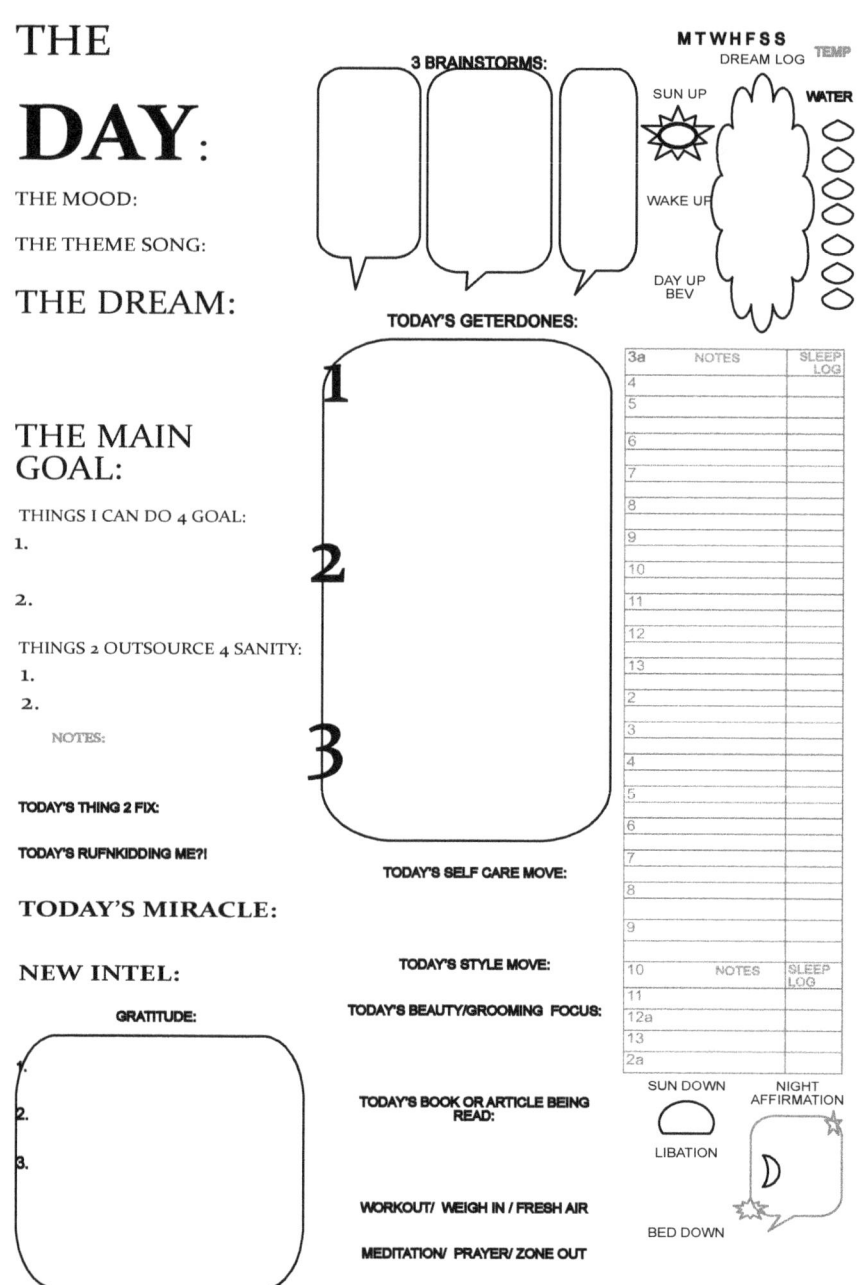

THE
DAY:

THE MOOD:

THE THEME SONG:

THE DREAM:

THE MAIN GOAL:

THINGS I CAN DO 4 GOAL:
1.
2.

THINGS 2 OUTSOURCE 4 SANITY:
1.
2.

NOTES:

TODAY'S THING 2 FIX:

TODAY'S RUFNKIDDING ME?!

TODAY'S MIRACLE:

NEW INTEL:

GRATITUDE:
1.
2.
3.

THE
pregaming:

THE recap:

THE DAY:

THE MOOD:

THE THEME SONG:

THE DREAM:

THE MAIN GOAL:

THINGS I CAN DO 4 GOAL:
1.
2.

THINGS 2 OUTSOURCE 4 SANITY:
1.
2.

NOTES:

TODAY'S THING 2 FIX:

TODAY'S RUFNKIDDING ME?!

TODAY'S MIRACLE:

NEW INTEL:

GRATITUDE:
1.
2.
3.

3 BRAINSTORMS:

TODAY'S GETERDONES:
1
2
3

TODAY'S SELF CARE MOVE:

TODAY'S STYLE MOVE:

TODAY'S BEAUTY/GROOMING FOCUS:

TODAY'S BOOK OR ARTICLE BEING READ:

WORKOUT/ WEIGH IN / FRESH AIR

MEDITATION/ PRAYER/ ZONE OUT

M T W H F S S
DREAM LOG TEMP

SUN UP

WAKE UP

DAY UP BEV

WATER

NOTES | SLEEP LOG
3a
4
5
6
7
8
9
10
11
12
13
2
3
4
5
6
7
8
9
10 NOTES SLEEP LOG
11
12a
13
2a

SUN DOWN

LIBATION

BED DOWN

NIGHT AFFIRMATION

THE
pregaming:

THE recap:

THE
DAY:

THE MOOD:

THE THEME SONG:

THE DREAM:

THE MAIN GOAL:

THINGS I CAN DO 4 GOAL:
1.

2.

THINGS 2 OUTSOURCE 4 SANITY:
1.
2.

NOTES:

TODAY'S THING 2 FIX:

TODAY'S RUFNKIDDING ME?!

TODAY'S MIRACLE:

NEW INTEL:

GRATITUDE:

1.
2.
3.

3 BRAINSTORMS:

TODAY'S GETERDONES:

1

2

3

TODAY'S SELF CARE MOVE:

TODAY'S STYLE MOVE:

TODAY'S BEAUTY/GROOMING FOCUS:

TODAY'S BOOK OR ARTICLE BEING READ:

WORKOUT/ WEIGH IN / FRESH AIR

MEDITATION/ PRAYER/ ZONE OUT

M T W H F S S
DREAM LOG TEMP
SUN UP
WATER
WAKE UP
DAY UP BEV

3a	NOTES	SLEEP LOG
4		
5		
6		
7		
8		
9		
10		
11		
12		
13		
2		
3		
4		
5		
6		
7		
8		
9		
10	NOTES	SLEEP LOG
11		
12a		
13		
2a		

SUN DOWN

NIGHT AFFIRMATION

LIBATION

BED DOWN

THE
pregaming:

THE recap:

THE pregaming:

THE recap:

THE
DAY:

THE MOOD:

THE THEME SONG:

THE DREAM:

THE MAIN GOAL:

THINGS I CAN DO 4 GOAL:
1.
2.

THINGS 2 OUTSOURCE 4 SANITY:
1.
2.

NOTES:

TODAY'S THING 2 FIX:

TODAY'S RUFNKIDDING ME?!

TODAY'S MIRACLE:

NEW INTEL:

GRATITUDE:
1.
2.
3.

3 BRAINSTORMS:

TODAY'S GETERDONES:

1

2

3

TODAY'S SELF CARE MOVE:

TODAY'S STYLE MOVE:

TODAY'S BEAUTY/GROOMING FOCUS:

TODAY'S BOOK OR ARTICLE BEING READ:

WORKOUT/ WEIGH IN / FRESH AIR

MEDITATION/ PRAYER/ ZONE OUT

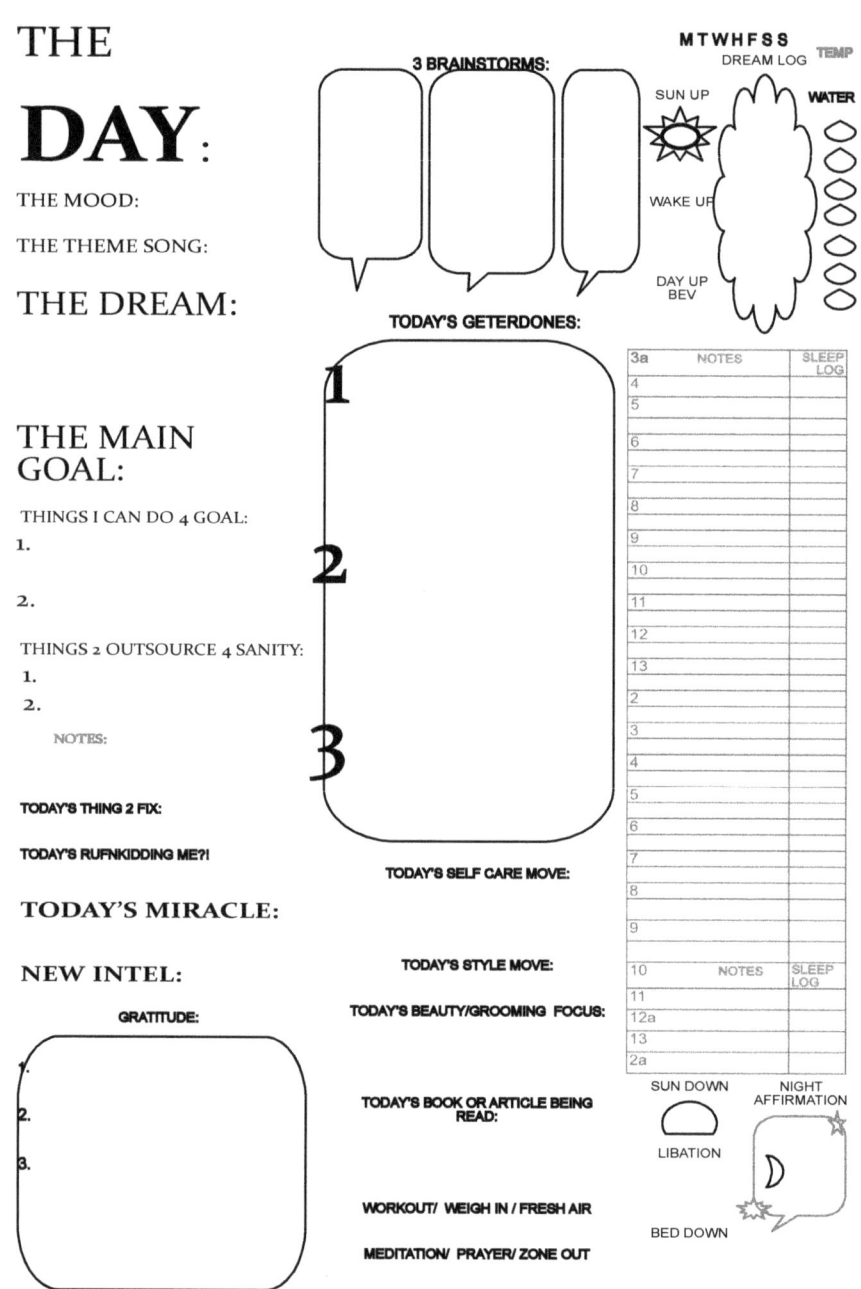

M T W H F S S
DREAM LOG   TEMP
SUN UP   WATER
WAKE UP
DAY UP BEV

NOTES | SLEEP LOG

SUN DOWN   NIGHT AFFIRMATION
LIBATION
BED DOWN

THE
pregaming:

THE recap:

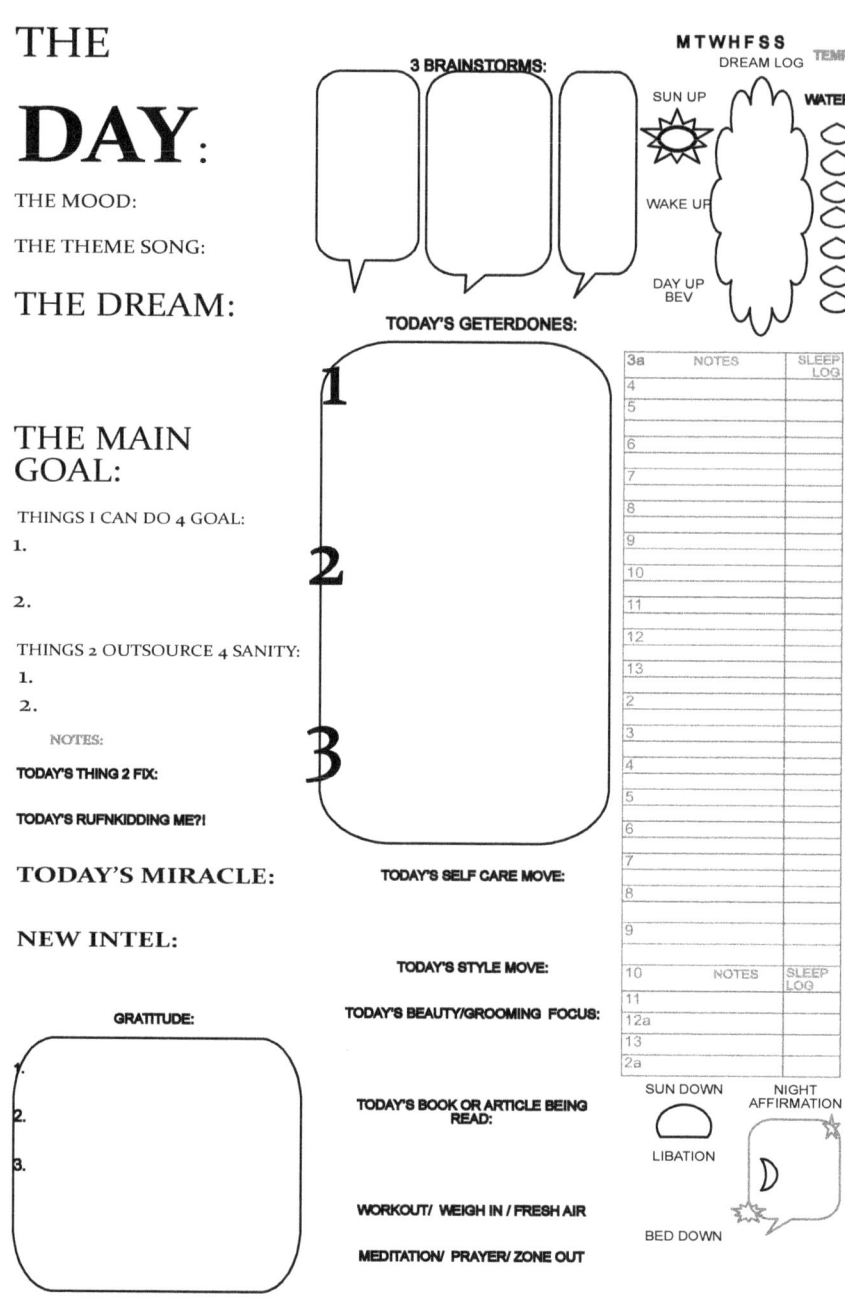

THE
pregaming:

THE recap:

THE
pregaming:

THE recap:

THE DAY:

THE MOOD:

THE THEME SONG:

THE DREAM:

THE MAIN GOAL:

THINGS I CAN DO 4 GOAL:
1.

2.

THINGS 2 OUTSOURCE 4 SANITY:
1.
2.

NOTES:

TODAY'S THING 2 FIX:

TODAY'S RUFNKIDDING ME?!

TODAY'S MIRACLE:

NEW INTEL:

GRATITUDE:
1.
2.
3.

3 BRAINSTORMS:

TODAY'S GETERDONES:
1
2
3

TODAY'S SELF CARE MOVE:

TODAY'S STYLE MOVE:

TODAY'S BEAUTY/GROOMING FOCUS:

TODAY'S BOOK OR ARTICLE BEING READ:

WORKOUT/ WEIGH IN / FRESH AIR

MEDITATION/ PRAYER/ ZONE OUT

M T W H F S S
DREAM LOG   TEMP
SUN UP
WATER
WAKE UP
DAY UP BEV

3a	NOTES	SLEEP LOG
4		
5		
6		
7		
8		
9		
10		
11		
12		
13		
2		
3		
4		
5		
6		
7		
8		
9		
10	NOTES	SLEEP LOG
11		
12a		
13		
2a		

SUN DOWN
LIBATION
BED DOWN
NIGHT AFFIRMATION

THE
pregaming:

THE recap:

THE DAY:

THE MOOD:

THE THEME SONG:

THE DREAM:

THE MAIN GOAL:

THINGS I CAN DO 4 GOAL:
1.
2.

THINGS 2 OUTSOURCE 4 SANITY:
1.
2.

NOTES:

TODAY'S THING 2 FIX:

TODAY'S RUFNKIDDING ME?!

TODAY'S MIRACLE:

NEW INTEL:

GRATITUDE:
1.
2.
3.

3 BRAINSTORMS:

TODAY'S GETERDONES:
1
2
3

TODAY'S SELF CARE MOVE:

TODAY'S STYLE MOVE:

TODAY'S BEAUTY/GROOMING FOCUS:

TODAY'S BOOK OR ARTICLE BEING READ:

WORKOUT/ WEIGH IN / FRESH AIR

MEDITATION/ PRAYER/ ZONE OUT

M T W H F S S
DREAM LOG   TEMP
SUN UP   WATER
WAKE UP
DAY UP BEV

	NOTES	SLEEP LOG
3a		
4		
5		
6		
7		
8		
9		
10		
11		
12		
13		
2		
3		
4		
5		
6		
7		
8		
9		
10	NOTES	SLEEP LOG
11		
12a		
13		
2a		

SUN DOWN   NIGHT AFFIRMATION

LIBATION

BED DOWN

THE
pregaming:

THE recap:

THE
DAY:

THE MOOD:

THE THEME SONG:

THE DREAM:

THE MAIN GOAL:

THINGS I CAN DO 4 GOAL:
1.

2.

THINGS 2 OUTSOURCE 4 SANITY:
1.
2.

NOTES:

TODAY'S THING 2 FIX:

TODAY'S RUFNKIDDING ME?!

TODAY'S MIRACLE:

NEW INTEL:

GRATITUDE:

1.

2.

3.

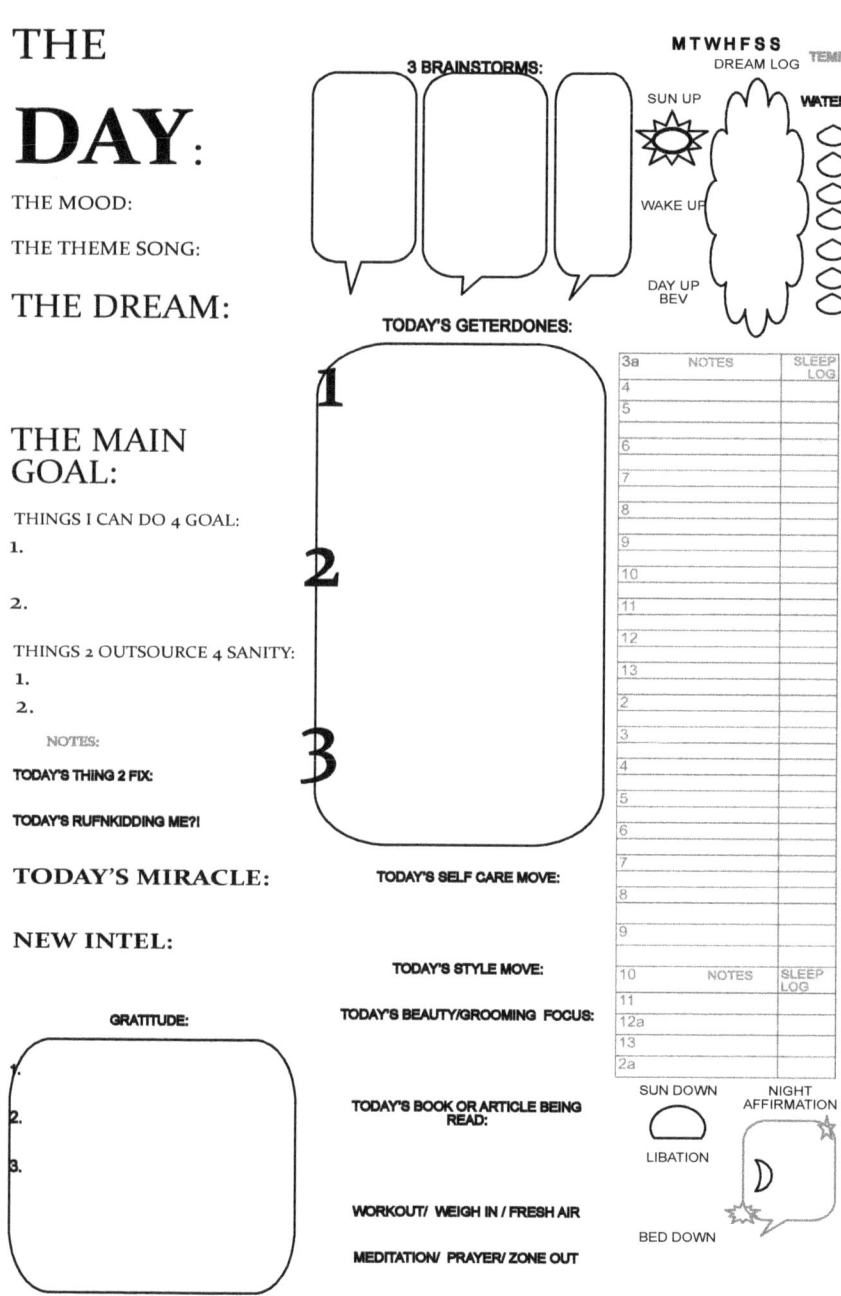

3 BRAINSTORMS:

TODAY'S GETERDONES:

1

2

3

TODAY'S SELF CARE MOVE:

TODAY'S STYLE MOVE:

TODAY'S BEAUTY/GROOMING FOCUS:

TODAY'S BOOK OR ARTICLE BEING READ:

WORKOUT/ WEIGH IN / FRESH AIR

MEDITATION/ PRAYER/ ZONE OUT

M T W H F S S
DREAM LOG TEMP
SUN UP
WAKE UP
DAY UP BEV
WATER

3a	NOTES	SLEEP LOG
4		
5		
6		
7		
8		
9		
10		
11		
12		
13		
2		
3		
4		
5		
6		
7		
8		
9		
10	NOTES	SLEEP LOG
11		
12a		
13		
2a		

SUN DOWN

LIBATION

BED DOWN

NIGHT AFFIRMATION

THE
pregaming:

THE recap:

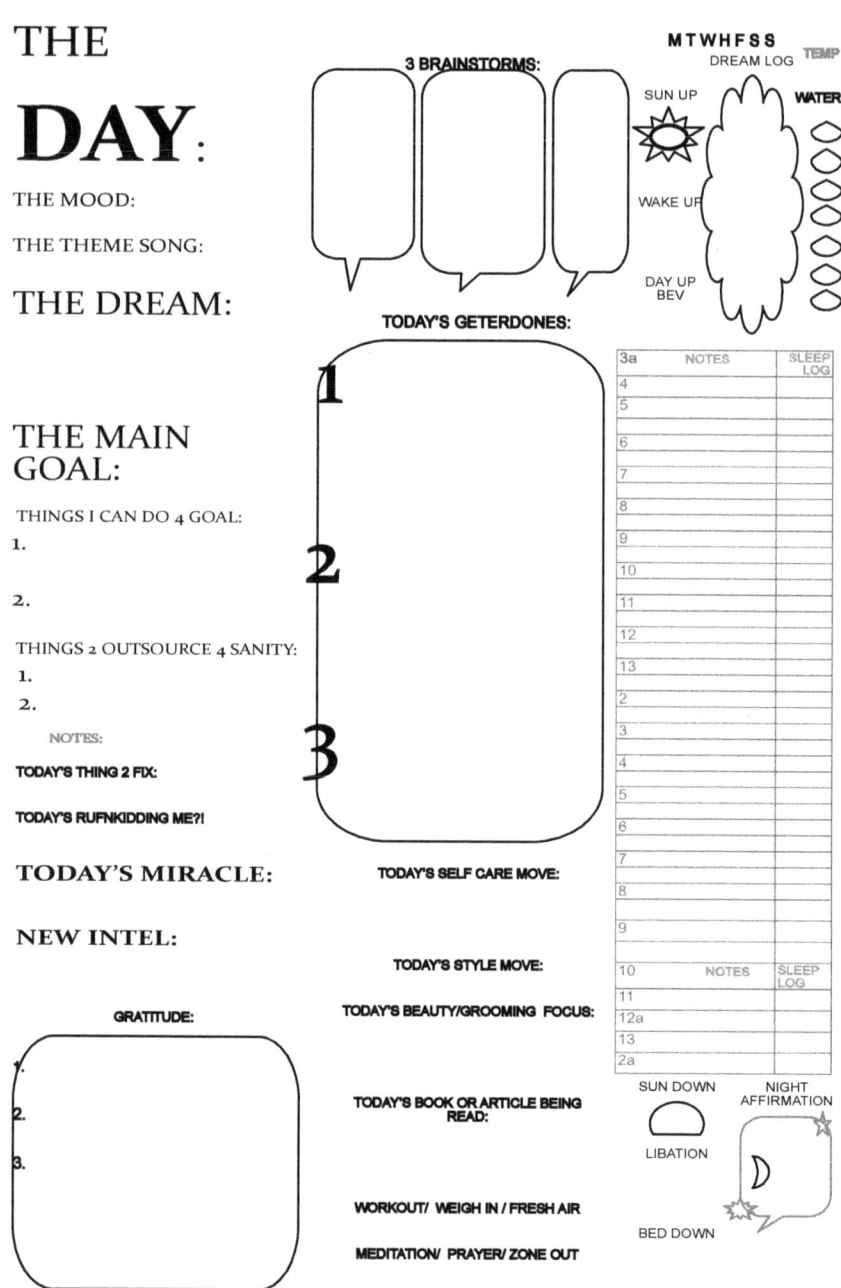

THE
pregaming:

THE recap:

THE
DAY:

THE MOOD:

THE THEME SONG:

THE DREAM:

THE MAIN GOAL:

THINGS I CAN DO 4 GOAL:
1.

2.

THINGS 2 OUTSOURCE 4 SANITY:
1.
2.

   NOTES:

TODAY'S THING 2 FIX:

TODAY'S RUFNKIDDING ME?!

TODAY'S MIRACLE:

NEW INTEL:

GRATITUDE:

1.

2.

3.

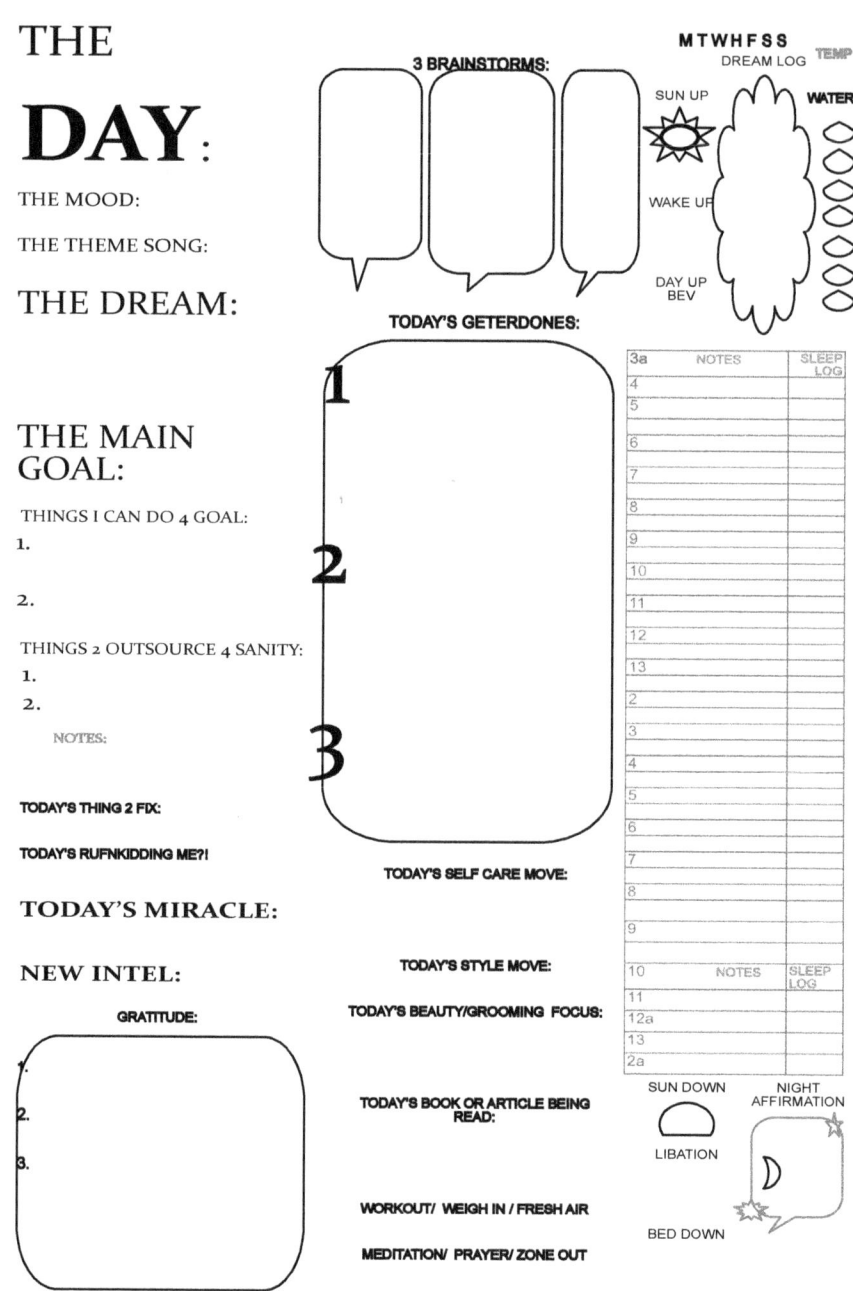

3 BRAINSTORMS:

TODAY'S GETERDONES:

1

2

3

TODAY'S SELF CARE MOVE:

TODAY'S STYLE MOVE:

TODAY'S BEAUTY/GROOMING FOCUS:

TODAY'S BOOK OR ARTICLE BEING READ:

WORKOUT/ WEIGH IN / FRESH AIR

MEDITATION/ PRAYER/ ZONE OUT

MTWHFSS
DREAM LOG   TEMP
SUN UP
WATER
WAKE UP
DAY UP BEV

3a	NOTES	SLEEP LOG
4		
5		
6		
7		
8		
9		
10		
11		
12		
13		
2		
3		
4		
5		
6		
7		
8		
9		
10	NOTES	SLEEP LOG
11		
12a		
13		
2a		

SUN DOWN   NIGHT AFFIRMATION

LIBATION

BED DOWN

THE
pregaming:

THE recap:

THE
DAY:

THE MOOD:

THE THEME SONG:

THE DREAM:

THE MAIN GOAL:

THINGS I CAN DO 4 GOAL:
1.

2.

THINGS 2 OUTSOURCE 4 SANITY:
1.
2.

NOTES:

TODAY'S THING 2 FIX:

TODAY'S RUFNKIDDING ME?!

TODAY'S MIRACLE:

NEW INTEL:

GRATITUDE:

1.

2.

3.

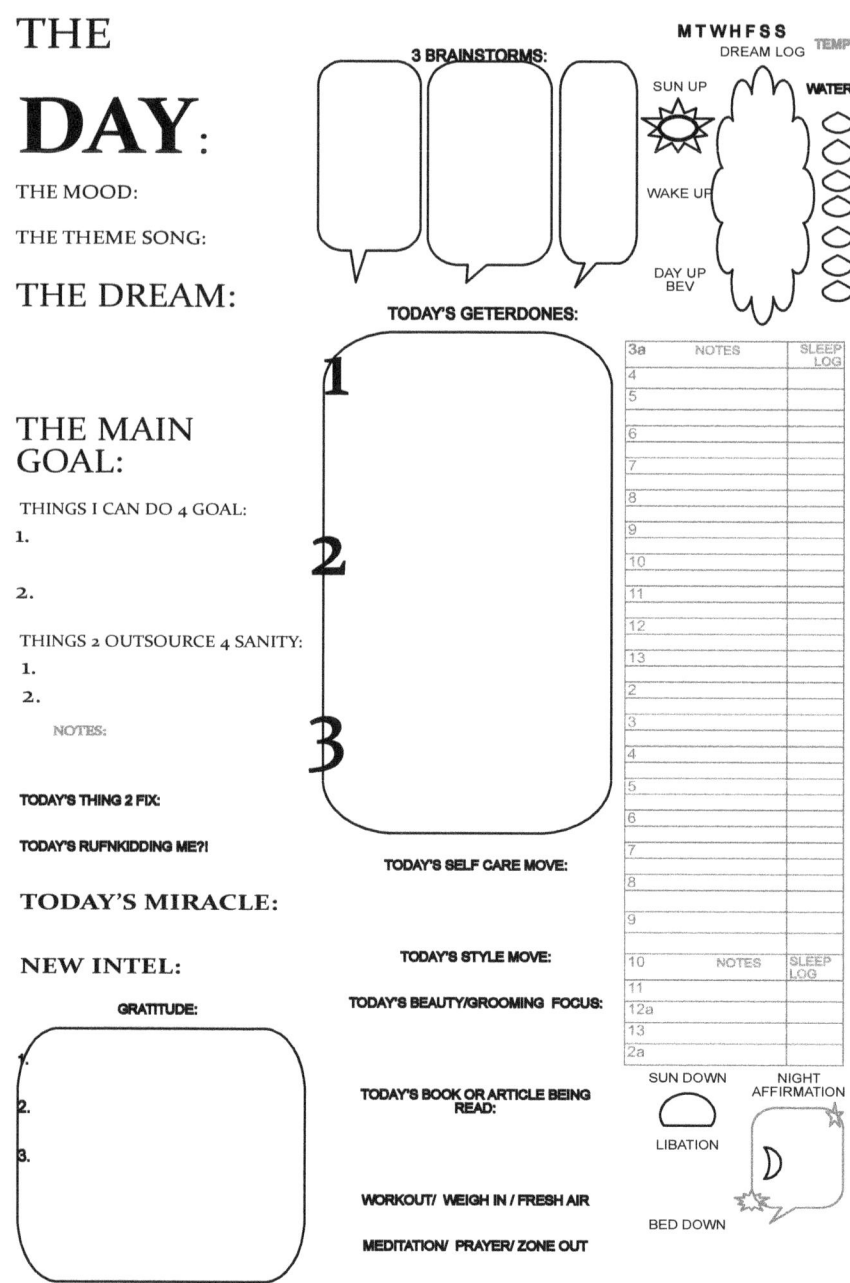

3 BRAINSTORMS:

TODAY'S GETERDONES:
1
2
3

TODAY'S SELF CARE MOVE:

TODAY'S STYLE MOVE:

TODAY'S BEAUTY/GROOMING FOCUS:

TODAY'S BOOK OR ARTICLE BEING READ:

WORKOUT/ WEIGH IN / FRESH AIR

MEDITATION/ PRAYER/ ZONE OUT

M T W H F S S
DREAM LOG   TEMP

SUN UP   WATER

WAKE UP

DAY UP BEV

3a	NOTES	SLEEP LOG
4		
5		
6		
7		
8		
9		
10		
11		
12		
13		
2		
3		
4		
5		
6		
7		
8		
9		
10	NOTES	SLEEP LOG
11		
12a		
13		
2a		

SUN DOWN   NIGHT AFFIRMATION

LIBATION

BED DOWN

THE
pregaming:

THE recap:

THE DAY:

THE MOOD:

THE THEME SONG:

THE DREAM:

THE MAIN GOAL:

THINGS I CAN DO 4 GOAL:
1.
2.

THINGS 2 OUTSOURCE 4 SANITY:
1.
2.

NOTES:

TODAY'S THING 2 FIX:

TODAY'S RUFNKIDDING ME?!

TODAY'S MIRACLE:

NEW INTEL:

GRATITUDE:
1.
2.
3.

3 BRAINSTORMS:

TODAY'S GETERDONES:
1
2
3

TODAY'S SELF CARE MOVE:

TODAY'S STYLE MOVE:

TODAY'S BEAUTY/GROOMING FOCUS:

TODAY'S BOOK OR ARTICLE BEING READ:

WORKOUT/ WEIGH IN / FRESH AIR

MEDITATION/ PRAYER/ ZONE OUT

M T W H F S S
DREAM LOG   TEMP

SUN UP   WATER

WAKE UP

DAY UP BEV

3a	NOTES	SLEEP LOG
4		
5		
6		
7		
8		
9		
10		
11		
12		
13		
2		
3		
4		
5		
6		
7		
8		
9		
10	NOTES	SLEEP LOG
11		
12a		
13		
2a		

SUN DOWN   NIGHT AFFIRMATION

LIBATION

BED DOWN

THE
pregaming:

THE recap:

THE
DAY:

THE MOOD:

THE THEME SONG:

THE DREAM:

THE MAIN GOAL:

THINGS I CAN DO 4 GOAL:
1.

2.

THINGS 2 OUTSOURCE 4 SANITY:
1.
2.

NOTES:

TODAY'S THING 2 FIX:

TODAY'S RUFNKIDDING ME?!

TODAY'S MIRACLE:

NEW INTEL:

GRATITUDE:
1.
2.
3.

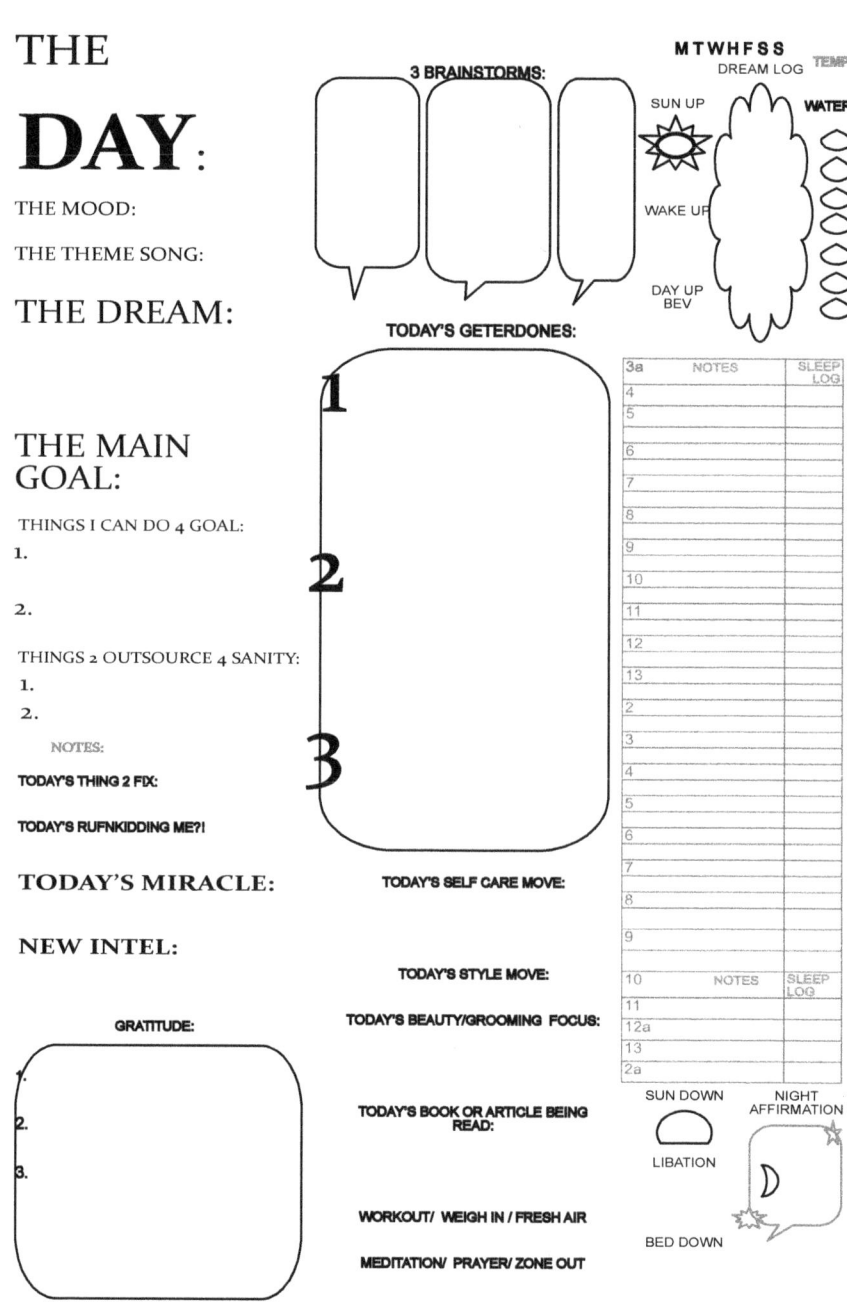

3 BRAINSTORMS:

TODAY'S GETERDONES:
1
2
3

TODAY'S SELF CARE MOVE:

TODAY'S STYLE MOVE:

TODAY'S BEAUTY/GROOMING FOCUS:

TODAY'S BOOK OR ARTICLE BEING READ:

WORKOUT/ WEIGH IN / FRESH AIR

MEDITATION/ PRAYER/ ZONE OUT

M T W H F S S
DREAM LOG   TEMP
SUN UP   WATER
WAKE UP
DAY UP BEV

3a	NOTES	SLEEP LOG
4		
5		
6		
7		
8		
9		
10		
11		
12		
13		
2		
3		
4		
5		
6		
7		
8		
9		
10	NOTES	SLEEP LOG
11		
12a		
13		
2a		

SUN DOWN   NIGHT AFFIRMATION
LIBATION
BED DOWN

THE
pregaming:

THE recap:

THE DAY:

THE MOOD:

THE THEME SONG:

THE DREAM:

THE MAIN GOAL:

THINGS I CAN DO 4 GOAL:
1.
2.

THINGS 2 OUTSOURCE 4 SANITY:
1.
2.

NOTES:

TODAY'S THING 2 FIX:

TODAY'S RUFNKIDDING ME?!

TODAY'S MIRACLE:

NEW INTEL:

GRATITUDE:
1.
2.
3.

3 BRAINSTORMS:

TODAY'S GETERDONES:
1.
2.
3.

TODAY'S SELF CARE MOVE:

TODAY'S STYLE MOVE:

TODAY'S BEAUTY/GROOMING FOCUS:

TODAY'S BOOK OR ARTICLE BEING READ:

WORKOUT/ WEIGH IN / FRESH AIR

MEDITATION/ PRAYER/ ZONE OUT

M T W H F S S
DREAM LOG TEMP
SUN UP
WAKE UP
DAY UP BEV
WATER

NOTES | SLEEP LOG
3a
4
5
6
7
8
9
10
11
12
13
2
3
4
5
6
7
8
9
10 NOTES SLEEP LOG
11
12a
13
2a

SUN DOWN
LIBATION
BED DOWN
NIGHT AFFIRMATION

THE
pregaming:

THE recap:

THE DAY:

THE MOOD:

THE THEME SONG:

THE DREAM:

THE MAIN GOAL:

THINGS I CAN DO 4 GOAL:
1.
2.

THINGS 2 OUTSOURCE 4 SANITY:
1.
2.

NOTES:

TODAY'S THING 2 FIX:

TODAY'S RUFNKIDDING ME?!

TODAY'S MIRACLE:

NEW INTEL:

GRATITUDE:
1.
2.
3.

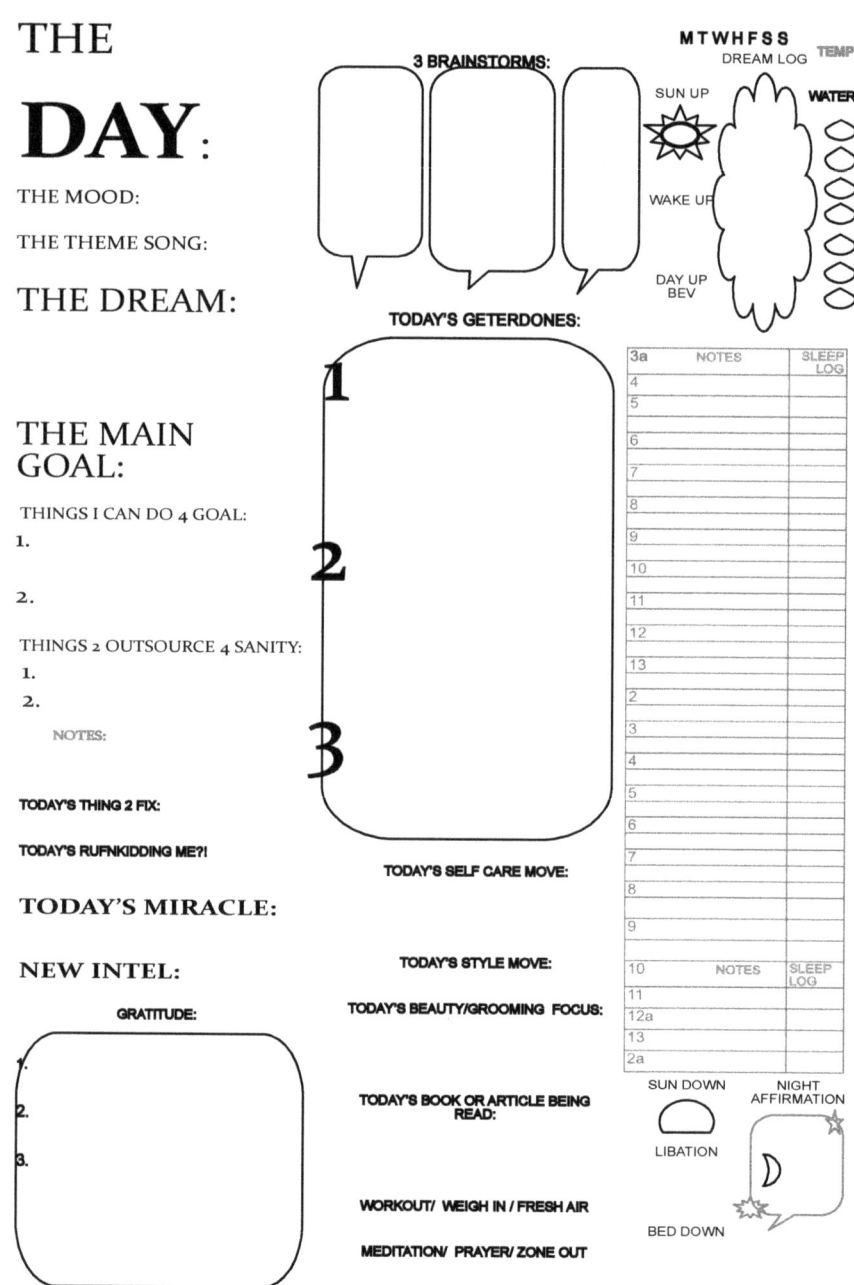

3 BRAINSTORMS:

TODAY'S GETERDONES:
1
2
3

TODAY'S SELF CARE MOVE:

TODAY'S STYLE MOVE:

TODAY'S BEAUTY/GROOMING FOCUS:

TODAY'S BOOK OR ARTICLE BEING READ:

WORKOUT/ WEIGH IN / FRESH AIR

MEDITATION/ PRAYER/ ZONE OUT

M T W H F S S
DREAM LOG   TEMP
SUN UP
WAKE UP
DAY UP BEV
WATER

SLEEP LOG — NOTES
3a, 4, 5, 6, 7, 8, 9, 10, 11, 12, 13, 2, 3, 4, 5, 6, 7, 8, 9, 10, 11, 12a, 13, 2a

SUN DOWN
LIBATION
BED DOWN
NIGHT AFFIRMATION

THE
pregaming:

THE recap:

THE
DAY:

THE MOOD:

THE THEME SONG:

THE DREAM:

THE MAIN GOAL:

THINGS I CAN DO 4 GOAL:
1.

2.

THINGS 2 OUTSOURCE 4 SANITY:
1.
2.

NOTES:

TODAY'S THING 2 FIX:

TODAY'S RUFNKIDDING ME?!

TODAY'S MIRACLE:

NEW INTEL:

GRATITUDE:

1.
2.
3.

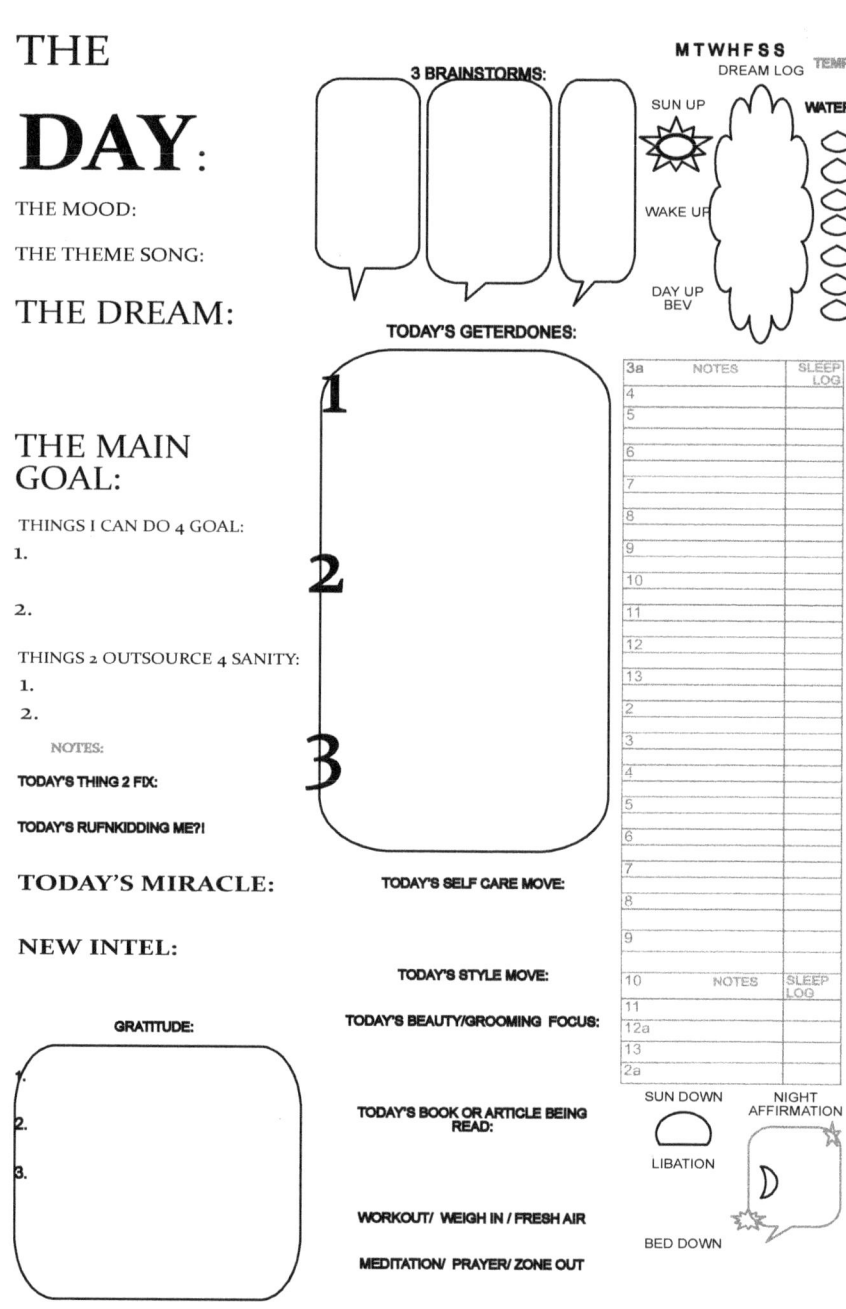

3 BRAINSTORMS:

TODAY'S GETERDONES:
1
2
3

TODAY'S SELF CARE MOVE:

TODAY'S STYLE MOVE:

TODAY'S BEAUTY/GROOMING FOCUS:

TODAY'S BOOK OR ARTICLE BEING READ:

WORKOUT/ WEIGH IN / FRESH AIR

MEDITATION/ PRAYER/ ZONE OUT

M T W H F S S
DREAM LOG   TEMP

SUN UP

WATER

WAKE UP

DAY UP BEV

3a	NOTES	SLEEP LOG
4		
5		
6		
7		
8		
9		
10		
11		
12		
13		
2		
3		
4		
5		
6		
7		
8		
9		
10	NOTES	SLEEP LOG
11		
12a		
13		
2a		

SUN DOWN

LIBATION

BED DOWN

NIGHT AFFIRMATION

THE
pregaming:

THE recap:

THE
DAY:

THE MOOD:

THE THEME SONG:

THE DREAM:

THE MAIN GOAL:

THINGS I CAN DO 4 GOAL:
1.

2.

THINGS 2 OUTSOURCE 4 SANITY:
1.
2.

NOTES:

TODAY'S THING 2 FIX:

TODAY'S RUFNKIDDING ME?!

TODAY'S MIRACLE:

NEW INTEL:

GRATITUDE:

1.

2.

3.

3 BRAINSTORMS:

TODAY'S GETERDONES:
1
2
3

TODAY'S SELF CARE MOVE:

TODAY'S STYLE MOVE:

TODAY'S BEAUTY/ GROOMING FOCUS:

TODAY'S BOOK OR ARTICLE BEING READ:

WORKOUT/ WEIGH IN / FRESH AIR

MEDITATION/ PRAYER/ ZONE OUT

M T W H F S S
DREAM LOG   TEMP
SUN UP
WAKE UP
DAY UP BEV
WATER

3a	NOTES	SLEEP LOG
4		
5		
6		
7		
8		
9		
10		
11		
12		
13		
2		
3		
4		
5		
6		
7		
8		
9		
10	NOTES	SLEEP LOG
11		
12a		
13		
2a		

SUN DOWN
LIBATION
NIGHT AFFIRMATION
BED DOWN

THE
pregaming:

THE recap:

THE
pregaming:

THE recap:

THE
DAY:

THE MOOD:

THE THEME SONG:

THE DREAM:

THE MAIN GOAL:

THINGS I CAN DO 4 GOAL:
1.

2.

THINGS 2 OUTSOURCE 4 SANITY:
1.
2.

NOTES:

TODAY'S THING 2 FIX:

TODAY'S RUFNKIDDING ME?!

TODAY'S MIRACLE:

NEW INTEL:

GRATITUDE:

1.
2.
3.

3 BRAINSTORMS:

TODAY'S GETERDONES:

1
2
3

TODAY'S SELF CARE MOVE:

TODAY'S STYLE MOVE:

TODAY'S BEAUTY/ GROOMING FOCUS:

TODAY'S BOOK OR ARTICLE BEING READ:

WORKOUT/ WEIGH IN / FRESH AIR

MEDITATION/ PRAYER/ ZONE OUT

M T W H F S S
DREAM LOG   TEMP
SUN UP   WATER
WAKE UP
DAY UP BEV

3a NOTES SLEEP LOG
4
5
6
7
8
9
10
11
12
13
2
3
4
5
6
7
8
9
10 NOTES SLEEP LOG
11
12a
13
2a

SUN DOWN   NIGHT AFFIRMATION

LIBATION

BED DOWN

THE
pregaming:

THE recap:

1	
2	
3	
4	
5	
6	
7	
8	
9	
10	
11	
12	
13	
14	
15	
16	
17	
18	
19	
20	
21	
22	
23	
24	
25	
26	
27	
28	
29	
30	
31	
date	Gratitude LOG

MONTH TWO.

JUST4FUN

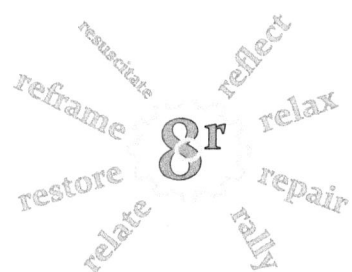

resuscitate
reflect
reframe
relax
8r
restore
repair
relate
rally

Recalibrate.
Rebrand.
Revamp.
Redo.
Recast.

Revise your reality.

174		285
369	Vibe	417
528	Tribe [Hertz]:	639
741		852
	963	

START
CYCLE
STOP

START
CYCLE
STOP

SEASON:
HARVEST   AUTUMN
WINTER   SPRING
    SUMMER
Seasonal focus:

NEW MOON:
FULL MOON:

HOLIDAYS:
This month's " I & i" DAY:
This month's "I & i" HOUR:

This month's HIGHEST TIMELINE log-line:

This month's affirmation:

This month's workout focus:

This month's physical challenge:

This month's shower & bathing meditation:

MONTH:
JAN FEB MAR
APR MAY JUN
JUL AUG SEP
OCT NOV DEC

Movie of your life

bigGOAL:
Aim to do's

bigTASK:
Gotta do's

PICK4 Impossible   PICK4 SANCTUARY   PICK4 SELF-CARE
Things 2 try: GETERDONES: GETERDONES:

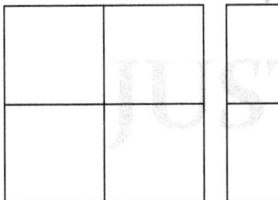
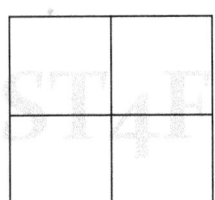
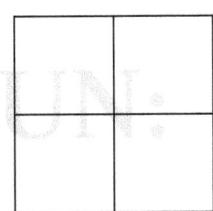

JUST4FUN:

New Moon Resonance

1. Imagine what you aim to Bring into your zone..
2. Set new intentions.
3. Journal & Meditate.
4. Scrub &/or soak your body.
5. Get out in some moonlight.

New/Things 2do.

Things 2do/Full.

1. Cleanse your space [Mental & physical].
2. Crystals! Charge 'em if ya got'em.
3. Celebrate any wins.
4. Release what no longer serves you.
5. Get out in some moonlight.

Full Moon Resonance

WHO ARE YOU   HOW DO YOU EXPRESS IT?

ideal
POINT
OF THE
MONTH:

[NECESSARY]
COUNTERPOINT
OF THE MONTH:

(EVERY POINT HAS A COUNTERPOINT)

ORDERED IN:

PICK 4 MOVIES 2 WATCH:

PICK 4 BOOKS 2 READ:

| THEME SONG | POET | FLOWER |
| COLOR | CRYSTAL | HERB |

Give yourself ONE day a week. One way or another. For you. Find a way.

THIS MONTH'S:
(capsule closet)
[Current rotation]

THIS MONTH'S dayUP Geterdone:

THIS MONTH'S b4BED Geterdone:

BUILD YOU UP BETTER HABIT TO IMPROVE:

GIVE IT UP OR REPLACE ?

WITH WHAT ?　　　HOW ?:

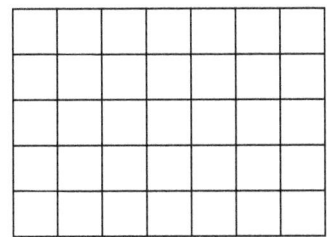

TREAT YOURSELF
Curious about it? LEARN IT

Wish you were able 2 do it? TRY IT

Place you want 2go? GO 2IT

Love to have it outside? TRY IT @HOME

 Otha Dailies

JUST4FUN FOCUS:
THING 2LOVE ABOUT YOU

SPIRIT SUBJECT 2 FOCUS: ON

ODD INTEREST 2DEEP DIVE:

BEAUTY FEATURE/FOCUS:

CLEAN UP NICE FOCUS:

STYLE FOCUS:

SMELL 2 LOVE:

SHAKE THAT ASS!/NOW MOovVE!!

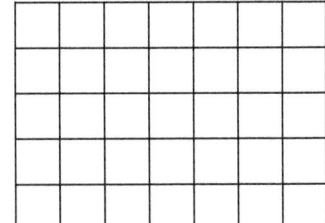

185

FIND/DO SOMETHING BEAUTIFUL

TRAVEL:
SCHEDULED　　STAY-CATION

THINGS2DOTHERE

DREAM TREK:

VISUALS

HABIT:

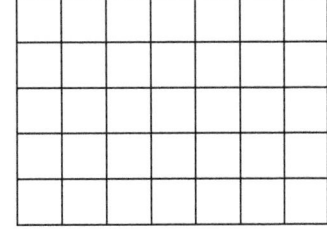

Project codename: Dawn: D-Day: Modus Operandi [M.O.]:	Magii Specialists Masterminds ("Who CAN shoot the dayum dawg?"): 1. 2. 3. 4.	KNOWN [Accessible] INTEL Gnosis needed [people, books, TEDx talks, documentaries, examples]:
How2Skin it Steps: E.g., Make a detailed supplies needed list	Dawn/M/D Day 8/22/23/ 9/13 / 10/1/23	New INTEL: issues & fixes as they arise: e.g., Delivery delays.

Project codename: Dawn: D-Day: Modus Operandi [M.O.]:	Magii Specialists Masterminds ("Who CAN shoot the dayum dawg?"): 1. 2. 3. 4.	KNOWN [Accessible] INTEL Gnosis needed [people, books, TEDx talks, documentaries, examples]:
How2Skin it Steps: E.g., Make a detailed supplies needed list	Dawn/M/D Day 8/22/23/ 9/13 / 10/1/23	New INTEL: issues & fixes as they arise: e.g., Delivery delays.

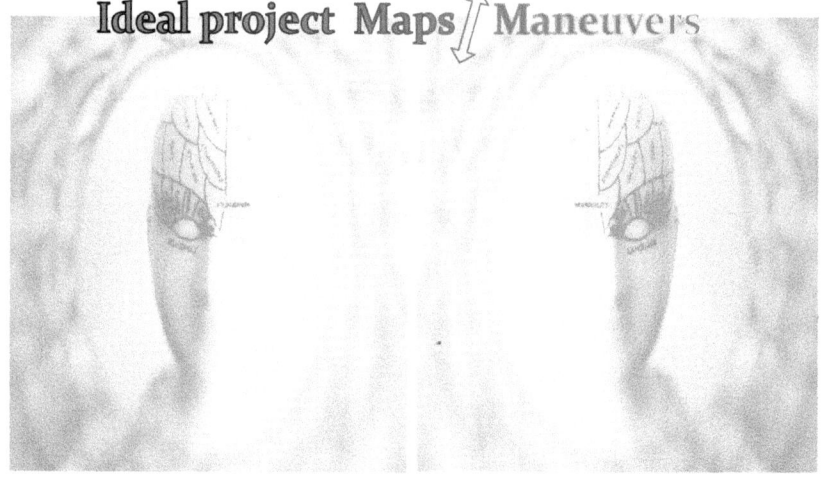

Ideal project Maps / Maneuvers

Ideal project Maps ↔ Maneuvers

Project codename:	Magii Specialists Masterminds ("Who CAN shoot the dayum dawg?"):	KNOWN [Accessible] INTEL Gnosis needed [people, books, TEDx talks, documentaries, examples]:	Project codename:	Magii Specialists Masterminds ("Who CAN shoot the dayum dawg?"):	KNOWN [Accessible] INTEL Gnosis needed [people, books, TEDx talks, documentaries, examples]:
Dawn: D-Day:	1.		Dawn: D-Day:	1.	
	2.			2.	
Modus Operandi [M.O.]:	3.		Modus Operandi [M.O.]:	3.	
	4.			4.	

How2Skin it Steps: E.g., Make a detailed supplies needed list	Dawn/M/D Day 8/22/23/ 9/13/ 10/1/23	New INTEL: issues & fixes as they arise: e.g., Delivery delays,	How2Skin it Steps: E.g., Make a detailed supplies needed list	Dawn/M/D Day 8/22/23/ 9/13/ 10/1/23	New INTEL: issues & fixes as they arise: e.g., Delivery delays,

THE WEEK:

THE vibe AIMED 4:

THE PLAYLIST:
1.
2.
3.

THE DREAM:

THE MAIN GOAL:

NOTES:

WEEK _____ OF 26

WEEKLY GREEN DRINK LOG ◯ ◯ ◯ ◯ ◯ ◯ ◯

THIS WEEK:

SELF CARE FOCUS

STYLE INSPO:

BEAUTY/GROOMING ZONE:

WORKOUT CHALLENGE FOCUS

MEDITATION/ FOCUS

PRAYER REQUEST

DECOMPRESSION TREAT

THIS WEEK'S WHATHAVEYOUS:

1.
2.
3.
4.
5.
6.
7.

7 THINGS YOU LOVE ABOUT YOU: (SELF PEP TALK)

1.
2.
3.
4.
5.
6.
7.

APPOINTMENTS	TIME & DATE	TYPE

WEEKLY DAY UP AFFIRMATION

THIS WEEK'S NIGHTLY AFFIRMATION

"I AM..."
(OF THE WEEK)

SPIRITUAL SHOTGUN:

What aspect of God, icon, archetype, angel, energy or spirit animal is riding out into the world *with* you this week?

LOVE ON OTHER'S LIST [L.O.O.L]

Who can you quietly do a cool thing for?

Aww~! Brain dump:

Sweethearts,
Did cool things,
Who are you FN with this week?

(FILL AS NEEDED)

Target Weekly meal plan:

Whole 30? Keto? Vegan? "All Thai, all week"? Paleo? Vegetarian? Carnivore?
Healthy Decadence?

Fast/ cleanse/ omad/ IF/ Juicing/ FODMAP

Grocery items 2 get 2 hit it:

...the WEEKend RIT[UAL]S:

How can you bless them for for blessing you?

Argh! brain dump:

The jerks, the K*rens,
The nonsense,
Who are you so not FN with this week?

How did you forgive them to fully let their energy go?

THE WEEK:

THE vibe AIMED 4:

THE PLAYLIST:
1.
2.
3.

THE DREAM:

THE MAIN GOAL:

NOTES:

WEEK OF 26

WEEKLY GREEN DRINK LOG

THIS WEEK:

SELF CARE FOCUS

STYLE INSPO:

BEAUTY/GROOMING ZONE:

WORKOUT CHALLENGE FOCUS

MEDITATION/ FOCUS

PRAYER REQUEST

DECOMPRESSION TREAT

THIS WEEK'S WHATHAVEYOUS:

1.
2.
3.
4.
5.
6.
7.

7 THINGS YOU LOVE ABOUT YOU: (SELF PEP TALK)

1.
2.
3.
4.
5.
6.
7.

APPOINTMENTS	TIME & DATE	TYPE

WEEKLY DAY UP AFFIRMATION

THIS WEEK'S NIGHTLY AFFIRMATION

"I AM..."
(OF THE WEEK)

SPIRITUAL SHOTGUN:
What aspect of God, icon, archetype, angel, energy or spirit animal is riding out into the world *with* you this week?

LOVE ON OTHER'S LIST [L.O.O.L]

Who can you quietly do a cool thing for?

Aww~! Brain dump:
Sweethearts,
Did cool things,
Who are you FN with this week?

(FILL AS NEEDED)

Target Weekly meal plan:
Whole 30? Keto? Vegan? "All Thai, all week"? Paleo? Vegetarian? Carnivore?
Healthy Decadence?

Fast/ cleanse/ omad/ IF/ Juicing/ FODMAP

Grocery items 2 get 2 hit it:

...the WEEKend RIT[UAL]S:

How can you bless them for for blessing you?

Argh! brain dump:
The jerks, the K*rens,
The nonsense,
Who are you so not FN with this week?

How did you forgive them to fully let their energy go?

THE WEEK:

THE vibe AIMED 4:

THE PLAYLIST:
1.
2.
3.

THE DREAM:

THE MAIN GOAL:

NOTES:

WEEK OF 26

WEEKLY GREEN DRINK LOG

THIS WEEK:

SELF CARE FOCUS

STYLE INSPO:

BEAUTY/GROOMING ZONE:

WORKOUT CHALLENGE FOCUS

MEDITATION/ FOCUS

PRAYER REQUEST

DECOMPRESSION TREAT

THIS WEEK'S WHATHAVEYOUS:
1.
2.
3.
4.
5.
6.
7.

7 THINGS YOU LOVE ABOUT YOU: (SELF PEP TALK)
1.
2.
3.
4.
5.
6.
7.

APPOINTMENTS	TIME & DATE	TYPE

WEEKLY DAY UP AFFIRMATION

THIS WEEK'S NIGHTLY AFFIRMATION

"I AM..."
(OF THE WEEK)

SPIRITUAL SHOTGUN:

What aspect of God, icon, archetype, angel, energy or spirit animal is riding out into the world *with* you this week?

LOVE ON OTHER'S LIST [L.O.O.L]

Who can you quietly do a cool thing for?

Aww~! Brain dump:

Sweethearts,
Did cool things,
Who are you FN with this week?

(FILL AS NEEDED)

Target Weekly meal plan:

Whole 30? Keto? Vegan? "All Thai, all week"? Paleo? Vegetarian? Carnivore? Healthy Decadence?

Fast/ cleanse/ omad/ IF/ Juicing/ FODMAP

Grocery items 2 get 2 hit it:

...the WEEKend RIT[UAL]S:

How can you bless them for for blessing you?

Argh! brain dump:

The jerks, the K*rens,
The nonsense,
Who are you so not FN with this week?

How did you forgive them to fully let their energy go?

THE WEEK:

THE vibe AIMED 4:

THE PLAYLIST:
1.
2.
3.

THE DREAM:

THE MAIN GOAL:

THIS WEEK'S WHATHAVEYOUS:
1.
2.
3.
4.
5.
6.
7.

NOTES:

WEEK   OF 26

WEEKLY GREEN DRINK LOG

THIS WEEK:

SELF CARE FOCUS

STYLE INSPO:

BEAUTY/GROOMING ZONE:

WORKOUT CHALLENGE FOCUS

MEDITATION/ FOCUS

PRAYER REQUEST

DECOMPRESSION TREAT

7 THINGS YOU LOVE ABOUT YOU: (SELF PEP TALK)
1.
2.
3.
4.
5.
6.
7.

APPOINTMENTS	TIME & DATE	TYPE

WEEKLY DAY UP AFFIRMATION

THIS WEEK'S NIGHTLY AFFIRMATION

"I AM"...
(OF THE WEEK)

SPIRITUAL SHOTGUN:

What aspect of God, icon, archetype, angel, energy or spirit animal is riding out into the world *with* you this week?

LOVE ON OTHER'S LIST [L.O.O.L]

Who can you quietly do a cool thing for?

Aww~! Brain dump:

Sweethearts,
Did cool things,
Who are you FN with this week?

(FILL AS NEEDED)

How can you bless them for for blessing you?

Argh! brain dump:

The jerks, the K*rens,
The nonsense,
Who are you so not FN with this week?

How did you forgive them **to** fully let their energy go?

Target Weekly meal plan:

Whole 30? Keto? Vegan? "All Thai, all week"? Paleo? Vegetarian? Carnivore?
Healthy Decadence?

Fast/ cleanse/ omad/ IF/ Juicing/ FODMAP

Grocery items 2 get 2 hit it:

...the WEEKend RIT[UAL]S:

THE WEEK:

THE vibe AIMED 4:

THE PLAYLIST:
1.
2.
3.

THE DREAM:

THE MAIN GOAL:

THIS WEEK'S WHATHAVEYOUS:
1.
2.
3.
4.
5.
6.
7.

NOTES:

WEEK OF 26

WEEKLY GREEN DRINK LOG

THIS WEEK:

SELF CARE FOCUS

STYLE INSPO:

BEAUTY/GROOMING ZONE:

WORKOUT CHALLENGE FOCUS

MEDITATION/ FOCUS

PRAYER REQUEST

DECOMPRESSION TREAT

7 THINGS YOU LOVE ABOUT YOU: (SELF PEP TALK)
1.
2.
3.
4.
5.
6.
7.

APPOINTMENTS	TIME & DATE	TYPE

WEEKLY DAY UP AFFIRMATION

THIS WEEK'S NIGHTLY AFFIRMATION

"I AM"...
(OF THE WEEK)

SPIRITUAL SHOTGUN:
What aspect of God, icon, archetype, angel, energy or spirit animal is riding out into the world *with* you this week?

LOVE ON OTHER'S LIST [L.O.O.L]

Who can you quietly do a cool thing for?

Aww~! Brain dump:

Sweethearts,
Did cool things,
Who are you FN with this week?

(FILL AS NEEDED)

How can you bless them for for blessing you?

Target Weekly meal plan:

Whole 30? Keto? Vegan? "All Thai, all week"? Paleo? Vegetarian? Carnivore?
Healthy Decadence?

Fast/ cleanse/ omad/ IF/ Juicing/ FODMAP

Argh! brain dump:

The jerks, the K*rens,
The nonsense,
Who are you so not FN with this week?

Grocery items 2 get 2 hit it:

How did you forgive them to fully let their energy go?

...the WEEKend RIT[UAL]S:

date	SIX WORD STORY LOG
1	
2	
3	
4	
5	
6	
7	
8	
9	
10	
11	
12	
13	
14	
15	
16	
17	
18	
19	
20	
21	
22	
23	
24	
25	
26	
27	
28	
29	
30	
31	

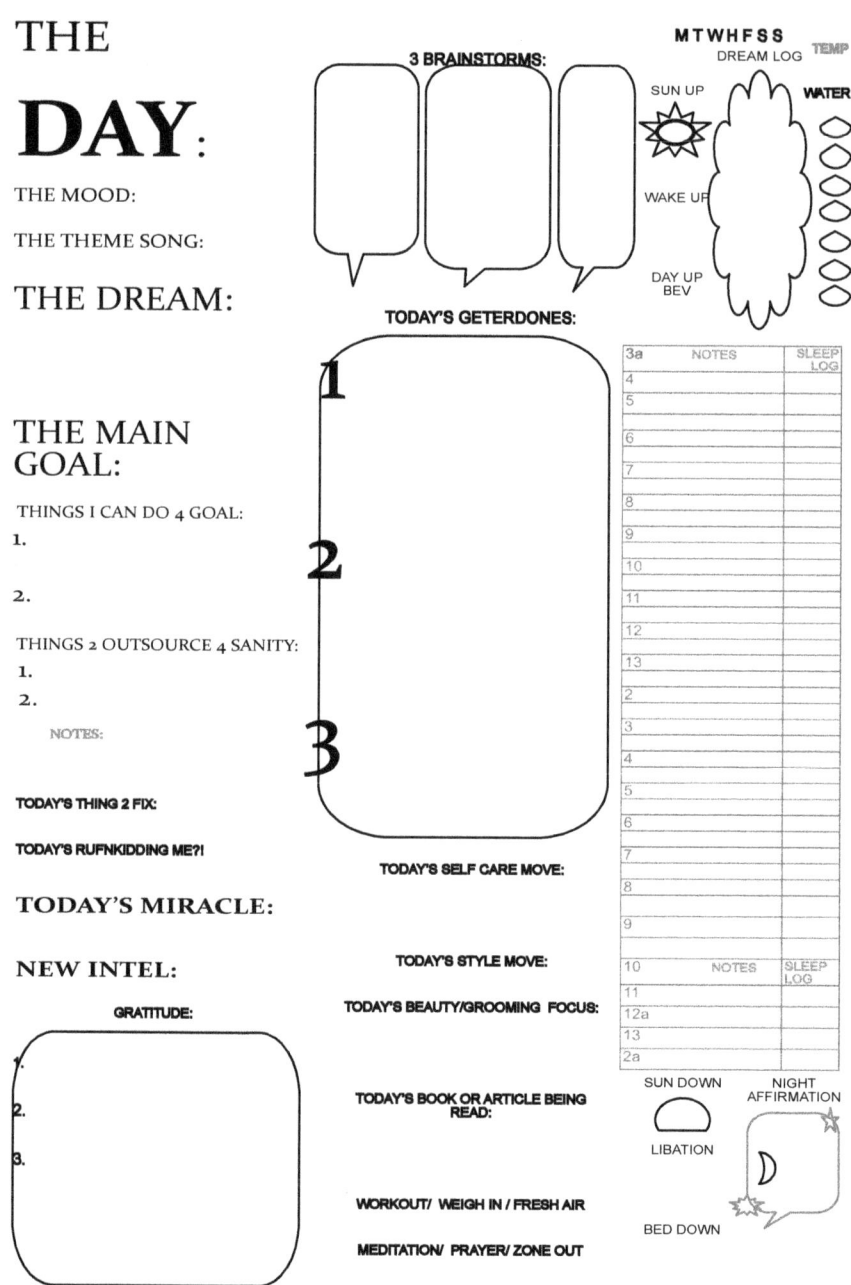

THE
pregaming:

THE recap:

THE
pregaming:

THE recap:

THE
pregaming:

THE recap:

THE
DAY:

THE MOOD:

THE THEME SONG:

THE DREAM:

THE MAIN GOAL:

THINGS I CAN DO 4 GOAL:
1.

2.

THINGS 2 OUTSOURCE 4 SANITY:
1.
2.

NOTES:

TODAY'S THING 2 FIX:

TODAY'S RUFNKIDDING ME?!

TODAY'S MIRACLE:

NEW INTEL:

GRATITUDE:

1.
2.
3.

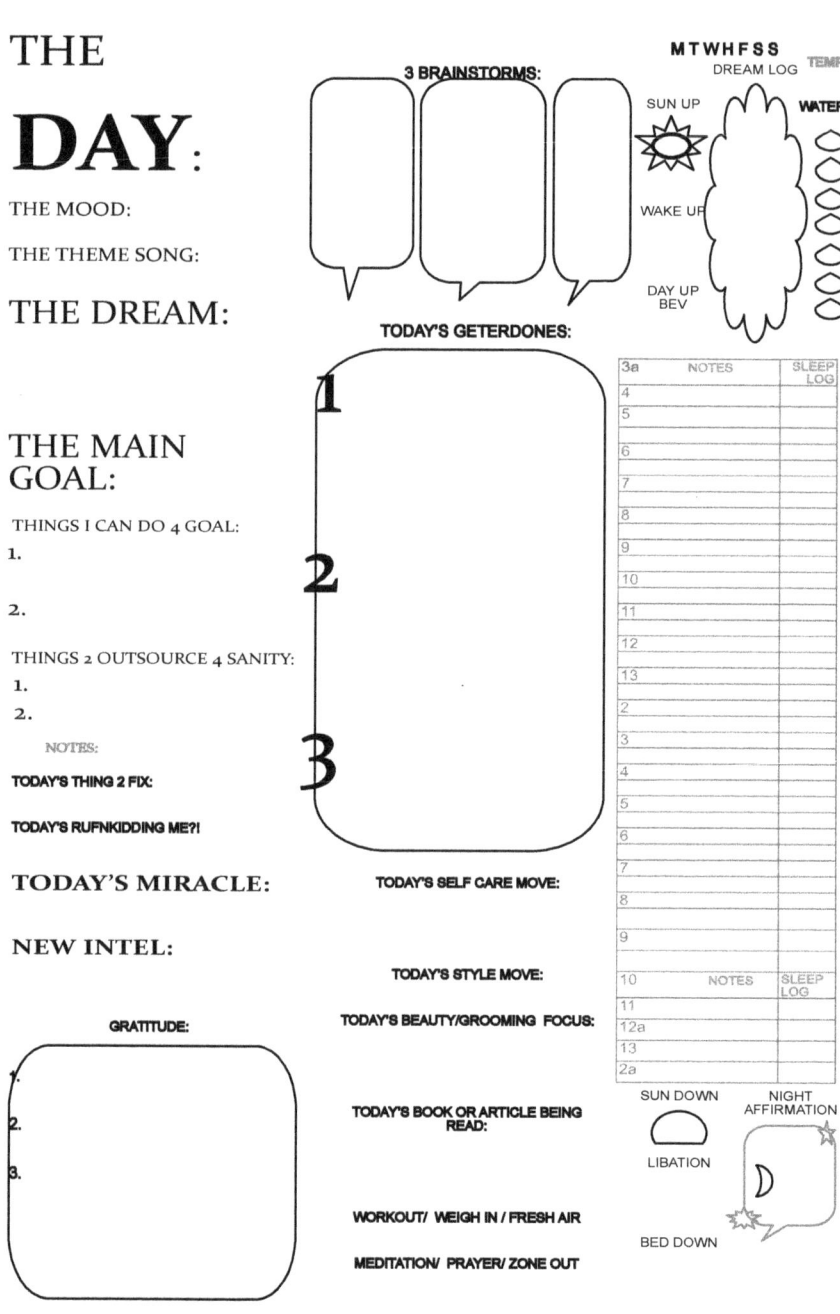

3 BRAINSTORMS:

TODAY'S GETERDONES:

1
2
3

TODAY'S SELF CARE MOVE:

TODAY'S STYLE MOVE:

TODAY'S BEAUTY/GROOMING FOCUS:

TODAY'S BOOK OR ARTICLE BEING READ:

WORKOUT/ WEIGH IN / FRESH AIR

MEDITATION/ PRAYER/ ZONE OUT

M T W H F S S
DREAM LOG   TEMP
SUN UP   WATER
WAKE UP
DAY UP BEV

3a NOTES SLEEP LOG
4
5
6
7
8
9
10
11
12
13
2
3
4
5
6
7
8
9
10 NOTES SLEEP LOG
11
12a
13
2a

SUN DOWN   NIGHT AFFIRMATION
LIBATION
BED DOWN

THE
pregaming:

THE recap:

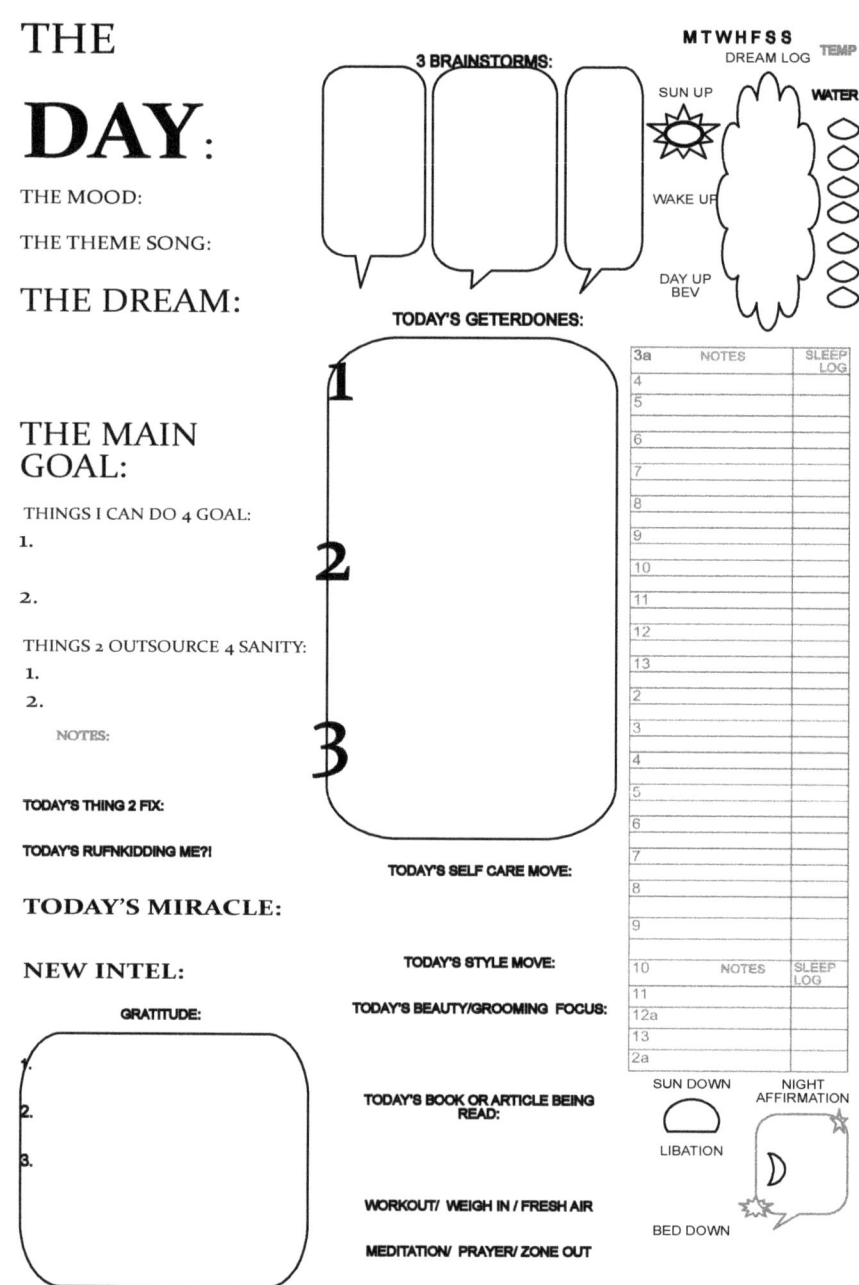

THE
pregaming:

THE recap:

THE pregaming:

THE recap:

THE pregaming:

THE recap:

THE DAY:

THE MOOD:

THE THEME SONG:

THE DREAM:

THE MAIN GOAL:

THINGS I CAN DO 4 GOAL:
1.
2.

THINGS 2 OUTSOURCE 4 SANITY:
1.
2.

NOTES:

TODAY'S THING 2 FIX:

TODAY'S RUFNKIDDING ME?!

TODAY'S MIRACLE:

NEW INTEL:

GRATITUDE:
1.
2.
3.

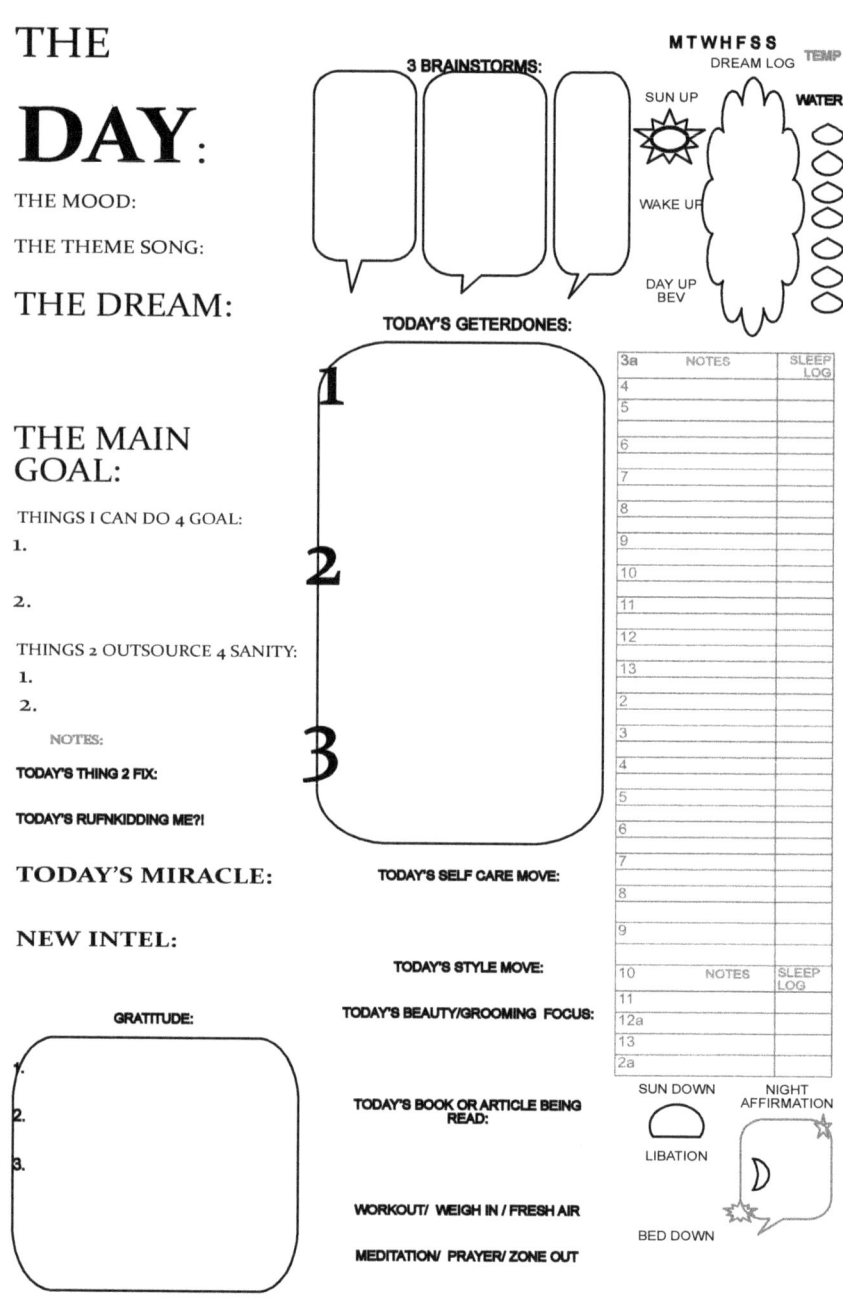

3 BRAINSTORMS:

TODAY'S GETERDONES:

1
2
3

TODAY'S SELF CARE MOVE:

TODAY'S STYLE MOVE:

TODAY'S BEAUTY/GROOMING FOCUS:

TODAY'S BOOK OR ARTICLE BEING READ:

WORKOUT/ WEIGH IN / FRESH AIR

MEDITATION/ PRAYER/ ZONE OUT

M T W H F S S
DREAM LOG   TEMP

SUN UP

WAKE UP

DAY UP BEV

WATER

3a NOTES SLEEP LOG
4
5
6
7
8
9
10
11
12
13
2
3
4
5
6
7
8
9
10 NOTES SLEEP LOG
11
12a
13
2a

SUN DOWN

LIBATION

NIGHT AFFIRMATION

BED DOWN

THE
pregaming:

THE recap:

THE DAY:

THE MOOD:

THE THEME SONG:

THE DREAM:

THE MAIN GOAL:

THINGS I CAN DO 4 GOAL:
1.
2.

THINGS 2 OUTSOURCE 4 SANITY:
1.
2.

   NOTES:

TODAY'S THING 2 FIX:

TODAY'S RUFNKIDDING ME?!

TODAY'S MIRACLE:

NEW INTEL:

GRATITUDE:
1.
2.
3.

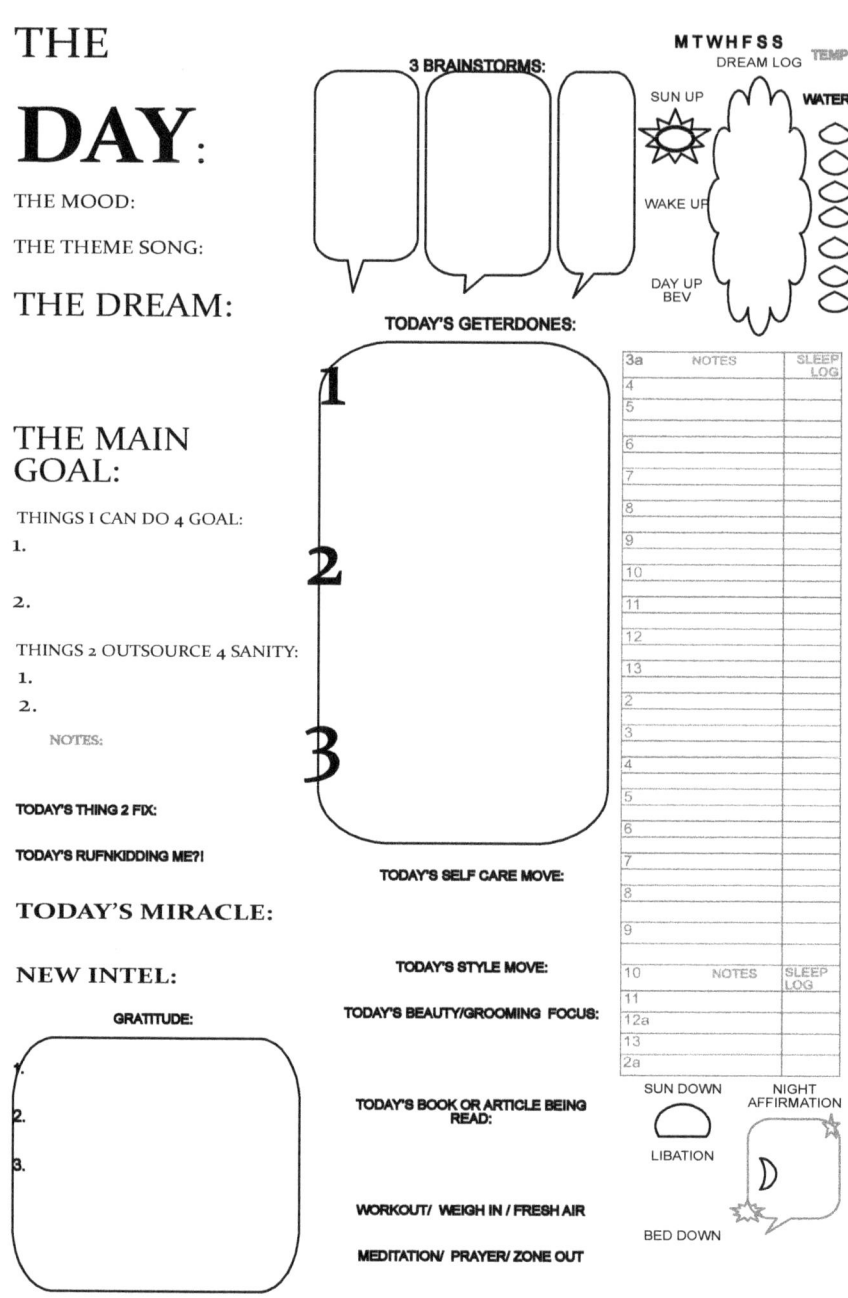

3 BRAINSTORMS:

TODAY'S GETERDONES:

1.

2.

3.

TODAY'S SELF CARE MOVE:

TODAY'S STYLE MOVE:

TODAY'S BEAUTY/GROOMING FOCUS:

TODAY'S BOOK OR ARTICLE BEING READ:

WORKOUT/ WEIGH IN / FRESH AIR

MEDITATION/ PRAYER/ ZONE OUT

M T W H F S S
DREAM LOG   TEMP
SUN UP
WATER
WAKE UP
DAY UP BEV

3a	NOTES	SLEEP LOG
4		
5		
6		
7		
8		
9		
10		
11		
12		
13		
2		
3		
4		
5		
6		
7		
8		
9		
10	NOTES	SLEEP LOG
11		
12a		
13		
2a		

SUN DOWN

LIBATION

NIGHT AFFIRMATION

BED DOWN

THE
pregaming:

THE recap:

THE
pregaming:

THE recap:

THE
pregaming:

THE recap:

THE
pregaming:

THE recap:

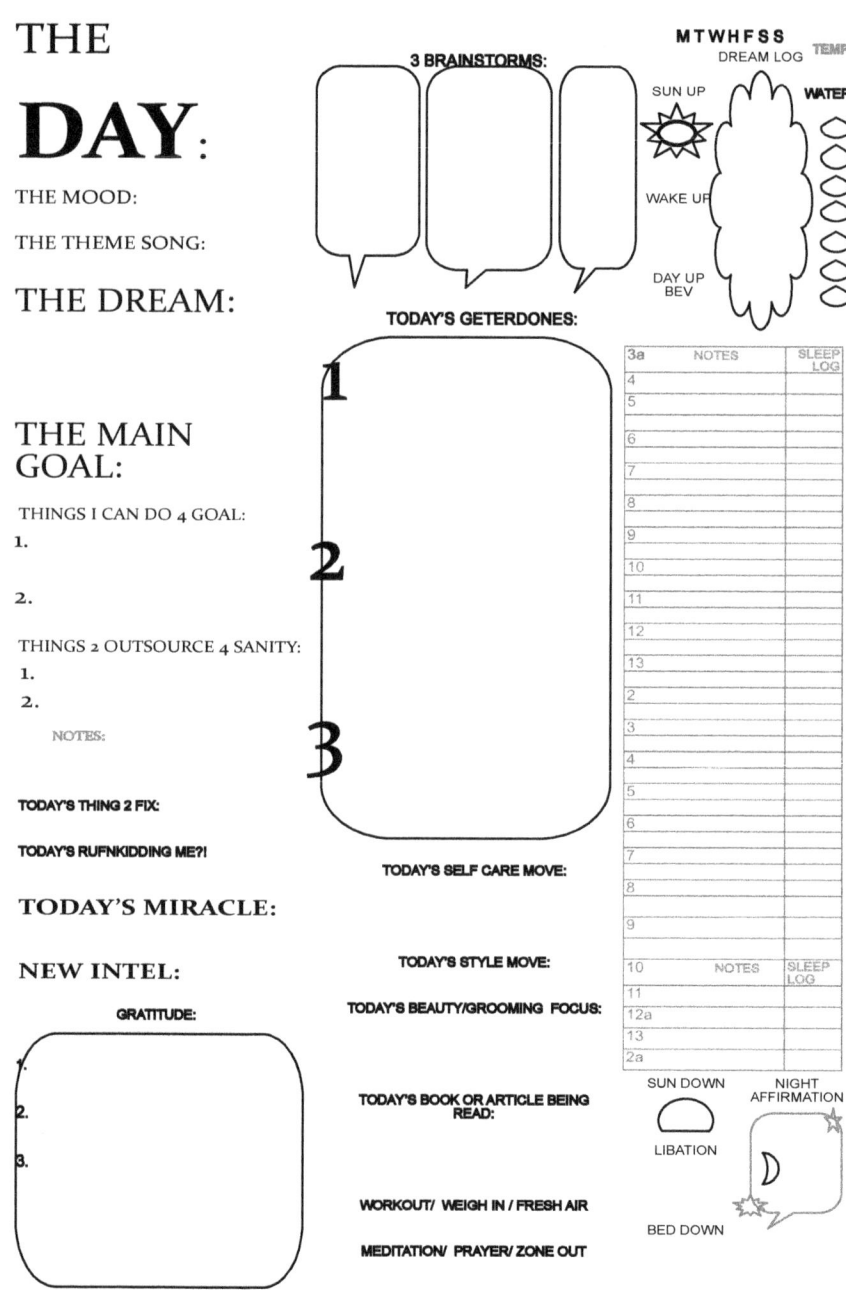

THE
pregaming:

THE recap:

THE

DAY:

THE MOOD:

THE THEME SONG:

THE DREAM:

THE MAIN GOAL:

THINGS I CAN DO 4 GOAL:
1.
2.

THINGS 2 OUTSOURCE 4 SANITY:
1.
2.

NOTES:

TODAY'S THING 2 FIX:

TODAY'S RUFNKIDDING ME?!

TODAY'S MIRACLE:

NEW INTEL:

GRATITUDE:
1.
2.
3.

THE pregaming:

THE recap:

THE
pregaming:

THE recap:

THE DAY:

THE MOOD:

THE THEME SONG:

THE DREAM:

THE MAIN GOAL:

THINGS I CAN DO 4 GOAL:
1.
2.

THINGS 2 OUTSOURCE 4 SANITY:
1.
2.

NOTES:

TODAY'S THING 2 FIX:

TODAY'S RUFNKIDDING ME?!

TODAY'S MIRACLE:

NEW INTEL:

GRATITUDE:
1.
2.
3.

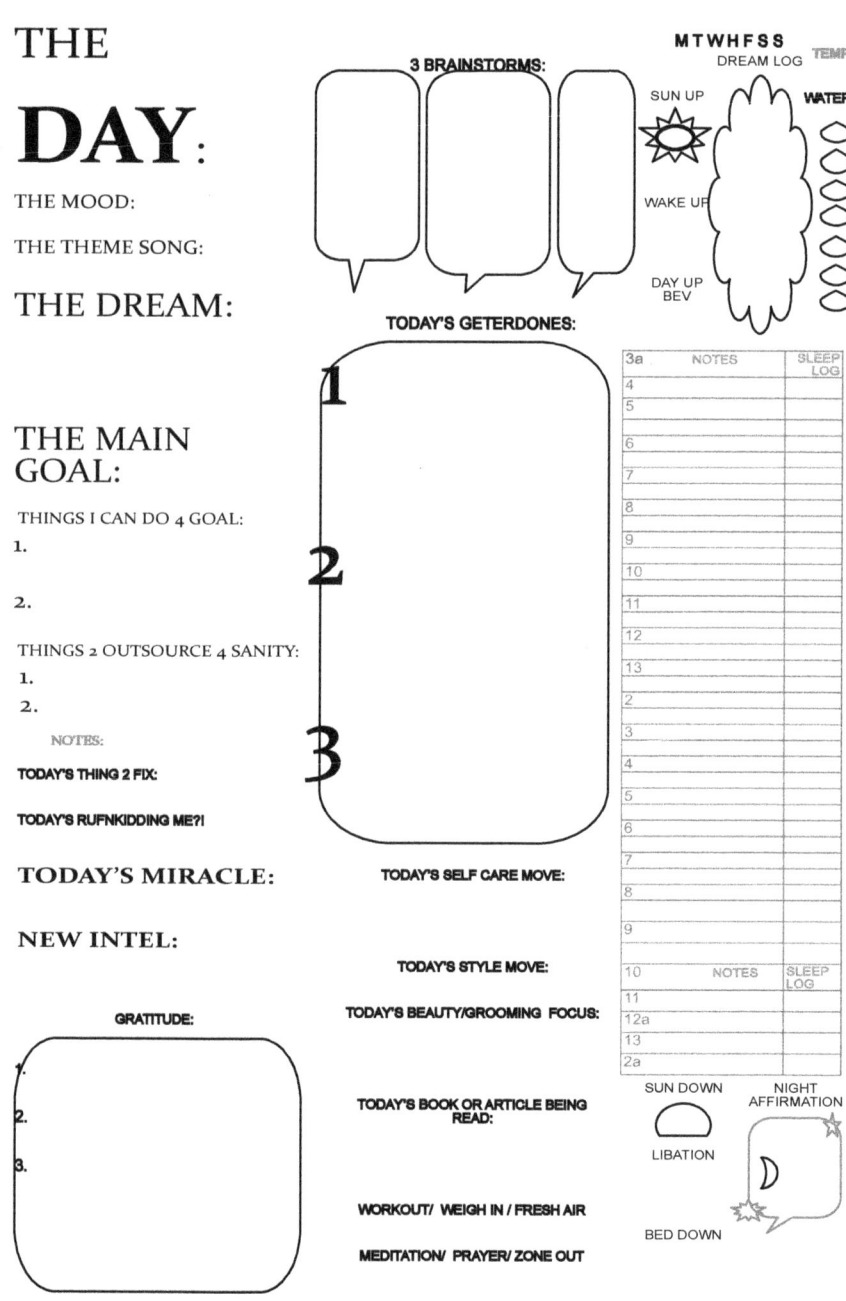

3 BRAINSTORMS:

TODAY'S GETERDONES:

1.
2.
3.

TODAY'S SELF CARE MOVE:

TODAY'S STYLE MOVE:

TODAY'S BEAUTY/GROOMING FOCUS:

TODAY'S BOOK OR ARTICLE BEING READ:

WORKOUT/ WEIGH IN / FRESH AIR

MEDITATION/ PRAYER/ ZONE OUT

M T W H F S S
DREAM LOG   TEMP
SUN UP   WATER
WAKE UP
DAY UP BEV

3a	NOTES	SLEEP LOG
4		
5		
6		
7		
8		
9		
10		
11		
12		
13		
2		
3		
4		
5		
6		
7		
8		
9		
10	NOTES	SLEEP LOG
11		
12a		
13		
2a		

SUN DOWN   NIGHT AFFIRMATION

LIBATION

BED DOWN

THE
pregaming:

THE recap:

THE
DAY:

THE MOOD:

THE THEME SONG:

THE DREAM:

THE MAIN GOAL:

THINGS I CAN DO 4 GOAL:
1.

2.

THINGS 2 OUTSOURCE 4 SANITY:
1.
2.
   NOTES:

TODAY'S THING 2 FIX:

TODAY'S RUFNKIDDING ME?!

TODAY'S MIRACLE:

NEW INTEL:

GRATITUDE:

1.

2.

3.

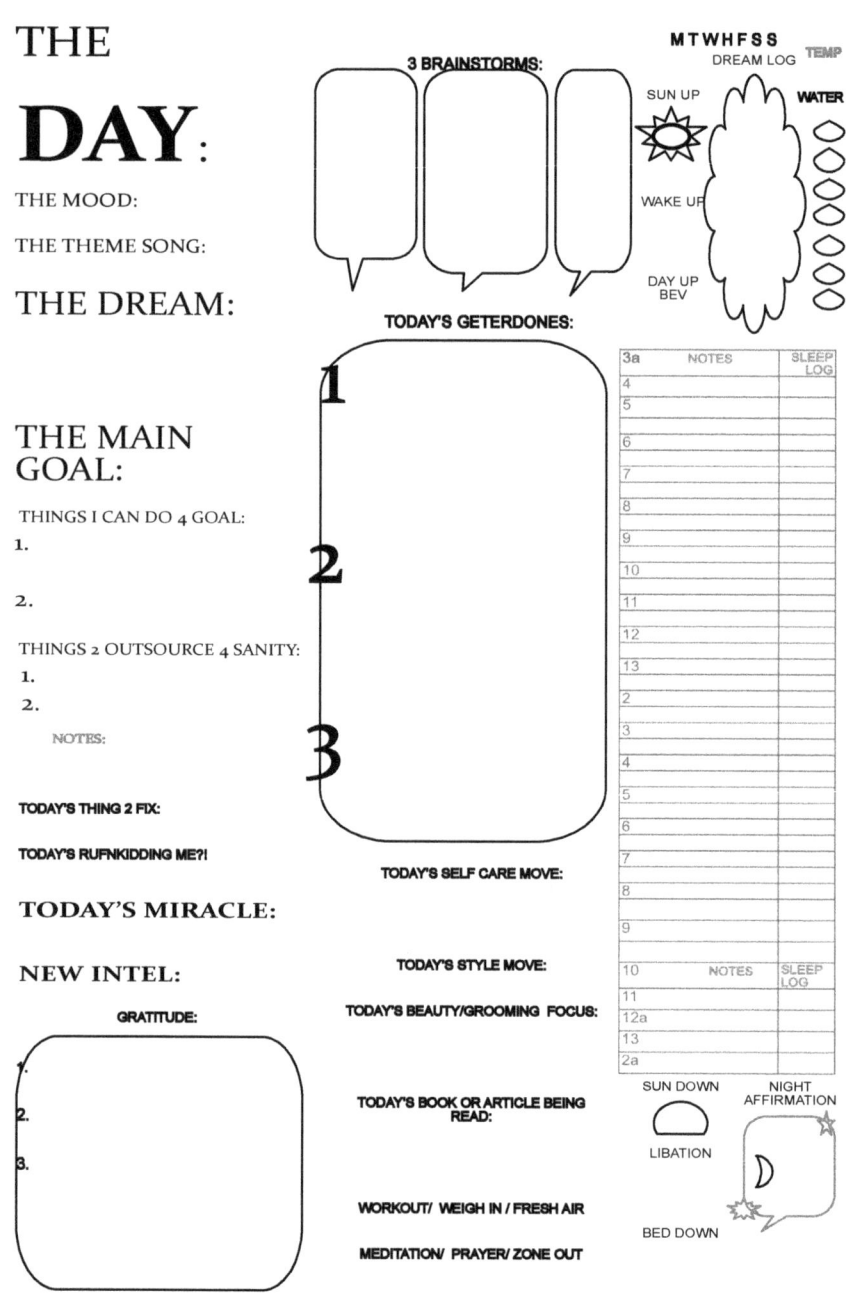

3 BRAINSTORMS:

TODAY'S GETERDONES:

1

2

3

TODAY'S SELF CARE MOVE:

TODAY'S STYLE MOVE:

TODAY'S BEAUTY/GROOMING FOCUS:

TODAY'S BOOK OR ARTICLE BEING READ:

WORKOUT/ WEIGH IN / FRESH AIR

MEDITATION/ PRAYER/ ZONE OUT

M T W H F S S
DREAM LOG   TEMP
SUN UP
WATER
WAKE UP
DAY UP BEV

	NOTES	SLEEP LOG
3a		
4		
5		
6		
7		
8		
9		
10		
11		
12		
13		
2		
3		
4		
5		
6		
7		
8		
9		
10	NOTES	SLEEP LOG
11		
12a		
13		
2a		

SUN DOWN   NIGHT AFFIRMATION

LIBATION

BED DOWN

THE
pregaming:

THE recap:

THE
pregaming:

THE recap:

THE
DAY:

THE MOOD:

THE THEME SONG:

THE DREAM:

THE MAIN GOAL:

THINGS I CAN DO 4 GOAL:
1.

2.

THINGS 2 OUTSOURCE 4 SANITY:
1.
2.

NOTES:

TODAY'S THING 2 FIX:

TODAY'S RUFNKIDDING ME?!

TODAY'S MIRACLE:

NEW INTEL:

GRATITUDE:
1.
2.
3.

3 BRAINSTORMS:

TODAY'S GETERDONES:
1
2
3

TODAY'S SELF CARE MOVE:

TODAY'S STYLE MOVE:

TODAY'S BEAUTY/GROOMING FOCUS:

TODAY'S BOOK OR ARTICLE BEING READ:

WORKOUT/ WEIGH IN / FRESH AIR

MEDITATION/ PRAYER/ ZONE OUT

M T W H F S S
DREAM LOG TEMP
SUN UP WATER
WAKE UP
DAY UP BEV

3a	NOTES	SLEEP LOG
4		
5		
6		
7		
8		
9		
10		
11		
12		
13		
2		
3		
4		
5		
6		
7		
8		
9		
10	NOTES	SLEEP LOG
11		
12a		
13		
2a		

SUN DOWN   NIGHT AFFIRMATION

LIBATION

BED DOWN

THE
pregaming:

THE recap:

THE DAY:

THE MOOD:

THE THEME SONG:

THE DREAM:

THE MAIN GOAL:

THINGS I CAN DO 4 GOAL:
1.
2.

THINGS 2 OUTSOURCE 4 SANITY:
1.
2.

NOTES:

TODAY'S THING 2 FIX:

TODAY'S RUFNKIDDING ME?!

TODAY'S MIRACLE:

NEW INTEL:

GRATITUDE:
1.
2.
3.

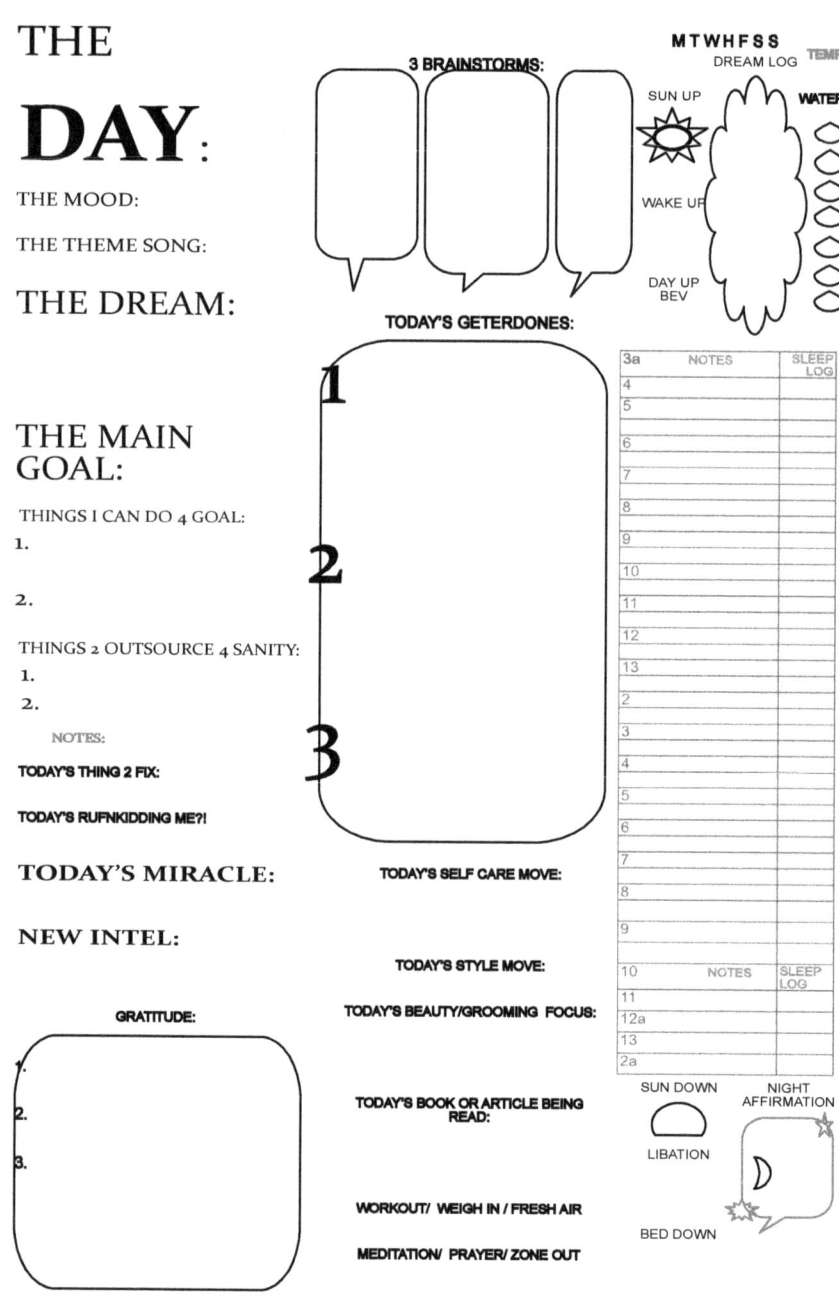

3 BRAINSTORMS:

TODAY'S GETERDONES:
1
2
3

TODAY'S SELF CARE MOVE:

TODAY'S STYLE MOVE:

TODAY'S BEAUTY/GROOMING FOCUS:

TODAY'S BOOK OR ARTICLE BEING READ:

WORKOUT/ WEIGH IN / FRESH AIR

MEDITATION/ PRAYER/ ZONE OUT

M T W H F S S
DREAM LOG TEMP

SUN UP

WAKE UP

DAY UP BEV

WATER

3a	NOTES	SLEEP LOG
4		
5		
6		
7		
8		
9		
10		
11		
12		
13		
2		
3		
4		
5		
6		
7		
8		
9		
10	NOTES	SLEEP LOG
11		
12a		
13		
2a		

SUN DOWN

LIBATION

NIGHT AFFIRMATION

BED DOWN

THE
pregaming:

THE recap:

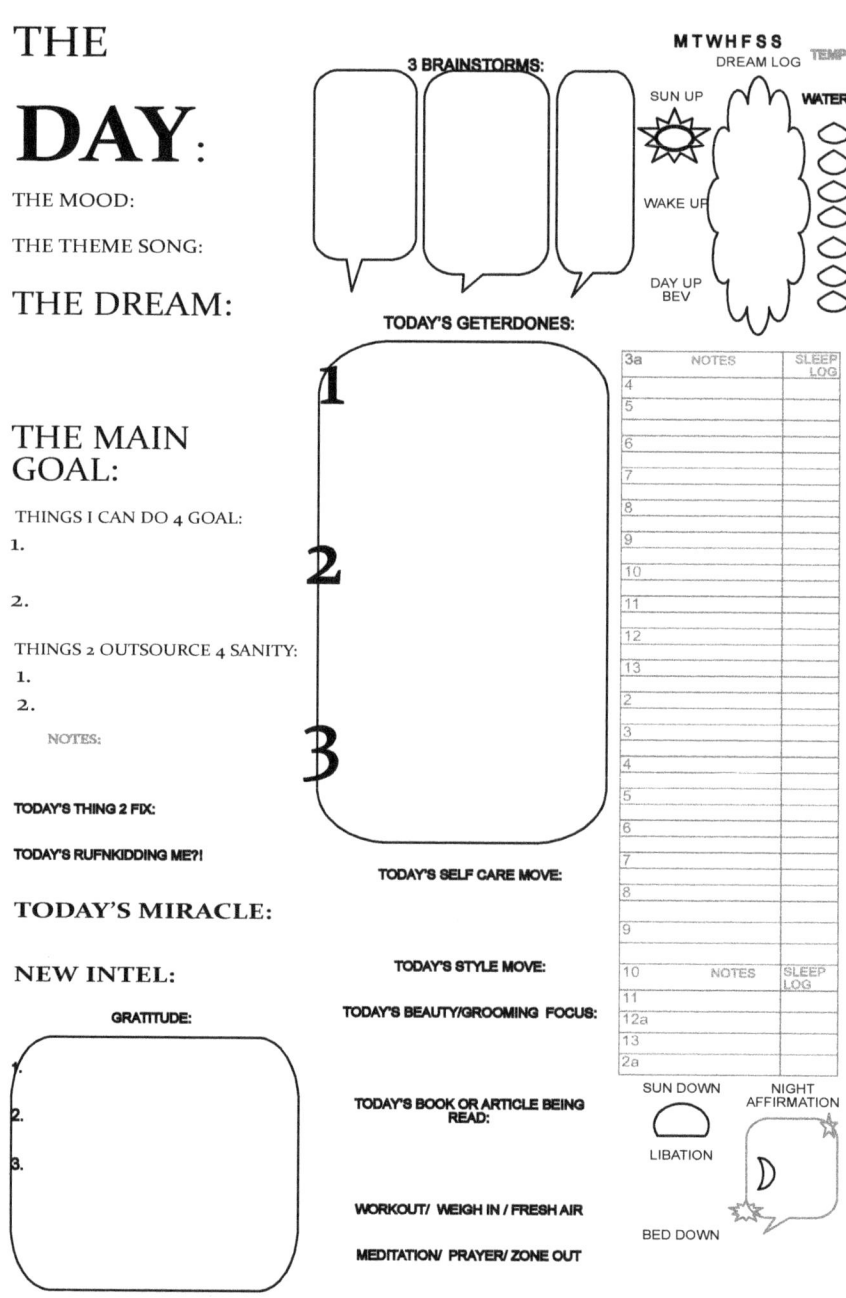

THE
pregaming:

THE recap:

THE DAY:

THE MOOD:

THE THEME SONG:

THE DREAM:

THE MAIN GOAL:

THINGS I CAN DO 4 GOAL:
1.
2.

THINGS 2 OUTSOURCE 4 SANITY:
1.
2.

NOTES:

TODAY'S THING 2 FIX:

TODAY'S RUFNKIDDING ME?!

TODAY'S MIRACLE:

NEW INTEL:

GRATITUDE:
1.
2.
3.

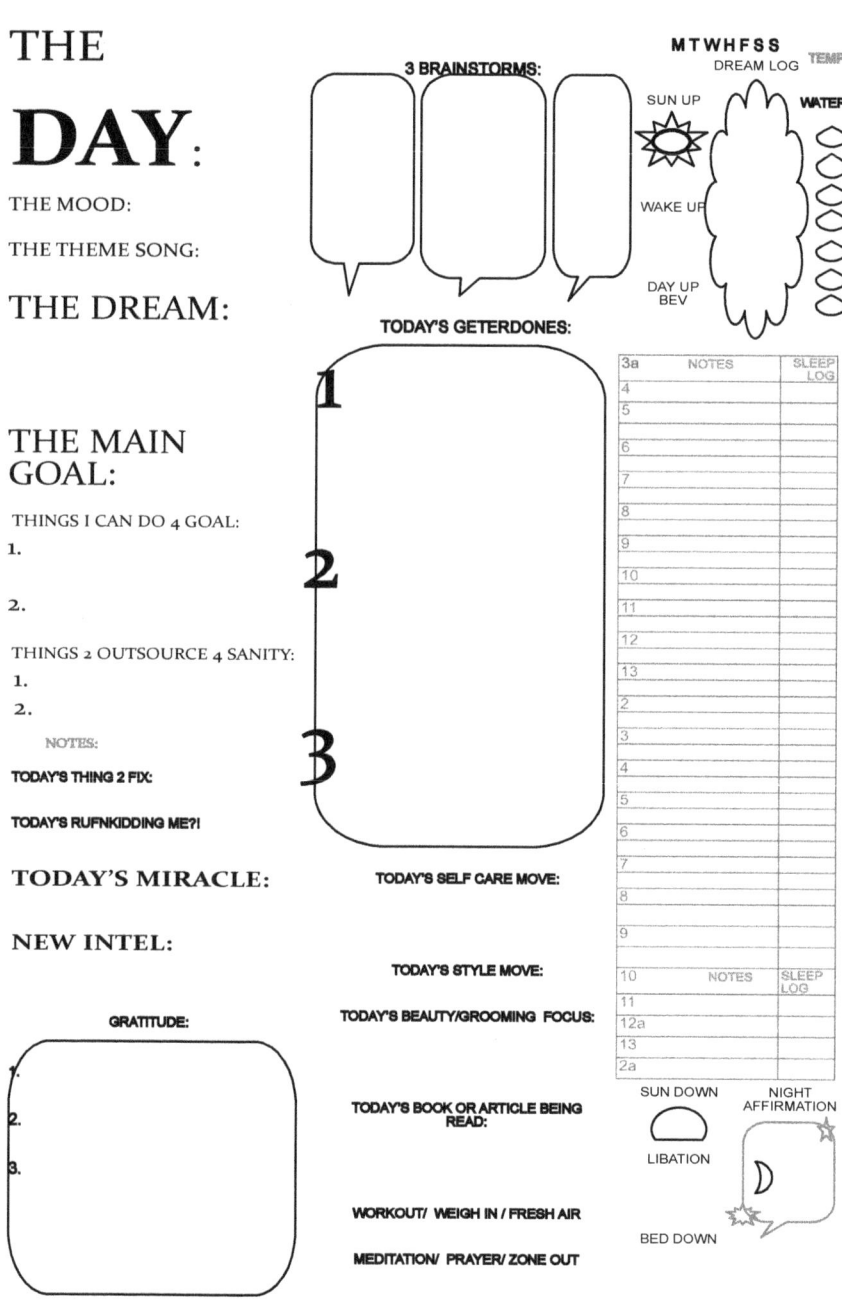

3 BRAINSTORMS:

TODAY'S GETERDONES:
1
2
3

TODAY'S SELF CARE MOVE:

TODAY'S STYLE MOVE:

TODAY'S BEAUTY/GROOMING FOCUS:

TODAY'S BOOK OR ARTICLE BEING READ:

WORKOUT/ WEIGH IN / FRESH AIR

MEDITATION/ PRAYER/ ZONE OUT

M T W H F S S
DREAM LOG   TEMP
SUN UP
WAKE UP
DAY UP BEV
WATER

	NOTES	SLEEP LOG
3a		
4		
5		
6		
7		
8		
9		
10		
11		
12		
13		
2		
3		
4		
5		
6		
7		
8		
9		
10	NOTES	SLEEP LOG
11		
12a		
13		
2a		

SUN DOWN

LIBATION

BED DOWN

NIGHT AFFIRMATION

THE
pregaming:

THE recap:

THE DAY:

THE MOOD:

THE THEME SONG:

THE DREAM:

THE MAIN GOAL:

THINGS I CAN DO 4 GOAL:
1.
2.

THINGS 2 OUTSOURCE 4 SANITY:
1.
2.

NOTES:

TODAY'S THING 2 FIX:

TODAY'S RUFNKIDDING ME?!

TODAY'S MIRACLE:

NEW INTEL:

GRATITUDE:
1.
2.
3.

3 BRAINSTORMS:

TODAY'S GETERDONES:
1
2
3

TODAY'S SELF CARE MOVE:

TODAY'S STYLE MOVE:

TODAY'S BEAUTY/GROOMING FOCUS:

TODAY'S BOOK OR ARTICLE BEING READ:

WORKOUT/ WEIGH IN / FRESH AIR

MEDITATION/ PRAYER/ ZONE OUT

MTWHFSS DREAM LOG — TEMP

SUN UP — WATER

WAKE UP

DAY UP BEV

NOTES — SLEEP LOG

3a
4
5
6
7
8
9
10
11
12
13
2
3
4
5
6
7
8
9
10 NOTES SLEEP LOG
11
12a
13
2a

SUN DOWN — LIBATION

NIGHT AFFIRMATION

BED DOWN

THE pregaming:

THE recap:

THE
DAY:

THE MOOD:

THE THEME SONG:

THE DREAM:

THE MAIN GOAL:

THINGS I CAN DO 4 GOAL:
1.
2.

THINGS 2 OUTSOURCE 4 SANITY:
1.
2.

NOTES:

TODAY'S THING 2 FIX:

TODAY'S RUFNKIDDING ME?!

TODAY'S MIRACLE:

NEW INTEL:

GRATITUDE:

1.
2.
3.

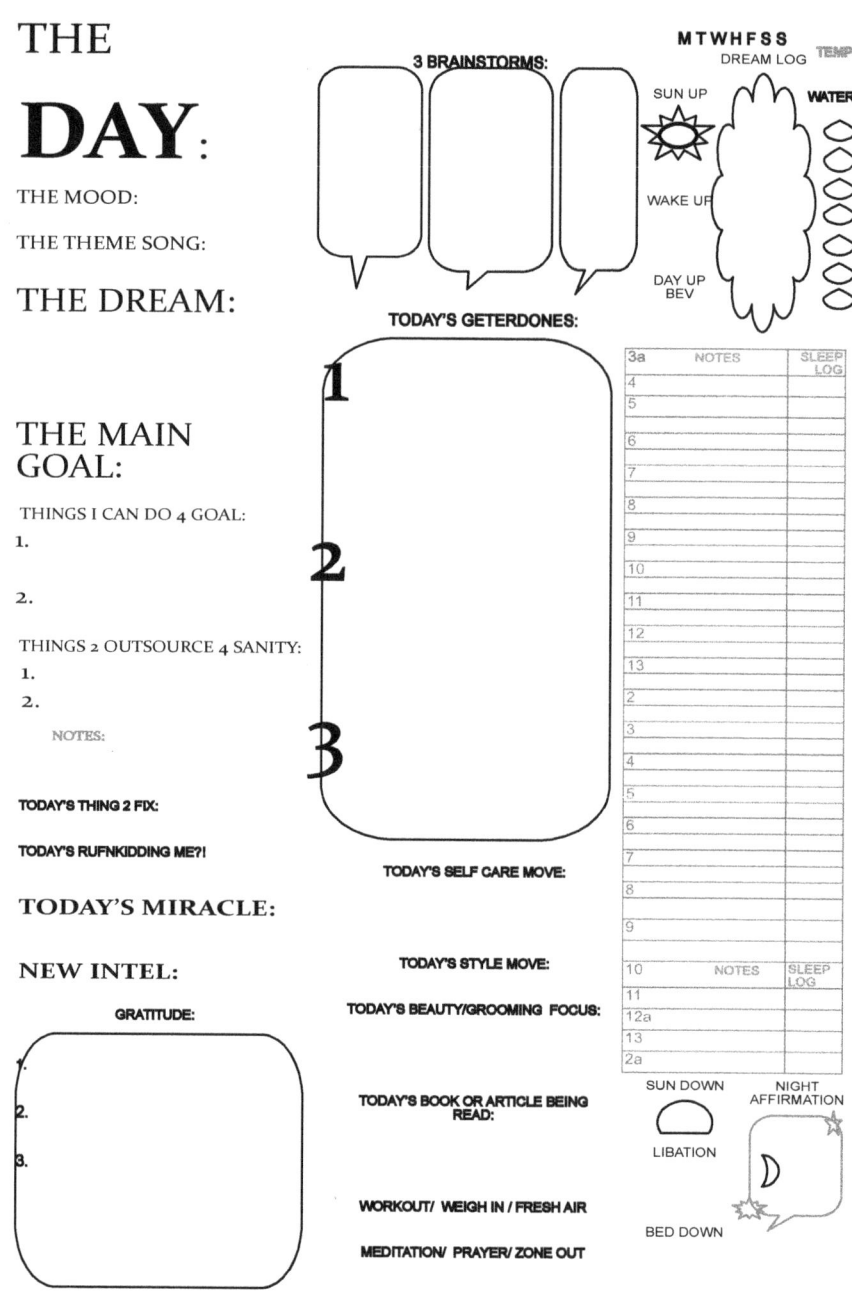

3 BRAINSTORMS:

TODAY'S GETERDONES:
1
2
3

TODAY'S SELF CARE MOVE:

TODAY'S STYLE MOVE:

TODAY'S BEAUTY/GROOMING FOCUS:

TODAY'S BOOK OR ARTICLE BEING READ:

WORKOUT/ WEIGH IN / FRESH AIR

MEDITATION/ PRAYER/ ZONE OUT

M T W H F S S
DREAM LOG   TEMP

SUN UP

WAKE UP

DAY UP BEV

WATER

NOTES | SLEEP LOG
3a
4
5
6
7
8
9
10
11
12
13
2
3
4
5
6
7
8
9
10 NOTES SLEEP LOG
11
12a
13
2a

SUN DOWN

LIBATION

NIGHT AFFIRMATION

BED DOWN

THE pregaming:

THE recap:

THE DAY:

THE MOOD:

THE THEME SONG:

THE DREAM:

THE MAIN GOAL:

THINGS I CAN DO 4 GOAL:
1.
2.

THINGS 2 OUTSOURCE 4 SANITY:
1.
2.

NOTES:

TODAY'S THING 2 FIX:

TODAY'S RUFNKIDDING ME?!

TODAY'S MIRACLE:

NEW INTEL:

GRATITUDE:
1.
2.
3.

3 BRAINSTORMS:

TODAY'S GETERDONES:
1
2
3

TODAY'S SELF CARE MOVE:

TODAY'S STYLE MOVE:

TODAY'S BEAUTY/GROOMING FOCUS:

TODAY'S BOOK OR ARTICLE BEING READ:

WORKOUT/ WEIGH IN / FRESH AIR

MEDITATION/ PRAYER/ ZONE OUT

M T W H F S S

DREAM LOG   TEMP

SUN UP

WAKE UP

DAY UP BEV

WATER

	NOTES	SLEEP LOG
3a		
4		
5		
6		
7		
8		
9		
10		
11		
12		
13		
2		
3		
4		
5		
6		
7		
8		
9		
10	NOTES	SLEEP LOG
11		
12a		
13		
2a		

SUN DOWN

LIBATION

NIGHT AFFIRMATION

BED DOWN

THE pregaming:

THE recap:

THE
pregaming:

THE recap:

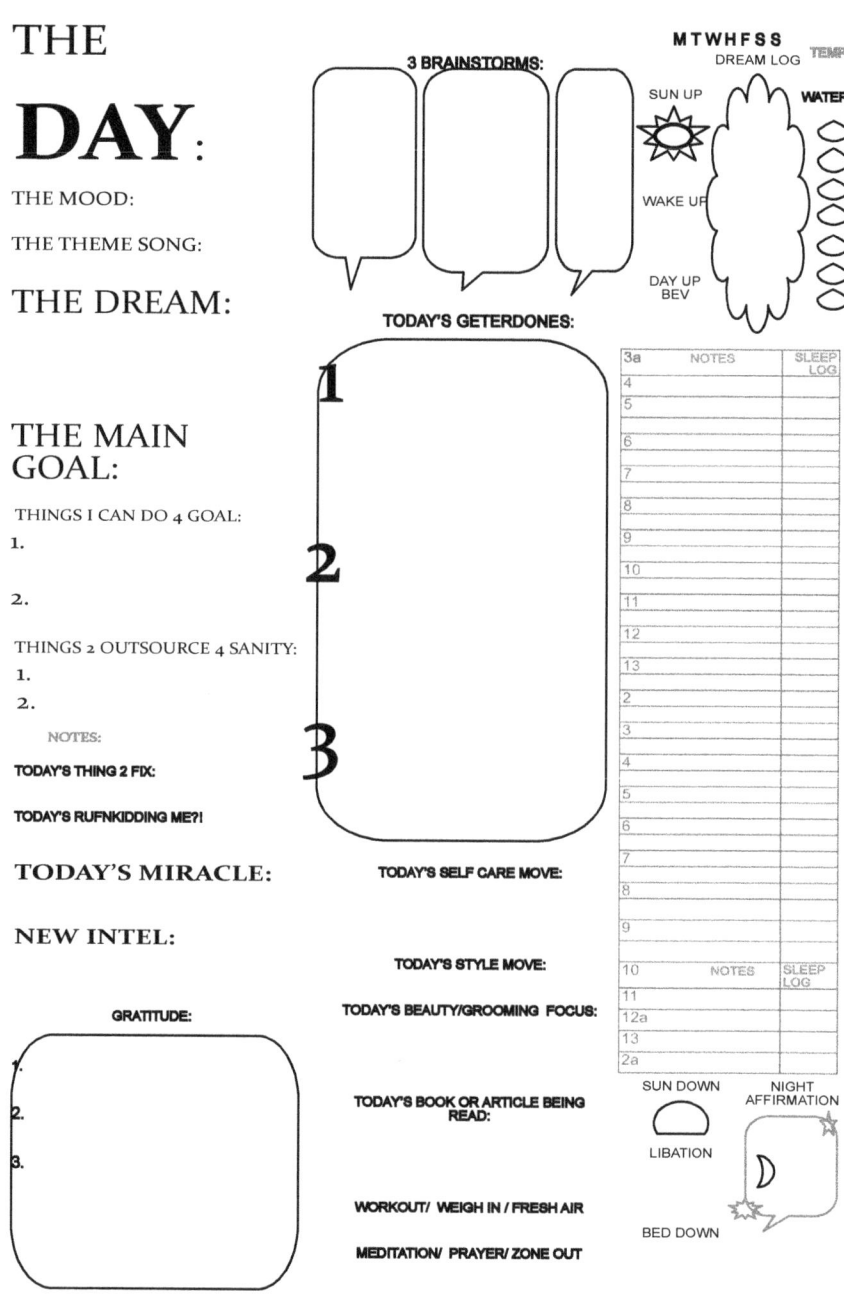

THE
pregaming:

THE recap:

THE
DAY:

THE MOOD:

THE THEME SONG:

THE DREAM:

THE MAIN GOAL:

THINGS I CAN DO 4 GOAL:
1.

2.

THINGS 2 OUTSOURCE 4 SANITY:
1.
2.

   NOTES:

TODAY'S THING 2 FIX:

TODAY'S RUFNKIDDING ME?!

TODAY'S MIRACLE:

NEW INTEL:

   GRATITUDE:

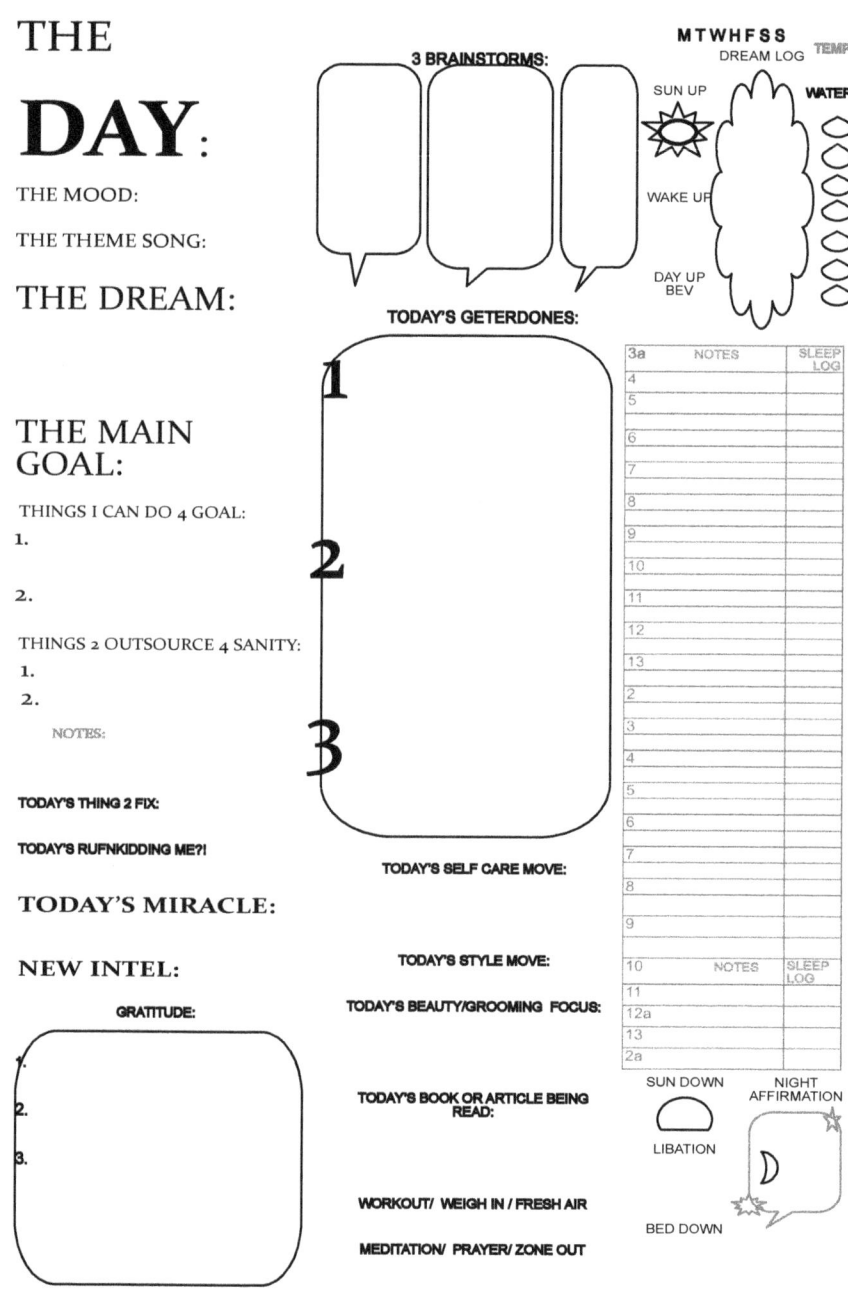

3 BRAINSTORMS:

TODAY'S GETERDONES:

1

2

3

TODAY'S SELF CARE MOVE:

TODAY'S STYLE MOVE:

TODAY'S BEAUTY/GROOMING FOCUS:

TODAY'S BOOK OR ARTICLE BEING READ:

WORKOUT/ WEIGH IN / FRESH AIR

MEDITATION/ PRAYER/ ZONE OUT

M T W H F S S
DREAM LOG   TEMP
SUN UP   WATER
WAKE UP
DAY UP BEV

SUN DOWN   NIGHT AFFIRMATION
LIBATION
BED DOWN

THE
pregaming:

THE recap:

THE DAY:

THE MOOD:

THE THEME SONG:

THE DREAM:

THE MAIN GOAL:

THINGS I CAN DO 4 GOAL:
1.
2.

THINGS 2 OUTSOURCE 4 SANITY:
1.
2.

NOTES:

TODAY'S THING 2 FIX:

TODAY'S RUFNKIDDING ME?!

TODAY'S MIRACLE:

NEW INTEL:

GRATITUDE:
1.
2.
3.

3 BRAINSTORMS:

TODAY'S GETERDONES:
1
2
3

TODAY'S SELF CARE MOVE:

TODAY'S STYLE MOVE:

TODAY'S BEAUTY/GROOMING FOCUS:

TODAY'S BOOK OR ARTICLE BEING READ:

WORKOUT/ WEIGH IN / FRESH AIR

MEDITATION/ PRAYER/ ZONE OUT

M T W H F S S
DREAM LOG   TEMP
SUN UP
WATER
WAKE UP
DAY UP BEV

3a	NOTES	SLEEP LOG
4		
5		
6		
7		
8		
9		
10		
11		
12		
13		
2		
3		
4		
5		
6		
7		
8		
9		
10	NOTES	SLEEP LOG
11		
12a		
13		
2a		

SUN DOWN   NIGHT AFFIRMATION
LIBATION
BED DOWN

THE pregaming:

THE recap:

THE
DAY:

THE MOOD:

THE THEME SONG:

THE DREAM:

THE MAIN GOAL:

THINGS I CAN DO 4 GOAL:
1.
2.

THINGS 2 OUTSOURCE 4 SANITY:
1.
2.

NOTES:

TODAY'S THING 2 FIX:

TODAY'S RUFNKIDDING ME?!

TODAY'S MIRACLE:

NEW INTEL:

GRATITUDE:
1.
2.
3.

3 BRAINSTORMS:

TODAY'S GETERDONES:
1
2
3

TODAY'S SELF CARE MOVE:

TODAY'S STYLE MOVE:

TODAY'S BEAUTY/GROOMING FOCUS:

TODAY'S BOOK OR ARTICLE BEING READ:

WORKOUT/ WEIGH IN / FRESH AIR

MEDITATION/ PRAYER/ ZONE OUT

M T W H F S S
DREAM LOG   TEMP
SUN UP
WAKE UP
DAY UP BEV
WATER

NOTES | SLEEP LOG
3a
4
5
6
7
8
9
10
11
12
13
2
3
4
5
6
7
8
9
10   NOTES   SLEEP LOG
11
12a
13
2a

SUN DOWN
LIBATION
NIGHT AFFIRMATION
BED DOWN

THE
pregaming:

THE recap:

THE pregaming:

THE recap:

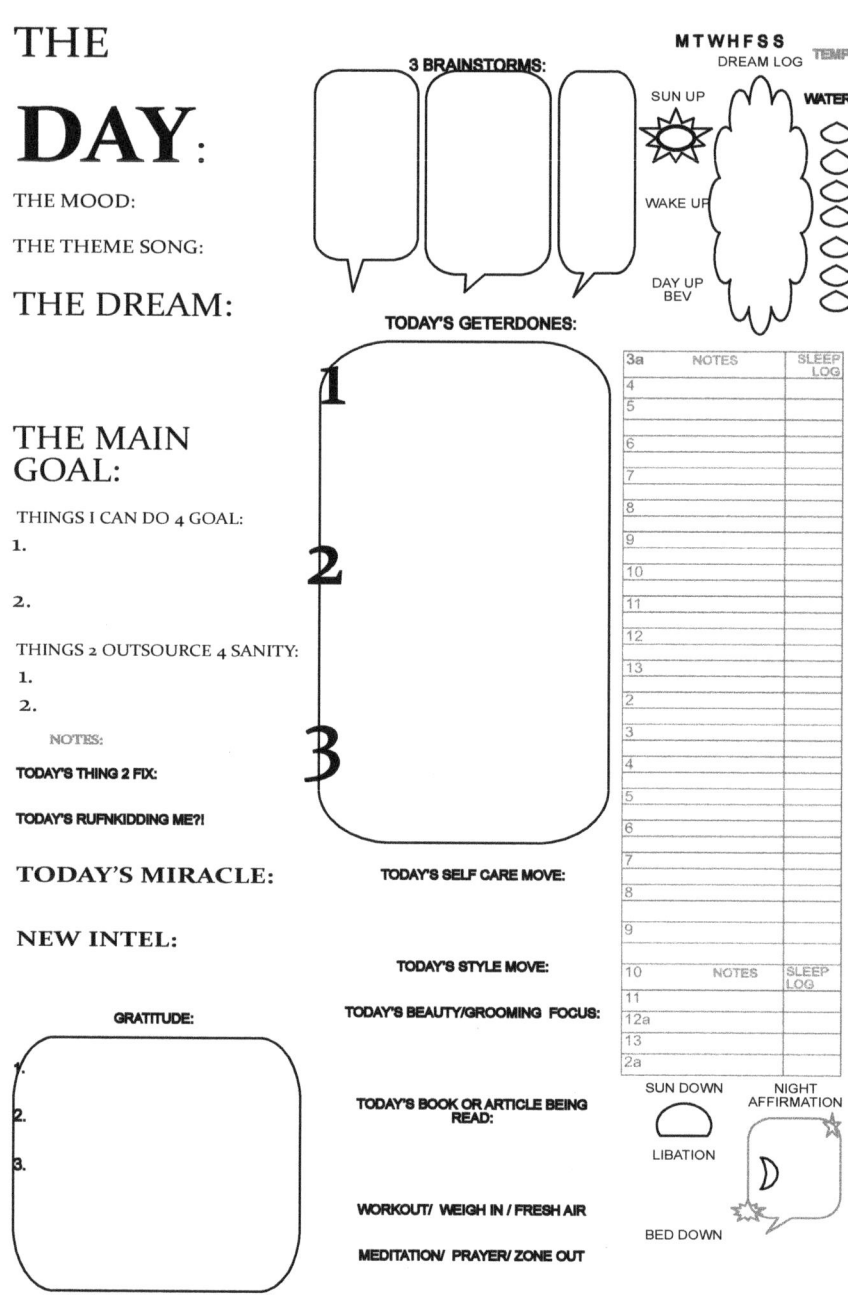

THE
pregaming:

THE recap:

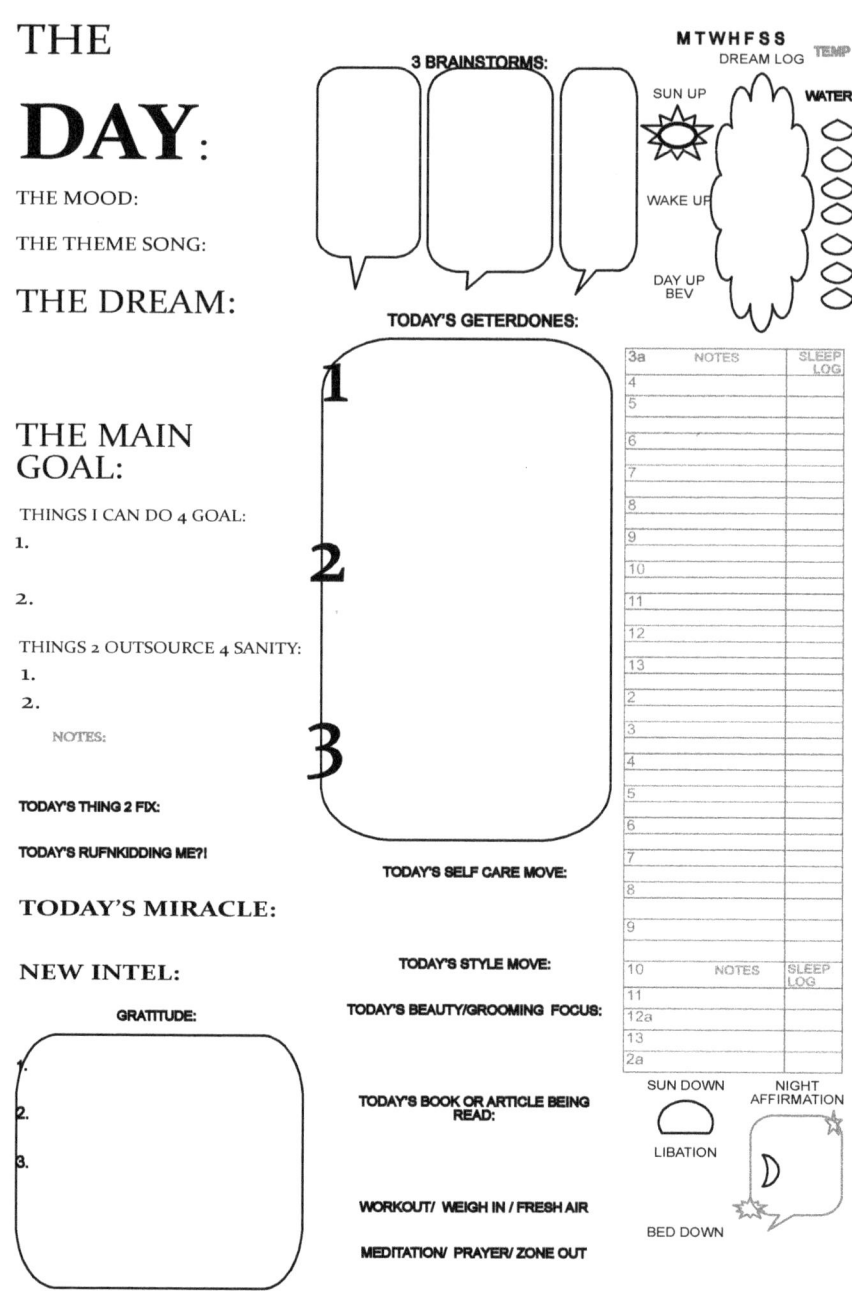

THE
pregaming:

THE recap:

THE
pregaming:

THE recap:

THE DAY:

THE MOOD:

THE THEME SONG:

THE DREAM:

THE MAIN GOAL:

THINGS I CAN DO 4 GOAL:
1.
2.

THINGS 2 OUTSOURCE 4 SANITY:
1.
2.

NOTES:

TODAY'S THING 2 FIX:

TODAY'S RUFNKIDDING ME?!

TODAY'S MIRACLE:

NEW INTEL:

GRATITUDE:
1.
2.
3.

3 BRAINSTORMS:

TODAY'S GETERDONES:
1
2
3

TODAY'S SELF CARE MOVE:

TODAY'S STYLE MOVE:

TODAY'S BEAUTY/GROOMING FOCUS:

TODAY'S BOOK OR ARTICLE BEING READ:

WORKOUT/ WEIGH IN / FRESH AIR

MEDITATION/ PRAYER/ ZONE OUT

M T W H F S S
DREAM LOG TEMP
SUN UP
WAKE UP
DAY UP BEV
WATER

3a NOTES SLEEP LOG
4
5
6
7
8
9
10
11
12
13
2
3
4
5
6
7
8
9
10 NOTES SLEEP LOG
11
12a
13
2a

SUN DOWN   NIGHT AFFIRMATION
LIBATION
BED DOWN

THE
pregaming:

THE recap:

THE
DAY:

THE MOOD:

THE THEME SONG:

THE DREAM:

THE MAIN GOAL:

THINGS I CAN DO 4 GOAL:
1.
2.

THINGS 2 OUTSOURCE 4 SANITY:
1.
2.

NOTES:

TODAY'S THING 2 FIX:

TODAY'S RUFNKIDDING ME?!

TODAY'S MIRACLE:

NEW INTEL:

GRATITUDE:
1.
2.
3.

3 BRAINSTORMS:

TODAY'S GETERDONES:
1
2
3

TODAY'S SELF CARE MOVE:

TODAY'S STYLE MOVE:

TODAY'S BEAUTY/GROOMING FOCUS:

TODAY'S BOOK OR ARTICLE BEING READ:

WORKOUT/ WEIGH IN / FRESH AIR

MEDITATION/ PRAYER/ ZONE OUT

M T W H F S S
DREAM LOG   TEMP
SUN UP
WAKE UP
DAY UP BEV
WATER

NOTES | SLEEP LOG
3a
4
5
6
7
8
9
10
11
12
13
2
3
4
5
6
7
8
9
10   NOTES   SLEEP LOG
11
12a
13
2a

SUN DOWN
LIBATION
BED DOWN
NIGHT AFFIRMATION

THE
pregaming:

THE recap:

THE
pregaming:

THE recap:

#	
1	
2	
3	
4	
5	
6	
7	
8	
9	
10	
11	
12	
13	
14	
15	
16	
17	
18	
19	
20	
21	
22	
23	
24	
25	
26	
27	
28	
29	
30	
31	
date	Gratitude LOG

MONTH THREE.

JUST₄FUN

resuscitate · reflect · reframe · relax · 8r · restore · repair · relate · rally

Recalibrate.

Rebrand.

Revamp.

Redo.

Recast.

Revise your reality.

START	174	285	START
CYCLE	369	Vibe Tribe [Hertz]:	417	CYCLE
STOP	528	639	STOP
	741	852	
	963		

SEASON:
HARVEST   AUTUMN
WINTER   SPRING
          SUMMER
Seasonal focus:

NEW MOON:
FULL MOON:

HOLIDAYS:
This month's " I & i" DAY:
This month's "I & i" HOUR:

This month's HIGHEST TIMELINE log-line:

This month's affirmation:

This month's workout focus:

This month's physical challenge:

This month's shower & bathing meditation:

MONTH:
JAN FEB MAR
APR MAY JUN
JUL AUG SEP
OCT NOV DEC

Movie of your life

bigGOAL:
Aim to do's

bigTASK:
Gotta do's

PICK4 Impossible   PICK4 SANCTUARY   PICK4 SELF-CARE
Things 2 try: GETERDONES: GETERDONES:

JUST4FUN:

New Moon Resonance

1. Imagine what you aim to Bring into your zone..
2. Set new intentions.
3. Journal & Meditate.
4. Scrub &/or soak your body.
5. Get out in some moonlight.

New/Things 2do.

Things 2do/Full.

1. Cleanse your space [Mental & physical].
2. Crystals! Charge 'em if ya got'em.
3. Celebrate any wins.
4. Release what no longer Serves you.
5. Get out in some moonlight.

Full Moon Resonance

WHO ARE YOU　　HOW DO YOU EXPRESS IT?

ideal
POINT
OF THE
MONTH:

[NECESSARY]
COUNTERPOINT
OF THE MONTH:

(EVERY POINT HAS A COUNTERPOINT)

ORDERED IN:

PICK 4 MOVIES 2 WATCH:

PICK 4 BOOKS 2 READ:

THEME SONG

POET

FLOWER

COLOR

CRYSTAL

HERB

Give yourself ONE day a week. One way or another. For you. Find a way.

THIS MONTH'S:
(capsule closet)
[Current rotation]

THIS MONTH'S dayUP Geterdone:

THIS MONTH'S b4BED Geterdone:

BUILD YOU UP BETTER HABIT TO IMPROVE:

GIVE IT UP OR REPLACE ?

WITH WHAT ?   HOW ?:

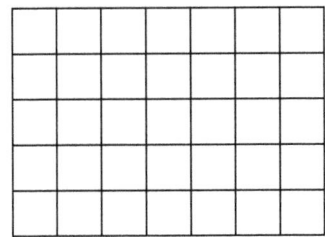

TREAT YOURSELF
Curious about it? LEARN IT

Wish you were able 2 do it? TRY IT

Place you want 2go? GO 2IT

Love to have it outside? TRY IT @HOME

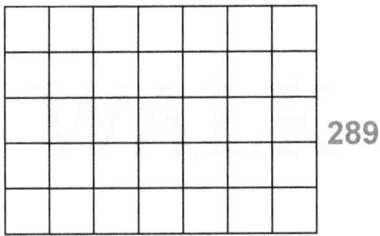

Otha Dailies

JUST4FUN FOCUS:

THING 2LOVE ABOUT YOU

SPIRIT SUBJECT 2 FOCUS: ON

ODD INTEREST 2DEEP DIVE:

BEAUTY FEATURE/FOCUS:

CLEAN UP NICE FOCUS:

STYLE FOCUS:

SMELL 2 LOVE:

SHAKE THAT ASS!/NOW MOovVE!!

289

FIND/DO SOMETHING BEAUTIFUL

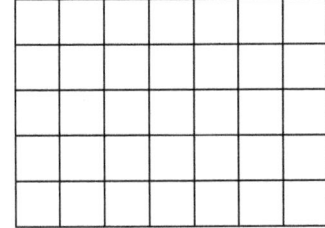

TRAVEL:
SCHEDULED   STAY-CATION

THINGS2DOTHERE

DREAM TREK:

VISUALS

HABIT:

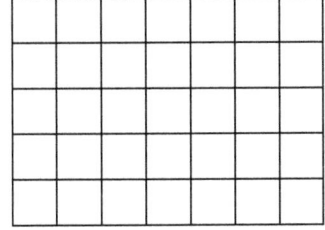

Project codename:	Magii Specialists Masterminds ("Who CAN shoot the dayum dawg?"):	KNOWN [Accessible] INTEL Gnosis needed [people, books, TEDx talks, documentaries, examples]:	Project codename:	Magii Specialists Masterminds ("Who CAN shoot the dayum dawg?"):	KNOWN [Accessible] INTEL Gnosis needed [people, books, TEDx talks, documentaries, examples]:
Dawn: D-Day: Modus Operandi [M.O.]:	1. 2. 3. 4.		Dawn: D-Day: Modus Operandi [M.O.]:	1. 2. 3. 4.	
How2Skin it Steps: E.g., Make a detailed supplies needed list	Dawn/M/D Day 8/22/23/ 9/13 / 10/1/23	New INTEL: issues & fixes as they arise: e.g., Delivery delays,	How2Skin it Steps: E.g., Make a detailed supplies needed list	Dawn/M/D Day 8/22/23/ 9/13 / 10/1/23	New INTEL: issues & fixes as they arise: e.g., Delivery delays,

Ideal project Maps / Maneuvers

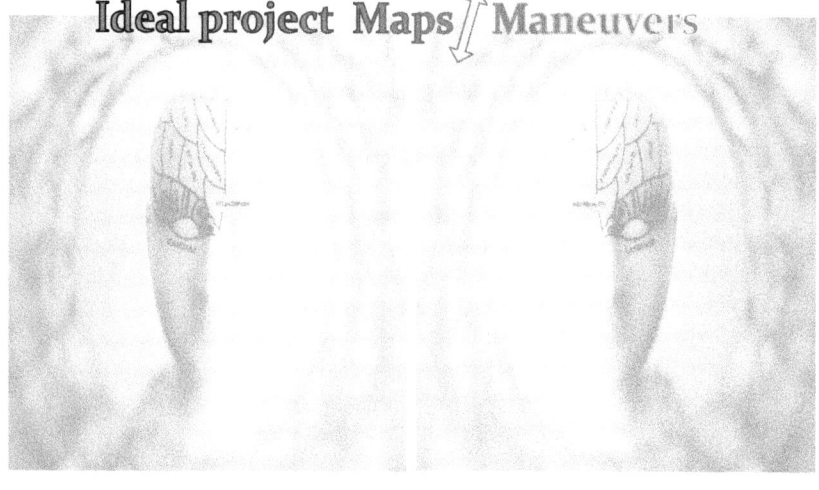

Ideal project Maps / Maneuvers

Project codename:	Magii Specialists Masterminds ("Who CAN shoot the dayum dawg?"):	KNOWN [Accessible] INTEL Gnosis needed [people, books, TEDx talks, documentaries, examples]:
	1.	
Dawn: D-Day:	2.	
Modus Operandi [M.O.]:	3.	
	4.	

How2Skin it Steps: E.g., Make a detailed supplies needed list	Dawn/M/D Day 8/22/23/ 9/13 / 10/1/23	New INTEL: issues & fixes as they arise: e.g., Delivery delays,

Project codename:	Magii Specialists Masterminds ("Who CAN shoot the dayum dawg?"):	KNOWN [Accessible] INTEL Gnosis needed [people, books, TEDx talks, documentaries, examples]:
	1.	
Dawn: D-Day:	2.	
Modus Operandi [M.O.]:	3.	
	4.	

How2Skin it Steps: E.g., Make a detailed supplies needed list	Dawn/M/D Day 8/22/23/ 9/13 / 10/1/23	New INTEL: issues & fixes as they arise: e.g., Delivery delays,

THE WEEK:

THE vibe AIMED 4:

THE PLAYLIST:
1.
2.
3.

THE DREAM:

THE MAIN GOAL:

NOTES:

WEEK   OF 26
WEEKLY GREEN DRINK LOG

THIS WEEK:

SELF CARE FOCUS

STYLE INSPO:

BEAUTY/GROOMING ZONE:

WORKOUT CHALLENGE FOCUS

MEDITATION/ FOCUS

PRAYER REQUEST

DECOMPRESSION TREAT

THIS WEEK'S WHATHAVEYOUS:

1.

2.

3.

4.

5.

6.

7.

APPOINTMENTS	TIME & DATE	TYPE

7 THINGS YOU LOVE ABOUT YOU: (SELF PEP TALK)

1.
2.
3.
4.
5.
6.
7.

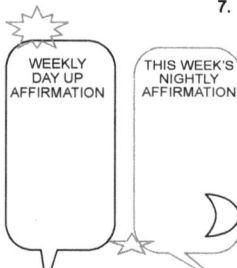

WEEKLY DAY UP AFFIRMATION

THIS WEEK'S NIGHTLY AFFIRMATION

"I AM..."
(OF THE WEEK)

SPIRITUAL SHOTGUN:
What aspect of God, icon, archetype, angel, energy or spirit animal is riding out into the world *with* you this week?

LOVE ON OTHER'S LIST [L.O.O.L]
Who can you quietly do a cool thing for?

Aww~! Brain dump:
Sweethearts,
Did cool things,
Who are you FN with this week?

(FILL AS NEEDED)

295

Target Weekly meal plan:
Whole 30? Keto? Vegan? "All Thai, all week"? Paleo? Vegetarian? Carnivore?
Healthy Decadence?

Fast/ cleanse/ omad/ IF/ Juicing/ FODMAP

How can you bless them for for blessing you?

Argh! brain dump:
The jerks, the K*rens,
The nonsense,
Who are you so not FN with this week?

Grocery items 2 get 2 hit it:

How did you forgive them to fully let their energy go?

...the WEEKend RIT[UAL]S:

THE WEEK:

THE vibe AIMED 4:

THE PLAYLIST:
1.
2.
3.

THE DREAM:

THE MAIN GOAL:

NOTES:

WEEK OF 26

WEEKLY GREEN DRINK LOG

THIS WEEK:

SELF CARE FOCUS

STYLE INSPO:

BEAUTY/GROOMING ZONE:

WORKOUT CHALLENGE FOCUS

MEDITATION/ FOCUS

PRAYER REQUEST

DECOMPRESSION TREAT

THIS WEEK'S WHATHAVEYOUS:

1.
2.
3.
4.
5.
6.
7.

APPOINTMENTS	TIME & DATE	TYPE

7 THINGS YOU LOVE ABOUT YOU: (SELF PEP TALK)

1.
2.
3.
4.
5.
6.
7.

WEEKLY DAY UP AFFIRMATION

THIS WEEK'S NIGHTLY AFFIRMATION

"I AM..."
(OF THE WEEK)

SPIRITUAL SHOTGUN:

What aspect of God, icon, archetype, angel, energy or spirit animal is riding out into the world *with* you this week?

LOVE ON OTHER'S LIST [L.O.O.L]

Who can you quietly do a cool thing for?

Aww~! Brain dump:

Sweethearts,
Did cool things,
Who are you FN with this week?

(FILL AS NEEDED)

How can you bless them for for blessing you?

Target Weekly meal plan:

Whole 30? Keto? Vegan? "All Thai, all week"? Paleo? Vegetarian? Carnivore?
Healthy Decadence?

Fast/ cleanse/ omad/ IF/ Juicing/ FODMAP

Argh! brain dump:

The jerks, the K*rens,
The nonsense,
Who are you so not FN with this week?

Grocery items 2 get 2 hit it:

How did you forgive them **to** fully let their energy go?

...the WEEKend RIT[UAL]S:

THE WEEK:

THE vibe AIMED 4:

THE PLAYLIST:
1.
2.
3.

THE DREAM:

THE MAIN GOAL:

THIS WEEK'S WHATHAVEYOUS:
1.
2.
3.
4.
5.
6.
7.

NOTES:

WEEK   OF 26

WEEKLY GREEN DRINK LOG

THIS WEEK:

SELF CARE FOCUS

STYLE INSPO:

BEAUTY/GROOMING ZONE:

WORKOUT CHALLENGE FOCUS

MEDITATION/ FOCUS

PRAYER REQUEST

DECOMPRESSION TREAT

7 THINGS YOU LOVE ABOUT YOU: (SELF PEP TALK)
1.
2.
3.
4.
5.
6.
7.

APPOINTMENTS	TIME & DATE	TYPE

WEEKLY DAY UP AFFIRMATION

THIS WEEK'S NIGHTLY AFFIRMATION

"I AM"...
(OF THE WEEK)

SPIRITUAL SHOTGUN:

What aspect of God, icon, archetype, angel, energy or spirit animal is riding out into the world *with* you this week?

LOVE ON OTHER'S LIST [L.O.O.L]

Who can you quietly do a cool thing for?

Aww~! Brain dump:

Sweethearts,
Did cool things,
Who are you FN with this week?

(FILL AS NEEDED)

Target Weekly meal plan:

Whole 30? Keto? Vegan? "All Thai, all week"? Paleo? Vegetarian? Carnivore? Healthy Decadence?

Fast/ cleanse/ omad/ IF/ Juicing/ FODMAP

Grocery items 2 get 2 hit it:

...the WEEKend RIT[UAL]S:

How can you bless them for for blessing you?

Argh! brain dump:

The jerks, the K*rens,
The nonsense,
Who are you so not FN with this week?

How did you forgive them **to** fully let their energy go?

THE WEEK:

THE vibe AIMED 4:

THE PLAYLIST:
1.
2.
3.

THE DREAM:

THE MAIN GOAL:

NOTES:

WEEK ___ OF 26

WEEKLY GREEN DRINK LOG

THIS WEEK:

SELF CARE FOCUS

STYLE INSPO:

BEAUTY/GROOMING ZONE:

WORKOUT CHALLENGE FOCUS

MEDITATION/ FOCUS

PRAYER REQUEST

DECOMPRESSION TREAT

THIS WEEK'S WHATHAVEYOUS:

1.
2.
3.
4.
5.
6.
7.

7 THINGS YOU LOVE ABOUT YOU: (SELF PEP TALK)

1.
2.
3.
4.
5.
6.
7.

APPOINTMENTS	TIME & DATE	TYPE

WEEKLY DAY UP AFFIRMATION

THIS WEEK'S NIGHTLY AFFIRMATION

"I AM..."
(OF THE WEEK)

SPIRITUAL SHOTGUN:
What aspect of God, icon, archetype, angel, energy or spirit animal is riding out into the world *with* you this week?

LOVE ON OTHER'S LIST [L.O.O.L]

Who can you quietly do a cool thing for?

Aww~! Brain dump:
Sweethearts,
Did cool things,
Who are you FN with this week?

(FILL AS NEEDED)

Target Weekly meal plan:
Whole 30? Keto? Vegan? "All Thai, all week"? Paleo? Vegetarian? Carnivore?
Healthy Decadence?

Fast/ cleanse/ omad/ IF/ Juicing/ FODMAP

Grocery items 2 get 2 hit it:

...the WEEKend RIT[UAL]S:

How can you bless them for for blessing you?

Argh! brain dump:
The jerks, the K*rens,
The nonsense,
Who are you so not FN with this week?

How did you forgive them **to** fully let their energy go?

THE WEEK:

THE vibe AIMED 4:

THE PLAYLIST:
1.
2.
3.

THE DREAM:

THE MAIN GOAL:

NOTES:

WEEK OF 26

WEEKLY GREEN DRINK LOG

THIS WEEK:

SELF CARE FOCUS

STYLE INSPO:

BEAUTY/GROOMING ZONE:

WORKOUT CHALLENGE FOCUS

MEDITATION/ FOCUS

PRAYER REQUEST

DECOMPRESSION TREAT

THIS WEEK'S WHATHAVEYOUS:
1.
2.
3.
4.
5.
6.
7.

APPOINTMENTS	TIME & DATE	TYPE

7 THINGS YOU LOVE ABOUT YOU: (SELF PEP TALK)
1.
2.
3.
4.
5.
6.
7.

WEEKLY DAY UP AFFIRMATION

THIS WEEK'S NIGHTLY AFFIRMATION

"I AM..."
(OF THE WEEK)

SPIRITUAL SHOTGUN:
What aspect of God, icon, archetype, angel, energy or spirit animal is riding out into the world *with* you this week?

LOVE ON OTHER'S LIST [L.O.O.L]
Who can you quietly do a cool thing for?

Aww~! Brain dump:
Sweethearts,
Did cool things,
Who are you FN with this week?

(FILL AS NEEDED)

How can you bless them for for blessing you?

Target Weekly meal plan:
Whole 30? Keto? Vegan? "All Thai, all week"? Paleo? Vegetarian? Carnivore? Healthy Decadence?

Fast/ cleanse/ omad/ IF/ Juicing/ FODMAP

Argh! brain dump:
The jerks, the K*rens,
The nonsense,
Who are you so not FN with this week?

Grocery items 2 get 2 hit it:

How did you forgive them **to** fully let their energy go?

...the WEEKend RIT[UAL]S:

date	SIX WORD STORY LOG
1	
2	
3	
4	
5	
6	
7	
8	
9	
10	
11	
12	
13	
14	
15	
16	
17	
18	
19	
20	
21	
22	
23	
24	
25	
26	
27	
28	
29	
30	
31	

305

THE
DAY:

THE MOOD:

THE THEME SONG:

THE DREAM:

THE MAIN GOAL:

THINGS I CAN DO 4 GOAL:
1.

2.

THINGS 2 OUTSOURCE 4 SANITY:
1.
2.

NOTES:

TODAY'S THING 2 FIX:

TODAY'S RUFNKIDDING ME?!

TODAY'S MIRACLE:

NEW INTEL:

GRATITUDE:

1.
2.
3.

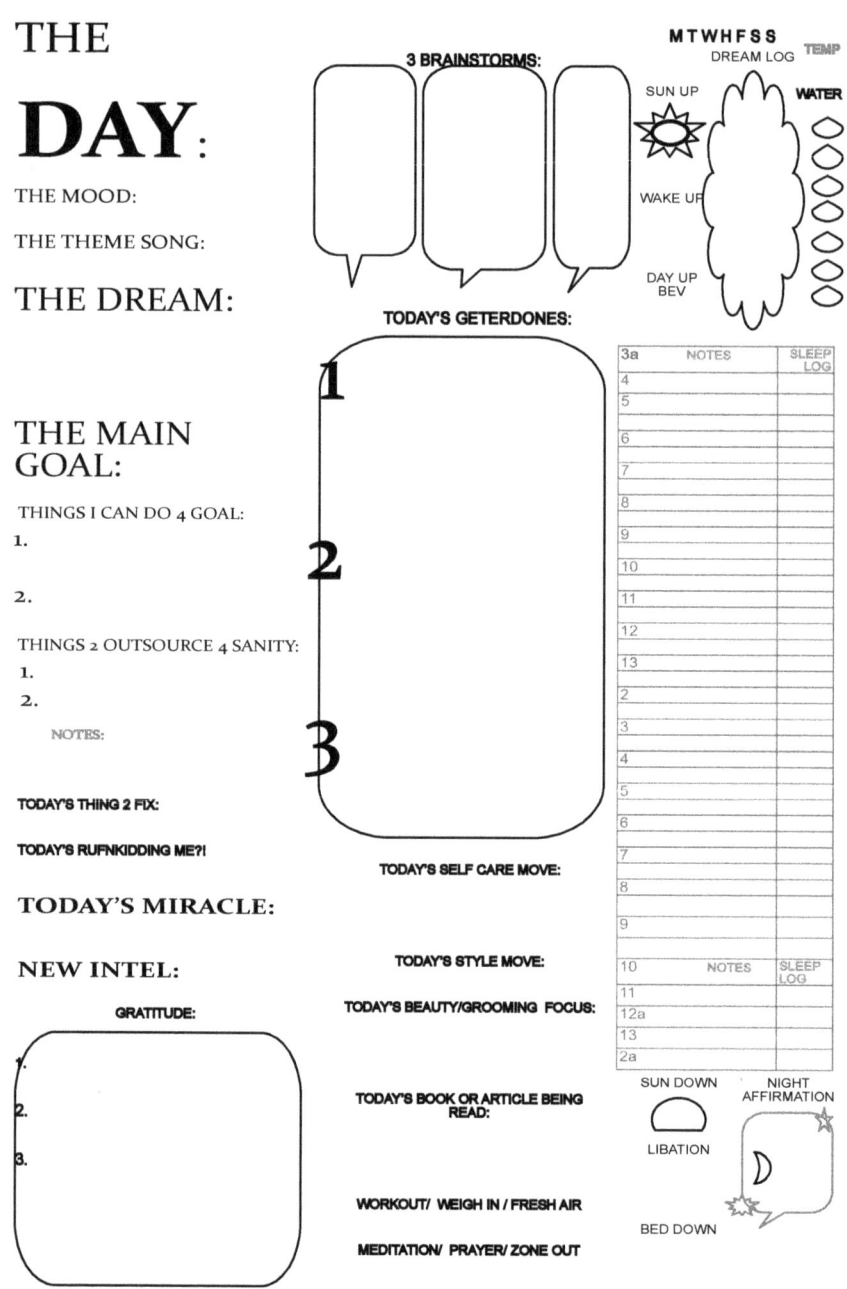

3 BRAINSTORMS:

TODAY'S GETERDONES:

1
2
3

TODAY'S SELF CARE MOVE:

TODAY'S STYLE MOVE:

TODAY'S BEAUTY/GROOMING FOCUS:

TODAY'S BOOK OR ARTICLE BEING READ:

WORKOUT/ WEIGH IN / FRESH AIR

MEDITATION/ PRAYER/ ZONE OUT

M T W H F S S
DREAM LOG   TEMP
SUN UP   WATER
WAKE UP
DAY UP BEV

3a NOTES SLEEP LOG
4
5
6
7
8
9
10
11
12
13
2
3
4
5
6
7
8
9
10 NOTES SLEEP LOG
11
12a
13
2a

SUN DOWN   NIGHT AFFIRMATION
LIBATION
BED DOWN

THE
pregaming:

THE recap:

THE pregaming:

THE recap:

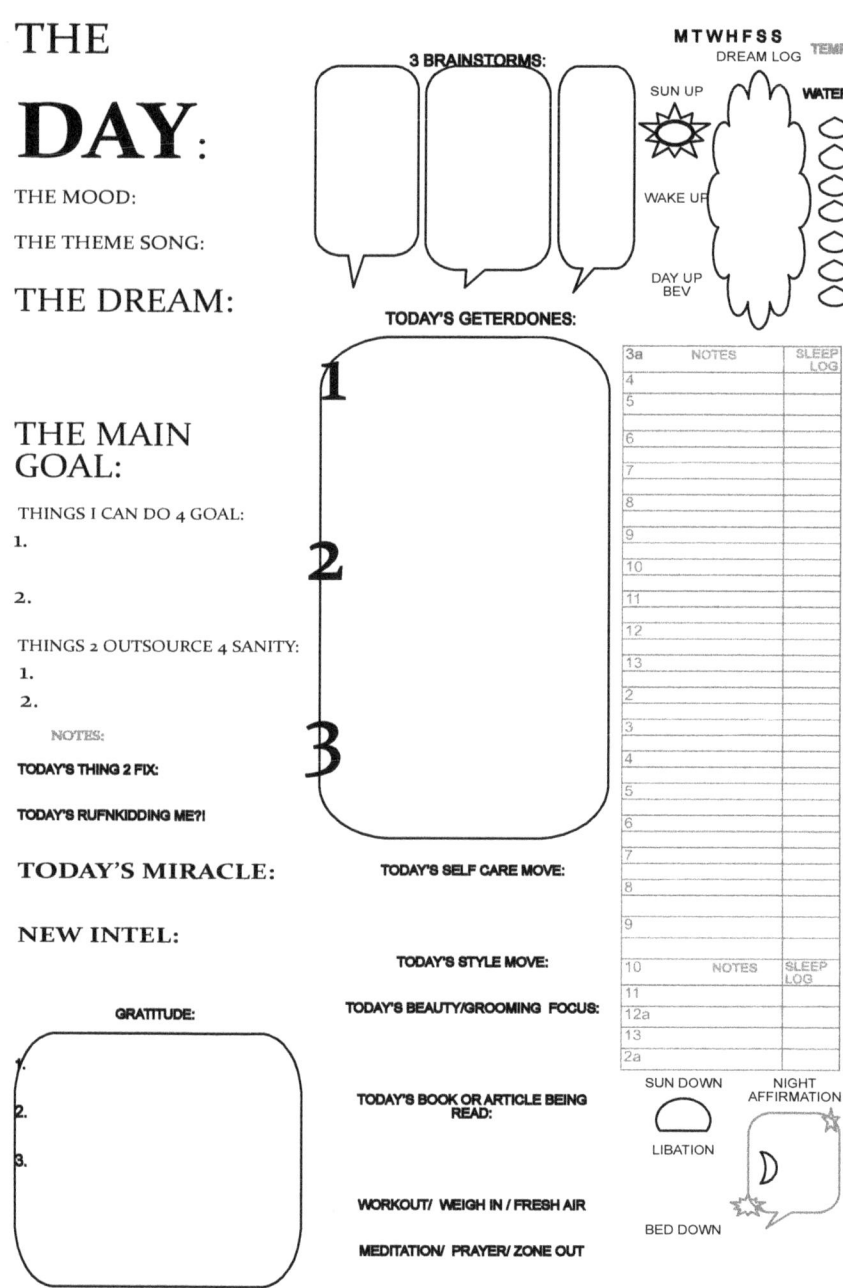

THE
pregaming:

THE recap:

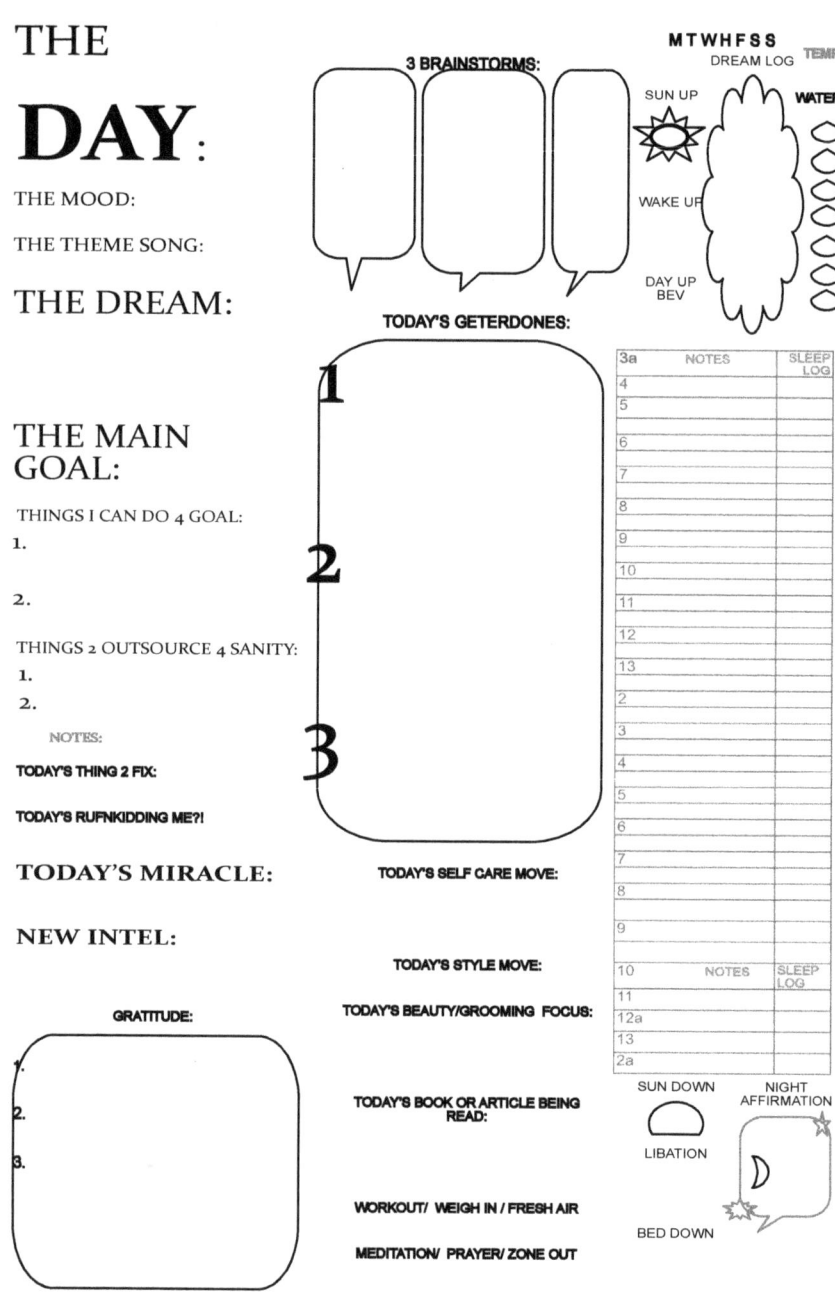

THE
pregaming:

THE recap:

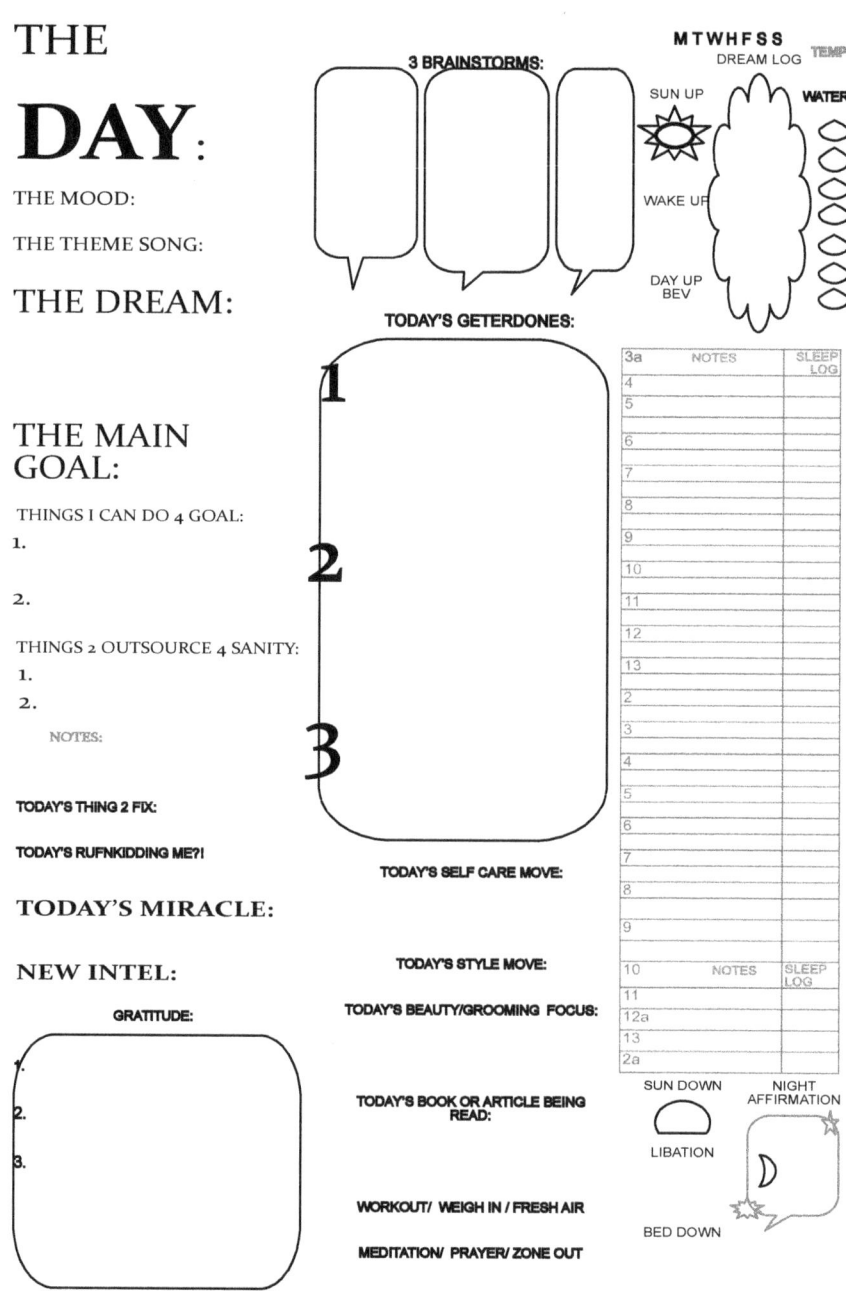

THE pregaming:

THE recap:

THE DAY:

THE MOOD:

THE THEME SONG:

THE DREAM:

THE MAIN GOAL:

THINGS I CAN DO 4 GOAL:
1.
2.

THINGS 2 OUTSOURCE 4 SANITY:
1.
2.

   NOTES:

TODAY'S THING 2 FIX:

TODAY'S RUFNKIDDING ME?!

TODAY'S MIRACLE:

NEW INTEL:

GRATITUDE:
1.
2.
3.

3 BRAINSTORMS:

TODAY'S GETERDONES:
1
2
3

TODAY'S SELF CARE MOVE:

TODAY'S STYLE MOVE:

TODAY'S BEAUTY/GROOMING FOCUS:

TODAY'S BOOK OR ARTICLE BEING READ:

WORKOUT/ WEIGH IN / FRESH AIR

MEDITATION/ PRAYER/ ZONE OUT

M T W H F S S
DREAM LOG   TEMP
SUN UP   WATER
WAKE UP
DAY UP BEV

3a	NOTES	SLEEP LOG
4		
5		
6		
7		
8		
9		
10		
11		
12		
13		
2		
3		
4		
5		
6		
7		
8		
9		
10	NOTES	SLEEP LOG
11		
12a		
13		
2a		

SUN DOWN   NIGHT AFFIRMATION

LIBATION

BED DOWN

THE
pregaming:

THE recap:

THE
pregaming:

THE recap:

THE DAY:

THE MOOD:

THE THEME SONG:

THE DREAM:

THE MAIN GOAL:

THINGS I CAN DO 4 GOAL:
1.
2.

THINGS 2 OUTSOURCE 4 SANITY:
1.
2.

NOTES:

TODAY'S THING 2 FIX:

TODAY'S RUFNKIDDING ME?!

TODAY'S MIRACLE:

NEW INTEL:

GRATITUDE:
1.
2.
3.

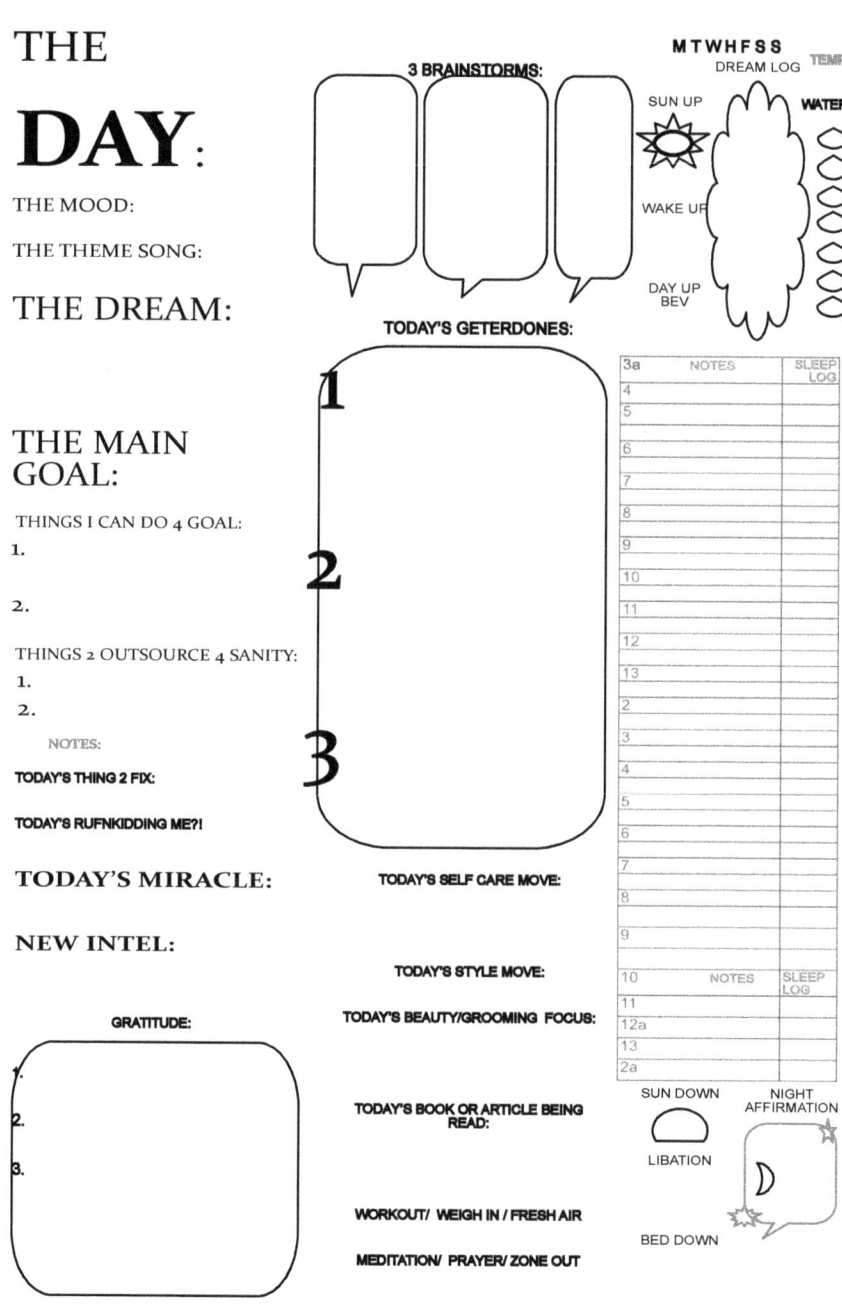

3 BRAINSTORMS:

TODAY'S GETERDONES:
1
2
3

TODAY'S SELF CARE MOVE:

TODAY'S STYLE MOVE:

TODAY'S BEAUTY/GROOMING FOCUS:

TODAY'S BOOK OR ARTICLE BEING READ:

WORKOUT/ WEIGH IN / FRESH AIR

MEDITATION/ PRAYER/ ZONE OUT

M T W H F S S
DREAM LOG TEMP
SUN UP WATER
WAKE UP
DAY UP BEV

NOTES SLEEP LOG
3a
4
5
6
7
8
9
10
11
12
13
2
3
4
5
6
7
8
9
10 NOTES SLEEP LOG
11
12a
13
2a

SUN DOWN NIGHT AFFIRMATION
LIBATION
BED DOWN

THE
pregaming:

THE recap:

THE
DAY:

THE MOOD:

THE THEME SONG:

THE DREAM:

THE MAIN GOAL:

THINGS I CAN DO 4 GOAL:
1.
2.

THINGS 2 OUTSOURCE 4 SANITY:
1.
2.

NOTES:

TODAY'S THING 2 FIX:

TODAY'S RUFNKIDDING ME?!

TODAY'S MIRACLE:

NEW INTEL:

GRATITUDE:

1.
2.
3.

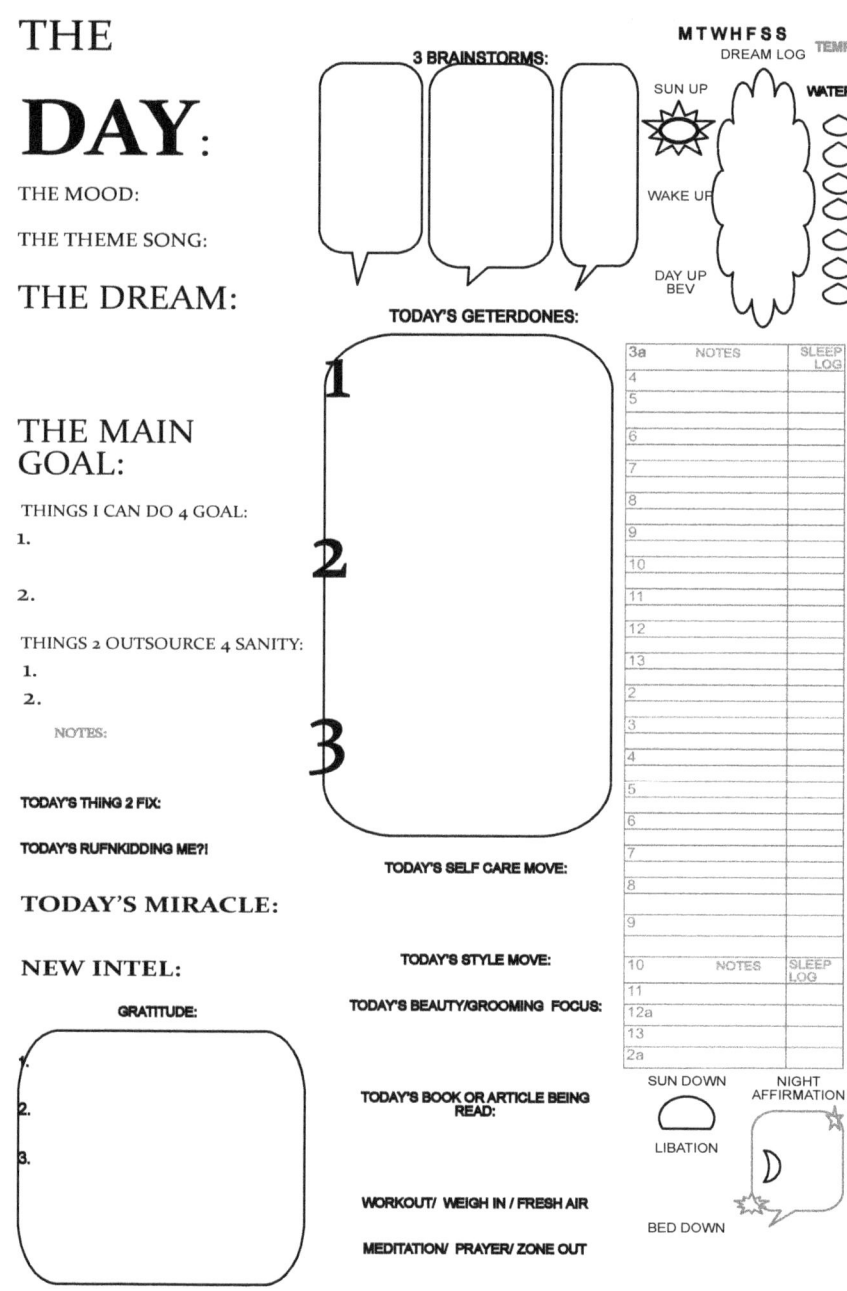

3 BRAINSTORMS:

TODAY'S GETERDONES:
1
2
3

TODAY'S SELF CARE MOVE:

TODAY'S STYLE MOVE:

TODAY'S BEAUTY/GROOMING FOCUS:

TODAY'S BOOK OR ARTICLE BEING READ:

WORKOUT/ WEIGH IN / FRESH AIR

MEDITATION/ PRAYER/ ZONE OUT

M T W H F S S
DREAM LOG TEMP

SUN UP
WAKE UP
DAY UP BEV

WATER

3a	NOTES	SLEEP LOG
4		
5		
6		
7		
8		
9		
10		
11		
12		
13		
2		
3		
4		
5		
6		
7		
8		
9		
10	NOTES	SLEEP LOG
11		
12a		
13		
2a		

SUN DOWN

LIBATION

BED DOWN

NIGHT AFFIRMATION

THE pregaming:

THE recap:

THE
DAY:

THE MOOD:

THE THEME SONG:

THE DREAM:

THE MAIN GOAL:

THINGS I CAN DO 4 GOAL:
1.
2.

THINGS 2 OUTSOURCE 4 SANITY:
1.
2.

   NOTES:

TODAY'S THING 2 FIX:

TODAY'S RUFNKIDDING ME?!

TODAY'S MIRACLE:

NEW INTEL:

GRATITUDE:

1.
2.
3.

3 BRAINSTORMS:

TODAY'S GETERDONES:

1
2
3

TODAY'S SELF CARE MOVE:

TODAY'S STYLE MOVE:

TODAY'S BEAUTY/GROOMING FOCUS:

TODAY'S BOOK OR ARTICLE BEING READ:

WORKOUT/ WEIGH IN / FRESH AIR

MEDITATION/ PRAYER/ ZONE OUT

M T W H F S S
DREAM LOG   TEMP
SUN UP   WATER
WAKE UP
DAY UP BEV

3a NOTES SLEEP LOG
4
5
6
7
8
9
10
11
12
13
2
3
4
5
6
7
8
9
10 NOTES SLEEP LOG
11
12a
13
2a

SUN DOWN   NIGHT AFFIRMATION
LIBATION
BED DOWN

THE pregaming:

THE recap:

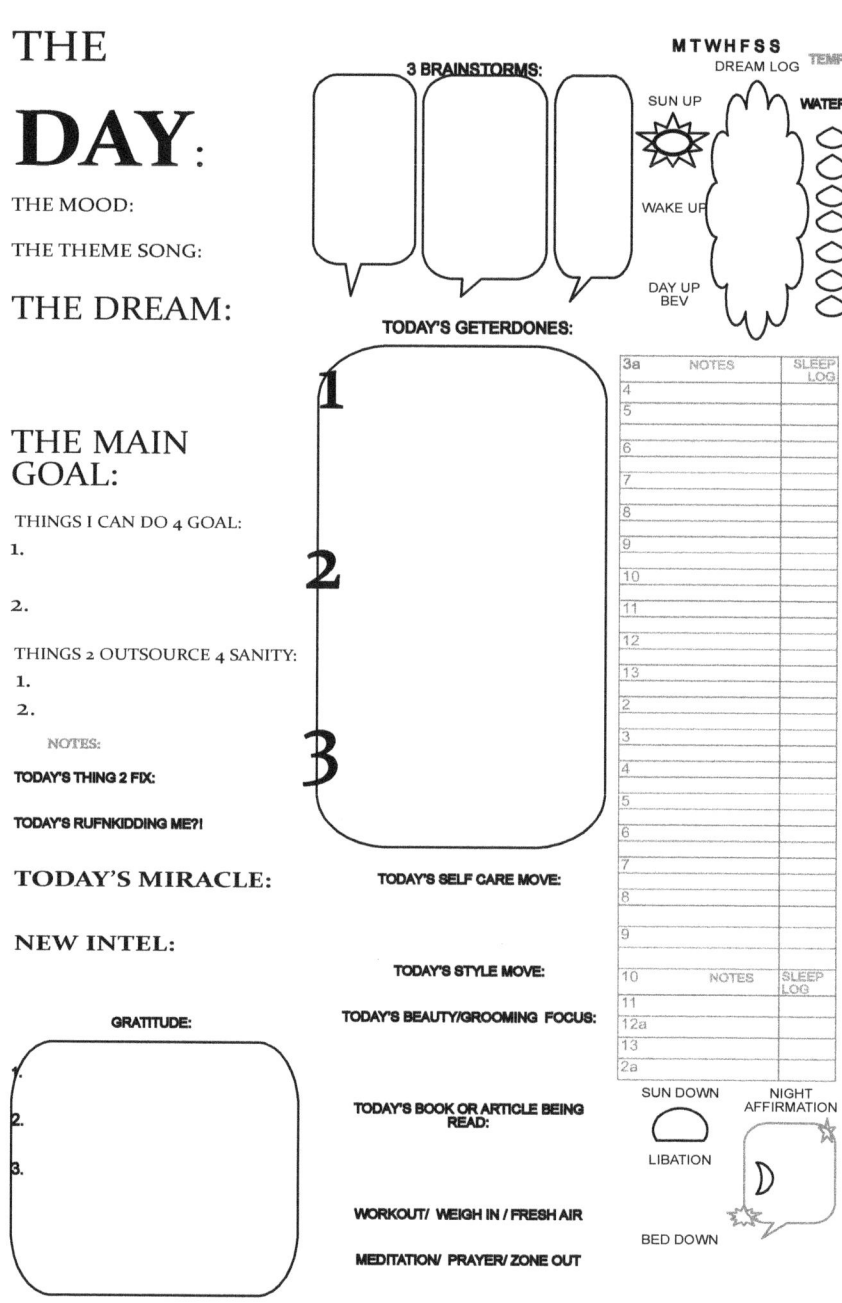

THE
pregaming:

THE recap:

THE pregaming:

THE recap:

THE
DAY:

THE MOOD:

THE THEME SONG:

THE DREAM:

THE MAIN GOAL:

THINGS I CAN DO 4 GOAL:
1.

2.

THINGS 2 OUTSOURCE 4 SANITY:
1.
2.

NOTES:

TODAY'S THING 2 FIX:

TODAY'S RUFNKIDDING ME?!

TODAY'S MIRACLE:

NEW INTEL:

GRATITUDE:

1.

2.

3.

3 BRAINSTORMS:

TODAY'S GETERDONES:

1

2

3

TODAY'S SELF CARE MOVE:

TODAY'S STYLE MOVE:

TODAY'S BEAUTY/GROOMING FOCUS:

TODAY'S BOOK OR ARTICLE BEING READ:

WORKOUT/ WEIGH IN / FRESH AIR

MEDITATION/ PRAYER/ ZONE OUT

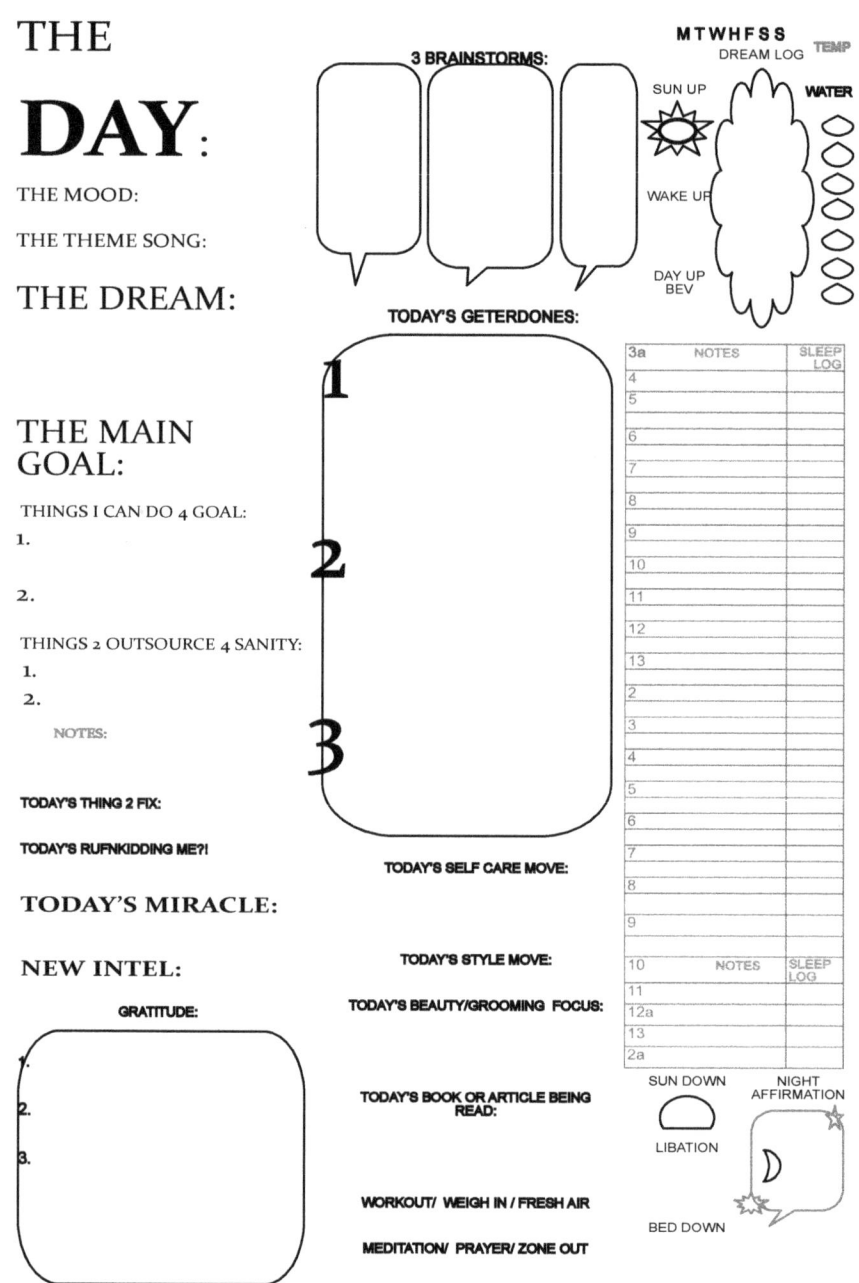

M T W H F S S
DREAM LOG   TEMP
SUN UP   WATER
WAKE UP
DAY UP
BEV

3a	NOTES	SLEEP LOG
4		
5		
6		
7		
8		
9		
10		
11		
12		
13		
2		
3		
4		
5		
6		
7		
8		
9		
10	NOTES	SLEEP LOG
11		
12a		
13		
2a		

SUN DOWN   NIGHT AFFIRMATION

LIBATION

BED DOWN

THE
pregaming:

THE recap:

THE
pregaming:

THE recap:

THE
pregaming:

THE recap:

THE
pregaming:

THE recap:

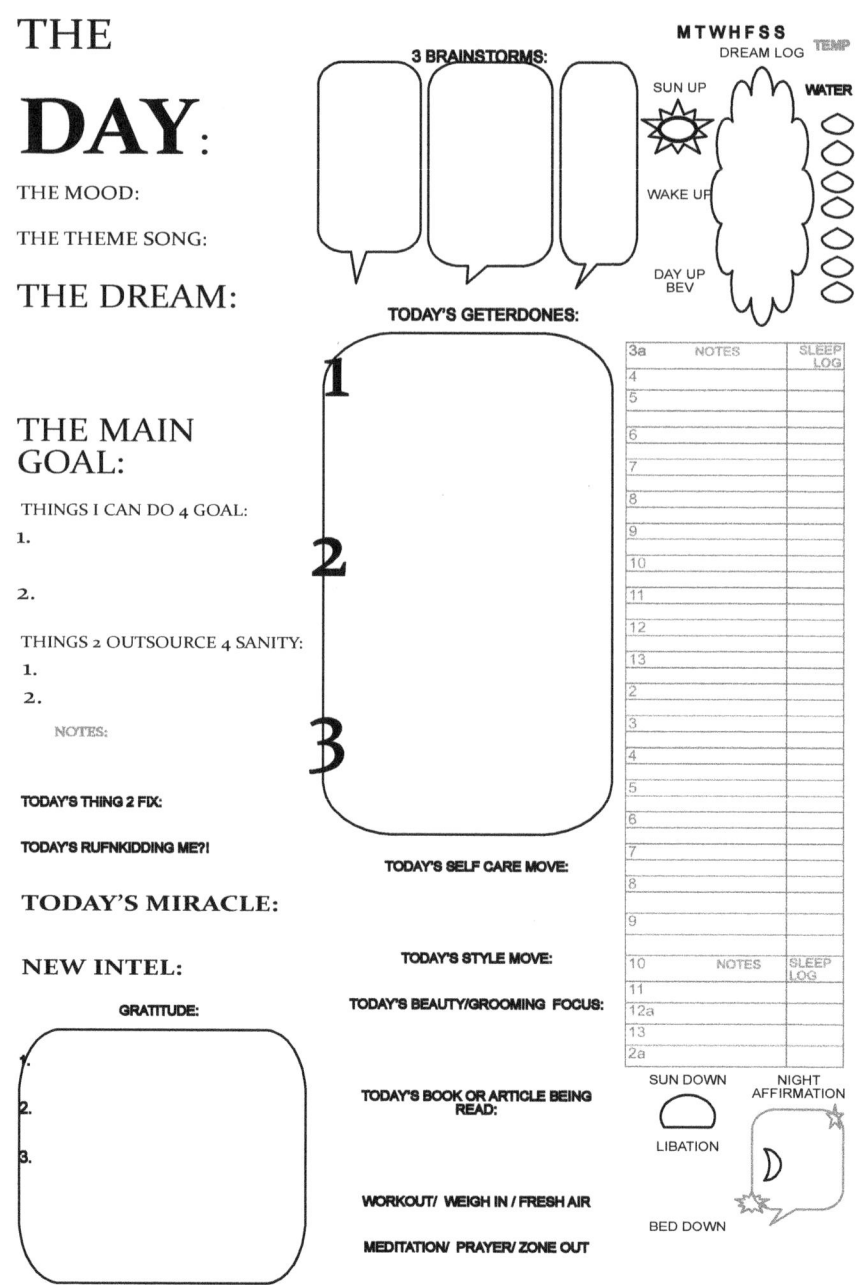

THE
pregaming:

THE recap:

THE DAY:

THE MOOD:

THE THEME SONG:

THE DREAM:

THE MAIN GOAL:

THINGS I CAN DO 4 GOAL:
1.
2.

THINGS 2 OUTSOURCE 4 SANITY:
1.
2.

NOTES:

TODAY'S THING 2 FIX:

TODAY'S RUFNKIDDING ME?!

TODAY'S MIRACLE:

NEW INTEL:

GRATITUDE:
1.
2.
3.

3 BRAINSTORMS:

TODAY'S GETERDONES:
1
2
3

TODAY'S SELF CARE MOVE:

TODAY'S STYLE MOVE:

TODAY'S BEAUTY/GROOMING FOCUS:

TODAY'S BOOK OR ARTICLE BEING READ:

WORKOUT/ WEIGH IN / FRESH AIR

MEDITATION/ PRAYER/ ZONE OUT

M T W H F S S
DREAM LOG   TEMP
SUN UP
WAKE UP
DAY UP BEV
WATER

3a	NOTES	SLEEP LOG
4		
5		
6		
7		
8		
9		
10		
11		
12		
13		
2		
3		
4		
5		
6		
7		
8		
9		
10	NOTES	SLEEP LOG
11		
12a		
13		
2a		

SUN DOWN

LIBATION

NIGHT AFFIRMATION

BED DOWN

THE
pregaming:

THE recap:

THE
pregaming:

THE recap:

THE DAY:

THE MOOD:

THE THEME SONG:

THE DREAM:

THE MAIN GOAL:

THINGS I CAN DO 4 GOAL:
1.
2.

THINGS 2 OUTSOURCE 4 SANITY:
1.
2.

NOTES:

TODAY'S THING 2 FIX:

TODAY'S RUFNKIDDING ME?!

TODAY'S MIRACLE:

NEW INTEL:

GRATITUDE:
1.
2.
3.

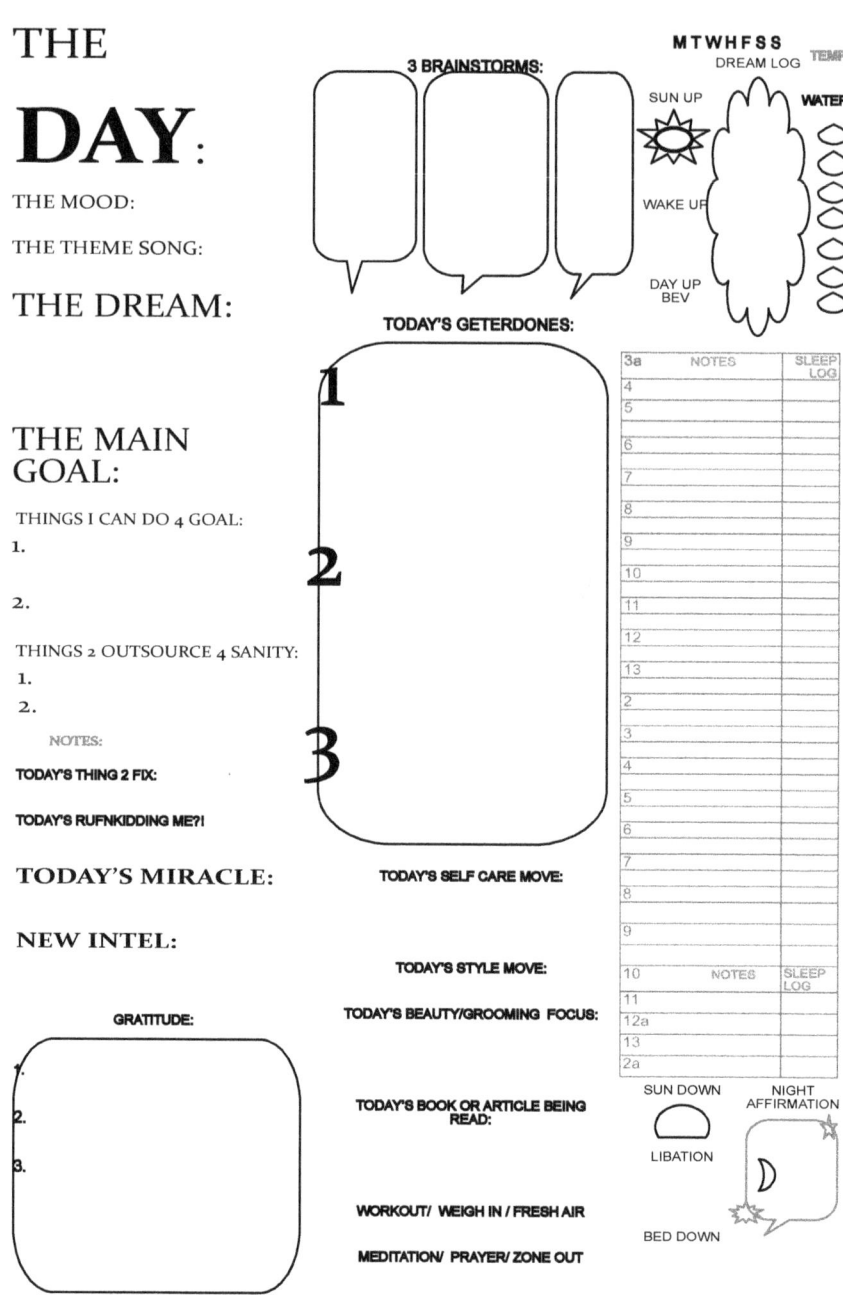

3 BRAINSTORMS:

TODAY'S GETERDONES:
1
2
3

TODAY'S SELF CARE MOVE:

TODAY'S STYLE MOVE:

TODAY'S BEAUTY/GROOMING FOCUS:

TODAY'S BOOK OR ARTICLE BEING READ:

WORKOUT/ WEIGH IN / FRESH AIR

MEDITATION/ PRAYER/ ZONE OUT

M T W H F S S
DREAM LOG   TEMP

SUN UP

WAKE UP

DAY UP BEV

WATER

3a	NOTES	SLEEP LOG
4		
5		
6		
7		
8		
9		
10		
11		
12		
13		
2		
3		
4		
5		
6		
7		
8		
9		
10	NOTES	SLEEP LOG
11		
12a		
13		
2a		

SUN DOWN

LIBATION

NIGHT AFFIRMATION

BED DOWN

THE
pregaming:

THE recap:

THE
DAY:

THE MOOD:

THE THEME SONG:

THE DREAM:

THE MAIN GOAL:

THINGS I CAN DO 4 GOAL:
1.

2.

THINGS 2 OUTSOURCE 4 SANITY:
1.
2.

   NOTES:

TODAY'S THING 2 FIX:

TODAY'S RUFNKIDDING ME?!

TODAY'S MIRACLE:

NEW INTEL:

GRATITUDE:

1.

2.

3.

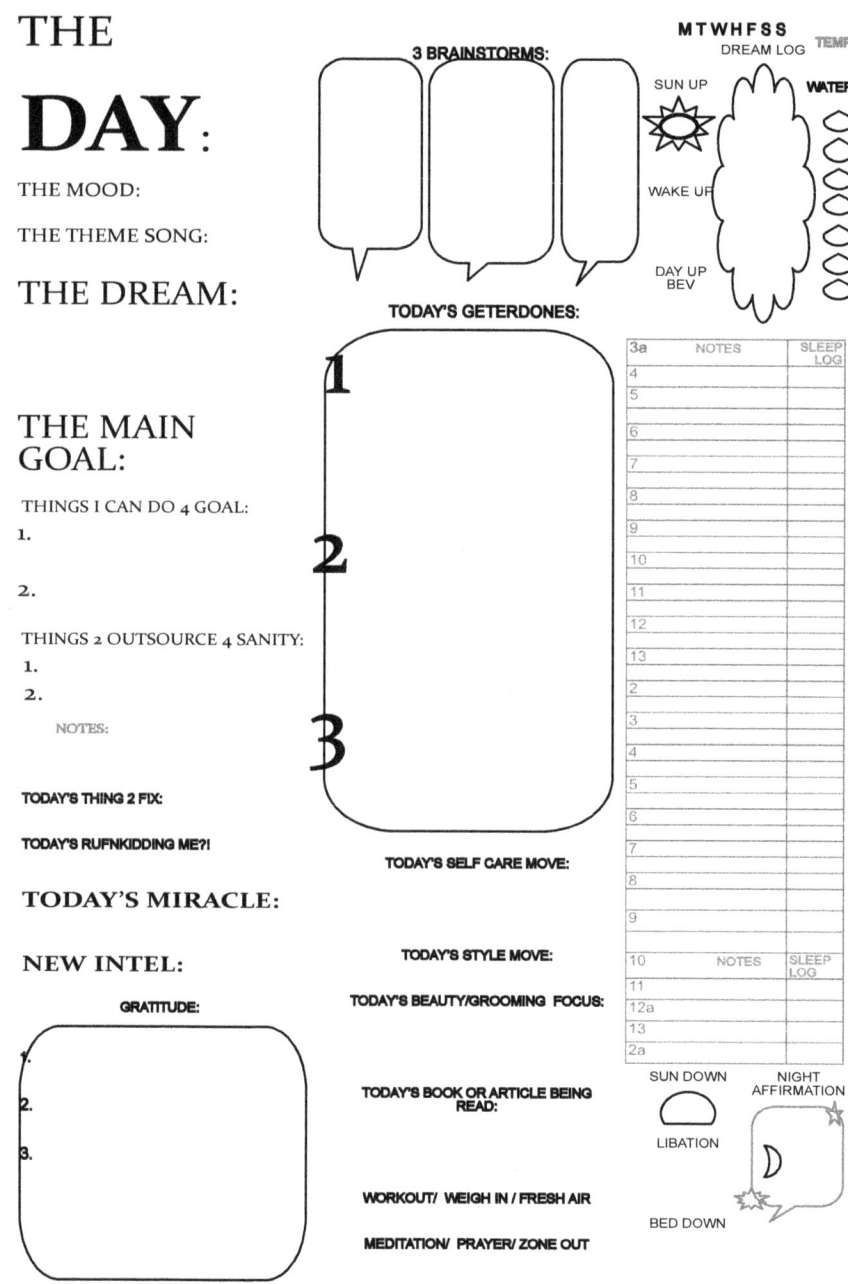

3 BRAINSTORMS:

TODAY'S GETERDONES:

1

2

3

TODAY'S SELF CARE MOVE:

TODAY'S STYLE MOVE:

TODAY'S BEAUTY/GROOMING FOCUS:

TODAY'S BOOK OR ARTICLE BEING READ:

WORKOUT/ WEIGH IN / FRESH AIR

MEDITATION/ PRAYER/ ZONE OUT

M T W H F S S
DREAM LOG   TEMP

SUN UP   WATER

WAKE UP

DAY UP BEV

3a	NOTES	SLEEP LOG
4		
5		
6		
7		
8		
9		
10		
11		
12		
13		
2		
3		
4		
5		
6		
7		
8		
9		
10	NOTES	SLEEP LOG
11		
12a		
13		
2a		

SUN DOWN   NIGHT AFFIRMATION

LIBATION

BED DOWN

THE pregaming:

THE recap:

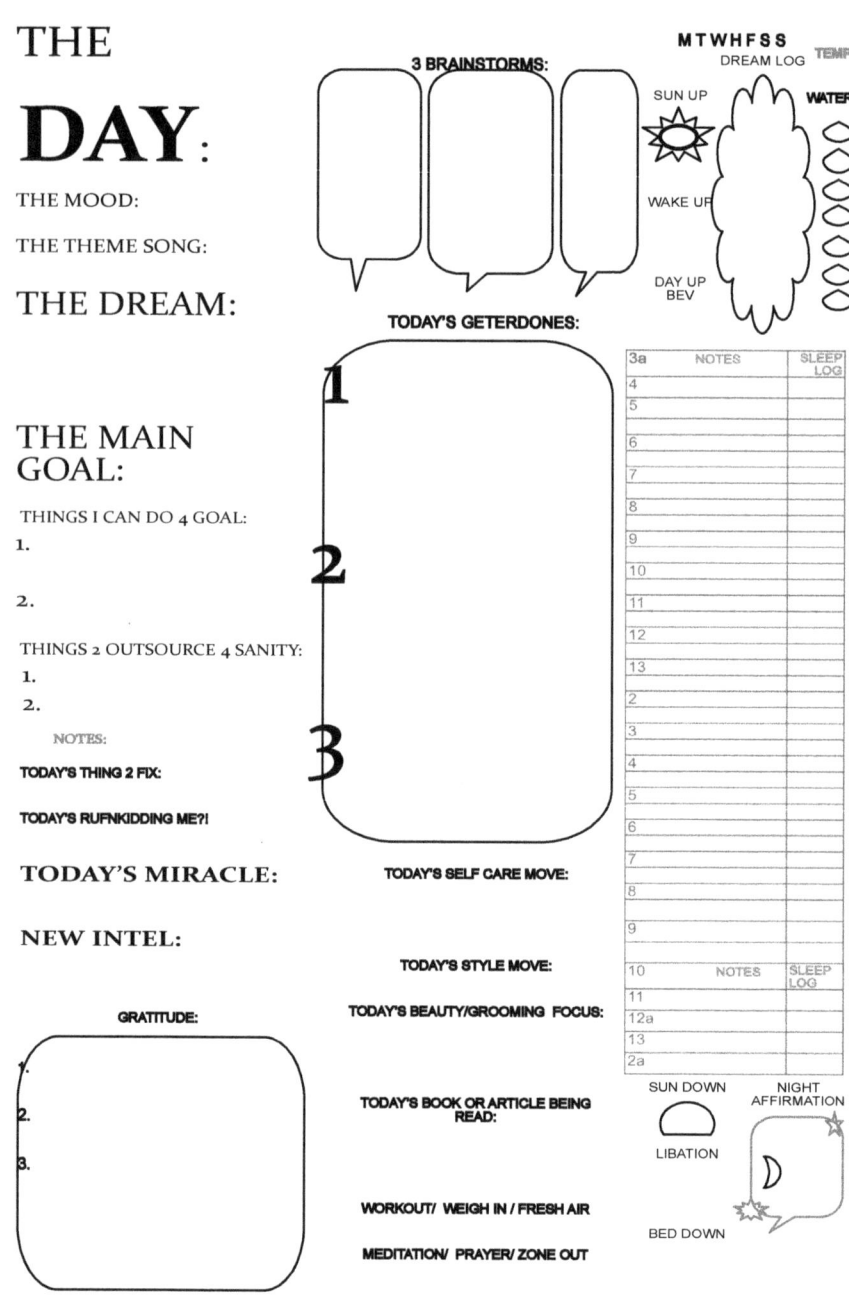

THE
pregaming:

THE recap:

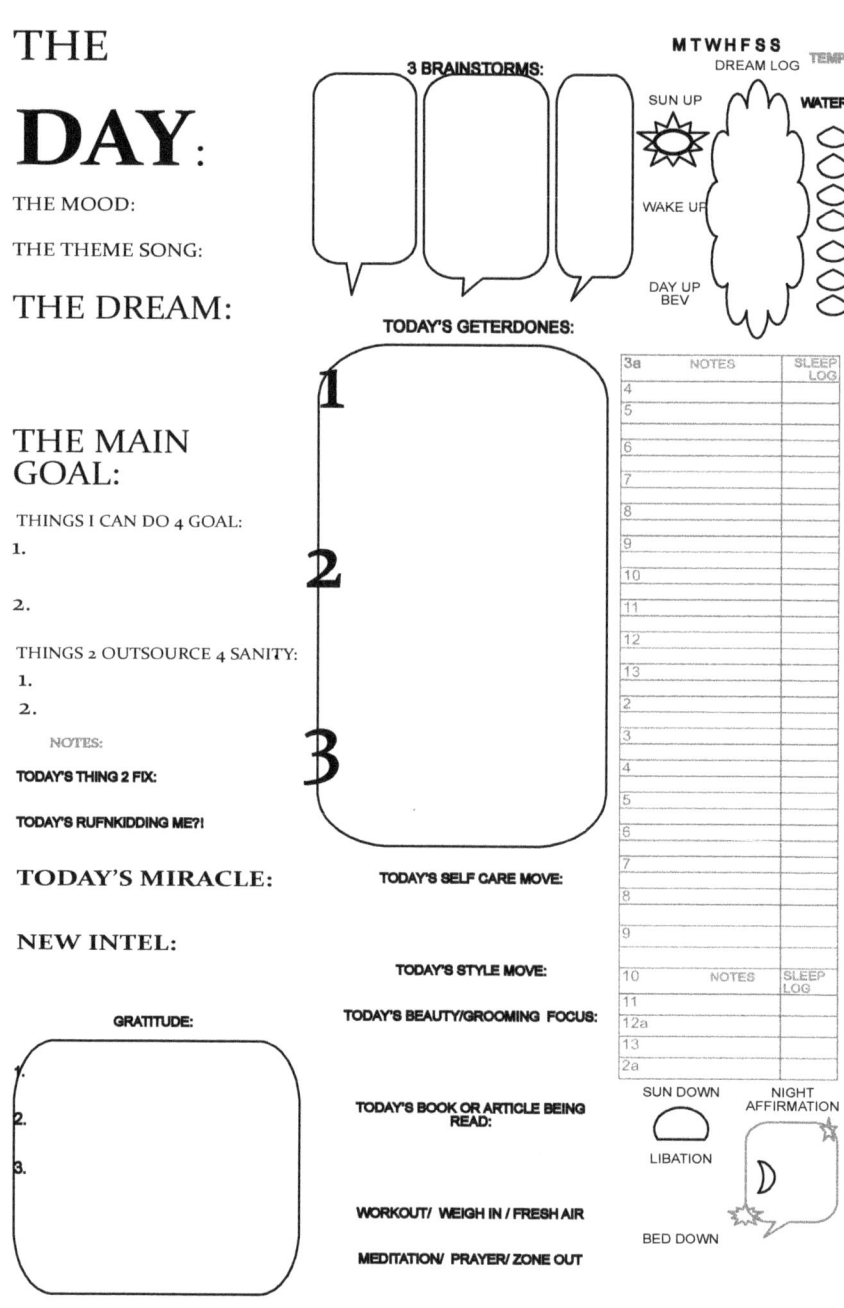

THE
pregaming:

THE recap:

THE
DAY:

THE MOOD:

THE THEME SONG:

THE DREAM:

THE MAIN GOAL:

THINGS I CAN DO 4 GOAL:
1.

2.

THINGS 2 OUTSOURCE 4 SANITY:
1.
2.

NOTES:

TODAY'S THING 2 FIX:

TODAY'S RUFNKIDDING ME?!

TODAY'S MIRACLE:

NEW INTEL:

GRATITUDE:

1.

2.

3.

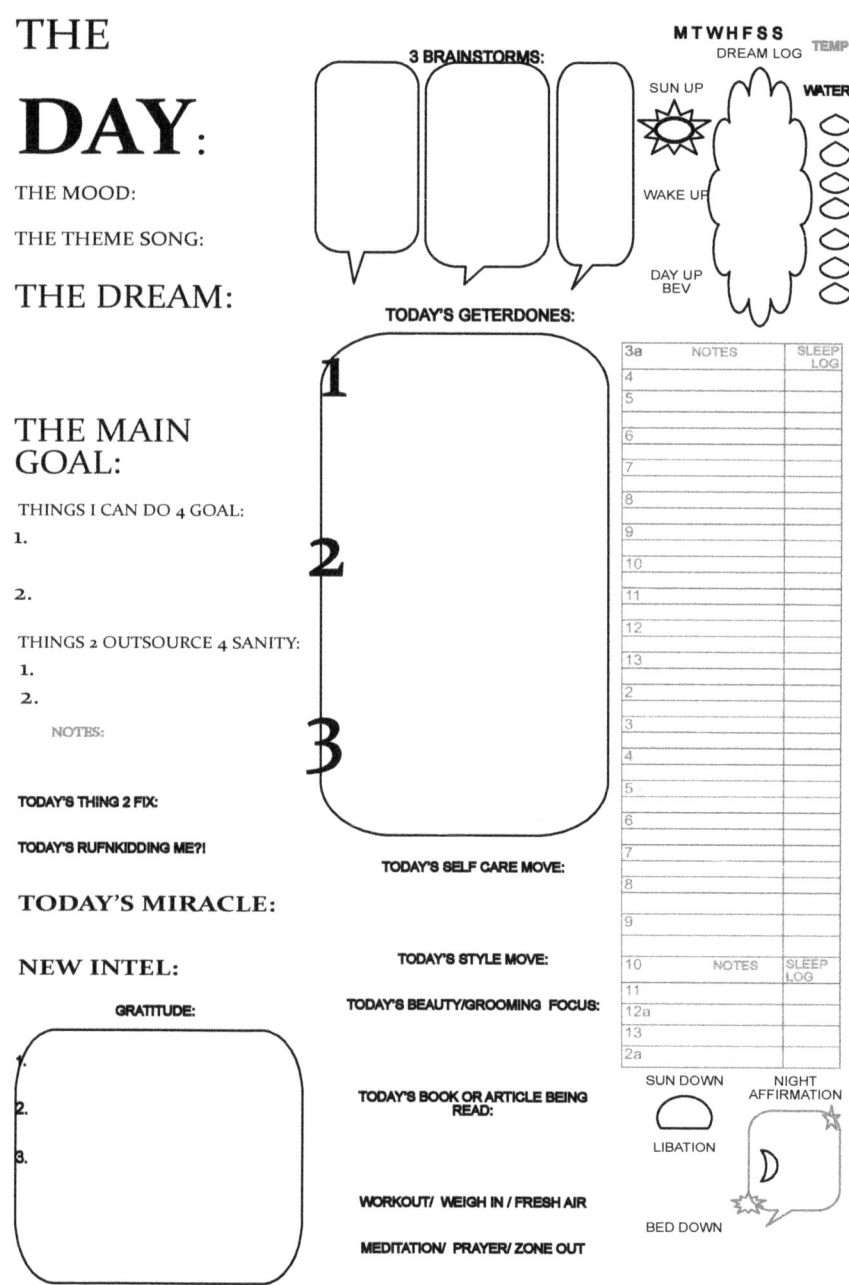

3 BRAINSTORMS:

TODAY'S GETERDONES:

1

2

3

TODAY'S SELF CARE MOVE:

TODAY'S STYLE MOVE:

TODAY'S BEAUTY/GROOMING FOCUS:

TODAY'S BOOK OR ARTICLE BEING READ:

WORKOUT/ WEIGH IN / FRESH AIR

MEDITATION/ PRAYER/ ZONE OUT

M T W H F S S
DREAM LOG   TEMP

SUN UP   WATER

WAKE UP

DAY UP BEV

3a	NOTES	SLEEP LOG
4		
5		
6		
7		
8		
9		
10		
11		
12		
13		
2		
3		
4		
5		
6		
7		
8		
9		
10	NOTES	SLEEP LOG
11		
12a		
13		
2a		

SUN DOWN   NIGHT AFFIRMATION

LIBATION

BED DOWN

THE
pregaming:

THE recap:

THE
DAY:

THE MOOD:

THE THEME SONG:

THE DREAM:

THE MAIN GOAL:

THINGS I CAN DO 4 GOAL:
1.
2.

THINGS 2 OUTSOURCE 4 SANITY:
1.
2.

NOTES:

TODAY'S THING 2 FIX:

TODAY'S RUFNKIDDING ME?!

TODAY'S MIRACLE:

NEW INTEL:

GRATITUDE:
1.
2.
3.

3 BRAINSTORMS:

TODAY'S GETERDONES:
1.
2.
3.

TODAY'S SELF CARE MOVE:

TODAY'S STYLE MOVE:

TODAY'S BEAUTY/GROOMING FOCUS:

TODAY'S BOOK OR ARTICLE BEING READ:

WORKOUT/ WEIGH IN / FRESH AIR

MEDITATION/ PRAYER/ ZONE OUT

M T W H F S S
DREAM LOG   TEMP
SUN UP
WAKE UP
DAY UP BEV
WATER

3a	NOTES	SLEEP LOG
4		
5		
6		
7		
8		
9		
10		
11		
12		
13		
2		
3		
4		
5		
6		
7		
8		
9		
10	NOTES	SLEEP LOG
11		
12a		
13		
2a		

SUN DOWN
LIBATION
BED DOWN
NIGHT AFFIRMATION

THE pregaming:

THE recap:

THE
DAY:

THE MOOD:

THE THEME SONG:

THE DREAM:

THE MAIN GOAL:

THINGS I CAN DO 4 GOAL:
1.

2.

THINGS 2 OUTSOURCE 4 SANITY:
1.
2.

NOTES:

TODAY'S THING 2 FIX:

TODAY'S RUFNKIDDING ME?!

TODAY'S MIRACLE:

NEW INTEL:

GRATITUDE:
1.
2.
3.

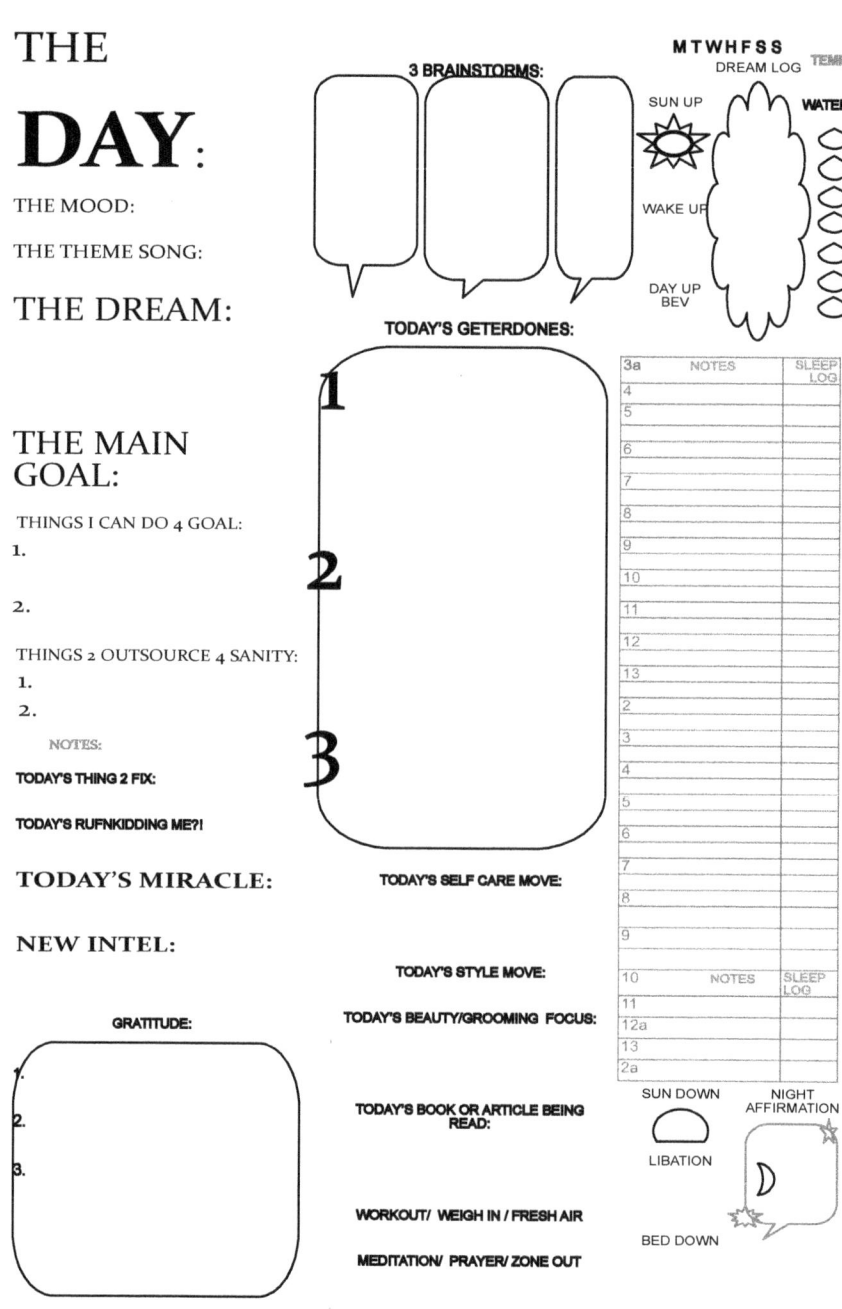

3 BRAINSTORMS:

TODAY'S GETERDONES:
1
2
3

TODAY'S SELF CARE MOVE:

TODAY'S STYLE MOVE:

TODAY'S BEAUTY/GROOMING FOCUS:

TODAY'S BOOK OR ARTICLE BEING READ:

WORKOUT/ WEIGH IN / FRESH AIR

MEDITATION/ PRAYER/ ZONE OUT

M T W H F S S
DREAM LOG   TEMP
SUN UP   WATER
WAKE UP
DAY UP BEV

	NOTES	SLEEP LOG
3a		
4		
5		
6		
7		
8		
9		
10		
11		
12		
13		
2		
3		
4		
5		
6		
7		
8		
9		
10	NOTES	SLEEP LOG
11		
12a		
13		
2a		

SUN DOWN

LIBATION

BED DOWN

NIGHT AFFIRMATION

THE
pregaming:

THE recap:

THE DAY:

THE MOOD:

THE THEME SONG:

THE DREAM:

THE MAIN GOAL:

THINGS I CAN DO 4 GOAL:
1.

2.

THINGS 2 OUTSOURCE 4 SANITY:
1.
2.

NOTES:

TODAY'S THING 2 FIX:

TODAY'S RUFNKIDDING ME?!

TODAY'S MIRACLE:

NEW INTEL:

GRATITUDE:
1.
2.
3.

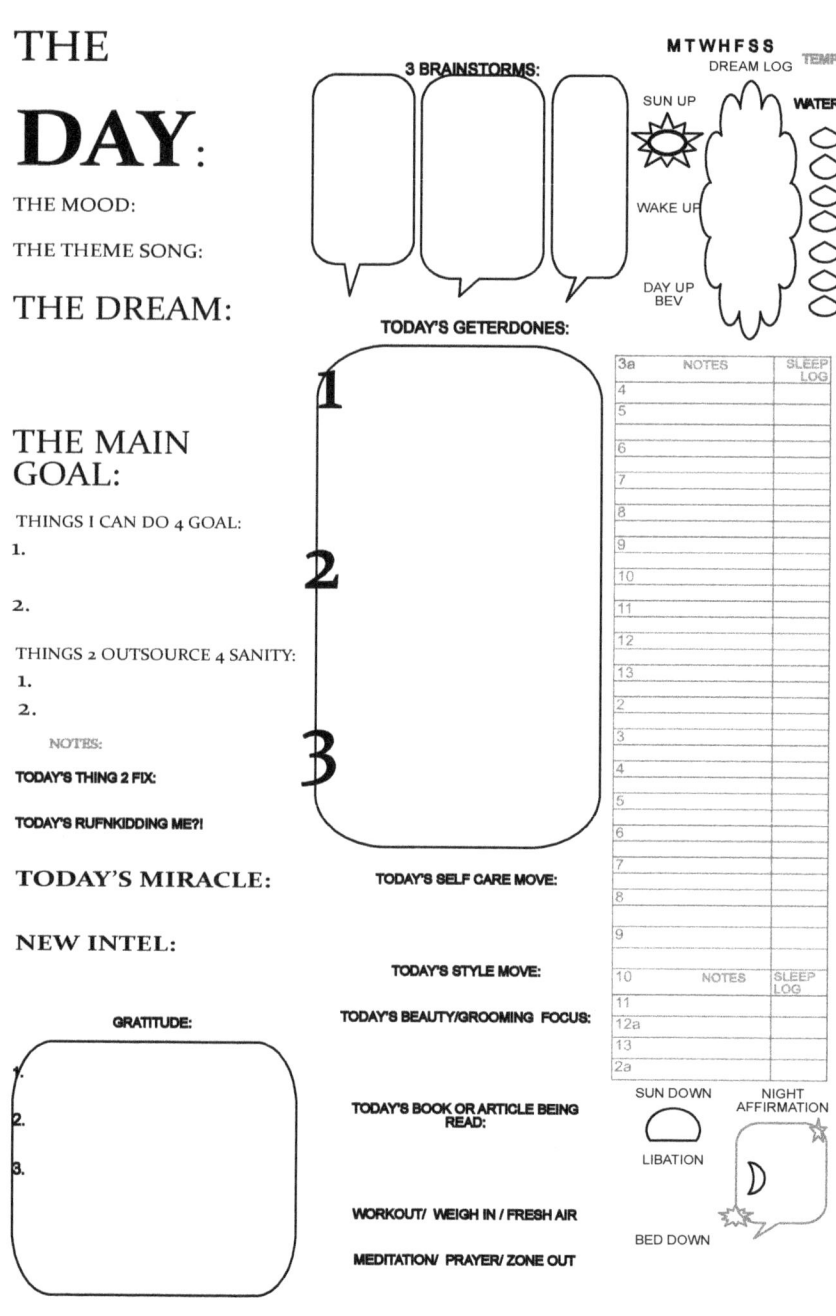

3 BRAINSTORMS:

TODAY'S GETERDONES:
1
2
3

TODAY'S SELF CARE MOVE:

TODAY'S STYLE MOVE:

TODAY'S BEAUTY/GROOMING FOCUS:

TODAY'S BOOK OR ARTICLE BEING READ:

WORKOUT/ WEIGH IN / FRESH AIR

MEDITATION/ PRAYER/ ZONE OUT

M T W H F S S
DREAM LOG   TEMP
SUN UP
WAKE UP
DAY UP BEV
WATER

NOTES | SLEEP LOG
3a
4
5
6
7
8
9
10
11
12
13
2
3
4
5
6
7
8
9
10 NOTES | SLEEP LOG
11
12a
13
2a

SUN DOWN
LIBATION
BED DOWN
NIGHT AFFIRMATION

THE
pregaming:

THE recap:

THE
DAY:

THE MOOD:

THE THEME SONG:

THE DREAM:

THE MAIN GOAL:

THINGS I CAN DO 4 GOAL:
1.

2.

THINGS 2 OUTSOURCE 4 SANITY:
1.
2.

NOTES:

TODAY'S THING 2 FIX:

TODAY'S RUFNKIDDING ME?!

TODAY'S MIRACLE:

NEW INTEL:

GRATITUDE:
1.
2.
3.

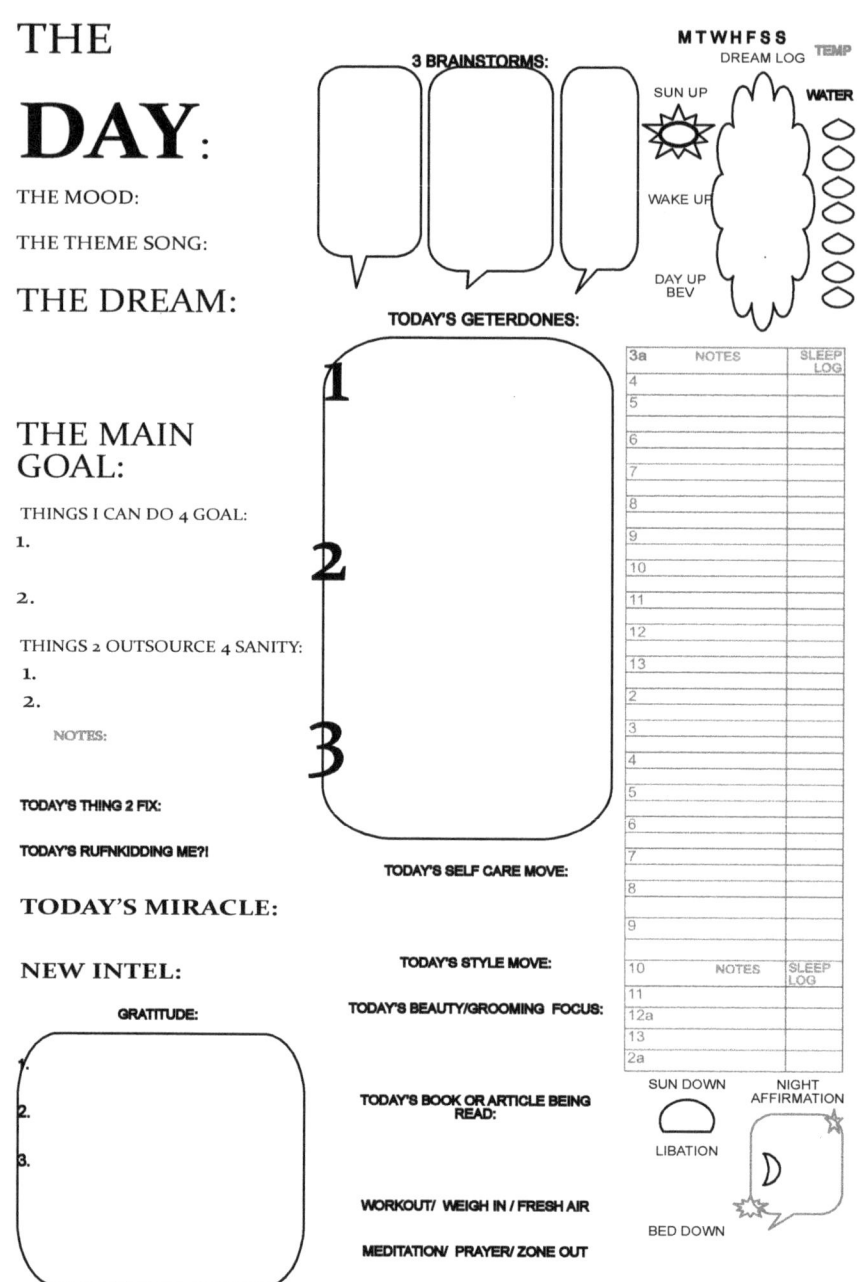

3 BRAINSTORMS:

TODAY'S GETERDONES:

1

2

3

TODAY'S SELF CARE MOVE:

TODAY'S STYLE MOVE:

TODAY'S BEAUTY/GROOMING FOCUS:

TODAY'S BOOK OR ARTICLE BEING READ:

WORKOUT/ WEIGH IN / FRESH AIR

MEDITATION/ PRAYER/ ZONE OUT

M T W H F S S
DREAM LOG   TEMP

SUN UP   WATER

WAKE UP

DAY UP BEV

NOTES   SLEEP LOG

SUN DOWN   NIGHT AFFIRMATION

LIBATION

BED DOWN

THE
pregaming:

THE recap:

THE
DAY:

THE MOOD:

THE THEME SONG:

THE DREAM:

THE MAIN GOAL:

THINGS I CAN DO 4 GOAL:
1.
2.

THINGS 2 OUTSOURCE 4 SANITY:
1.
2.

NOTES:

TODAY'S THING 2 FIX:

TODAY'S RUFNKIDDING ME?!

TODAY'S MIRACLE:

NEW INTEL:

GRATITUDE:

1.
2.
3.

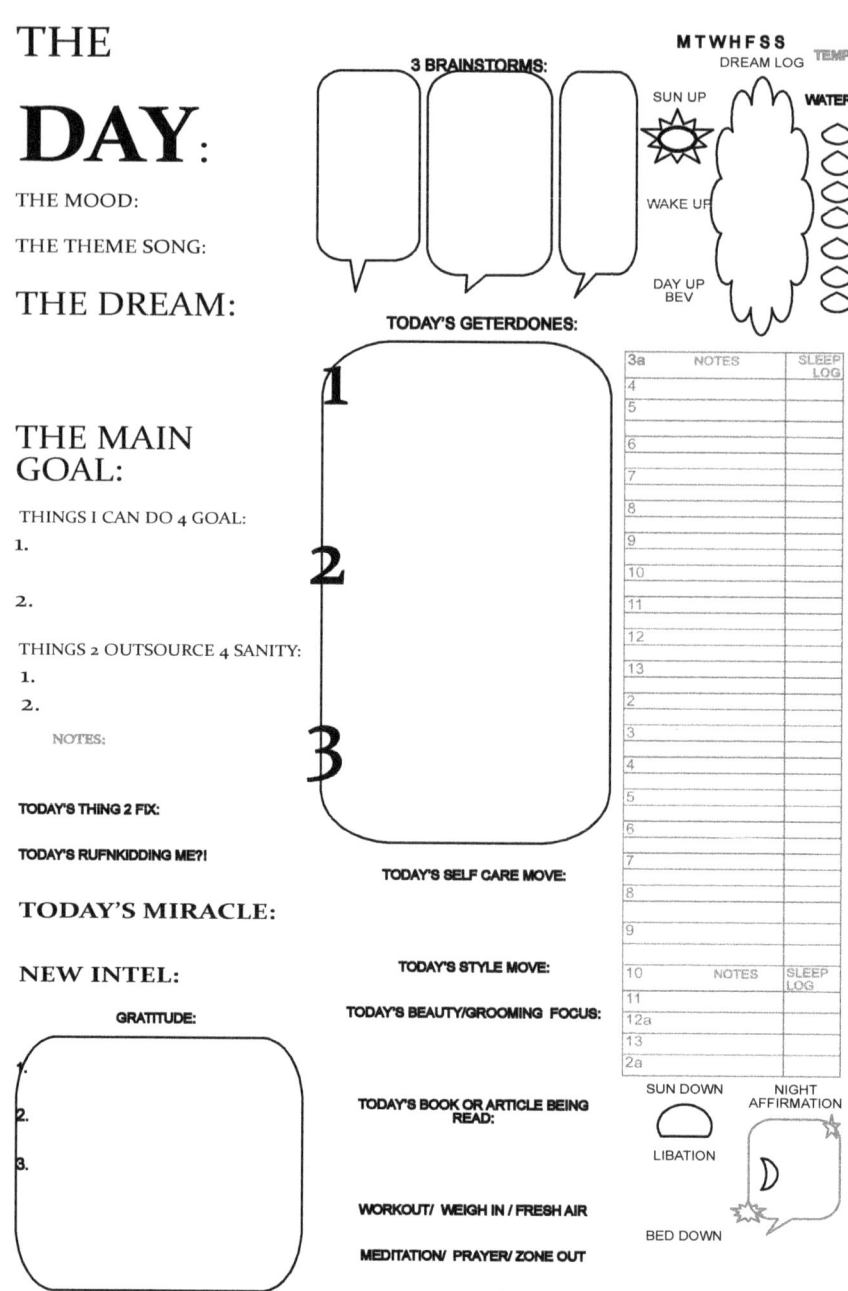

3 BRAINSTORMS:

TODAY'S GETERDONES:

1
2
3

TODAY'S SELF CARE MOVE:

TODAY'S STYLE MOVE:

TODAY'S BEAUTY/GROOMING FOCUS:

TODAY'S BOOK OR ARTICLE BEING READ:

WORKOUT/ WEIGH IN / FRESH AIR

MEDITATION/ PRAYER/ ZONE OUT

MTWHFSS
DREAM LOG   TEMP
SUN UP
WAKE UP
DAY UP BEV
WATER

NOTES | SLEEP LOG
3a
4
5
6
7
8
9
10
11
12
13
2
3
4
5
6
7
8
9
10   NOTES | SLEEP LOG
11
12a
13
2a

SUN DOWN
LIBATION
NIGHT AFFIRMATION
BED DOWN

THE pregaming:

THE recap:

THE DAY:

THE MOOD:

THE THEME SONG:

THE DREAM:

THE MAIN GOAL:

THINGS I CAN DO 4 GOAL:
1.
2.

THINGS 2 OUTSOURCE 4 SANITY:
1.
2.

NOTES:

TODAY'S THING 2 FIX:

TODAY'S RUFNKIDDING ME?!

TODAY'S MIRACLE:

NEW INTEL:

GRATITUDE:
1.
2.
3.

3 BRAINSTORMS:

TODAY'S GETERDONES:
1
2
3

TODAY'S SELF CARE MOVE:

TODAY'S STYLE MOVE:

TODAY'S BEAUTY/GROOMING FOCUS:

TODAY'S BOOK OR ARTICLE BEING READ:

WORKOUT/ WEIGH IN / FRESH AIR

MEDITATION/ PRAYER/ ZONE OUT

M T W H F S S
DREAM LOG   TEMP
SUN UP
WAKE UP
DAY UP BEV
WATER

	NOTES	SLEEP LOG
3a		
4		
5		
6		
7		
8		
9		
10		
11		
12		
13		
2		
3		
4		
5		
6		
7		
8		
9		
10	NOTES	SLEEP LOG
11		
12a		
13		
2a		

SUN DOWN
LIBATION
BED DOWN
NIGHT AFFIRMATION

THE
pregaming:

THE recap:

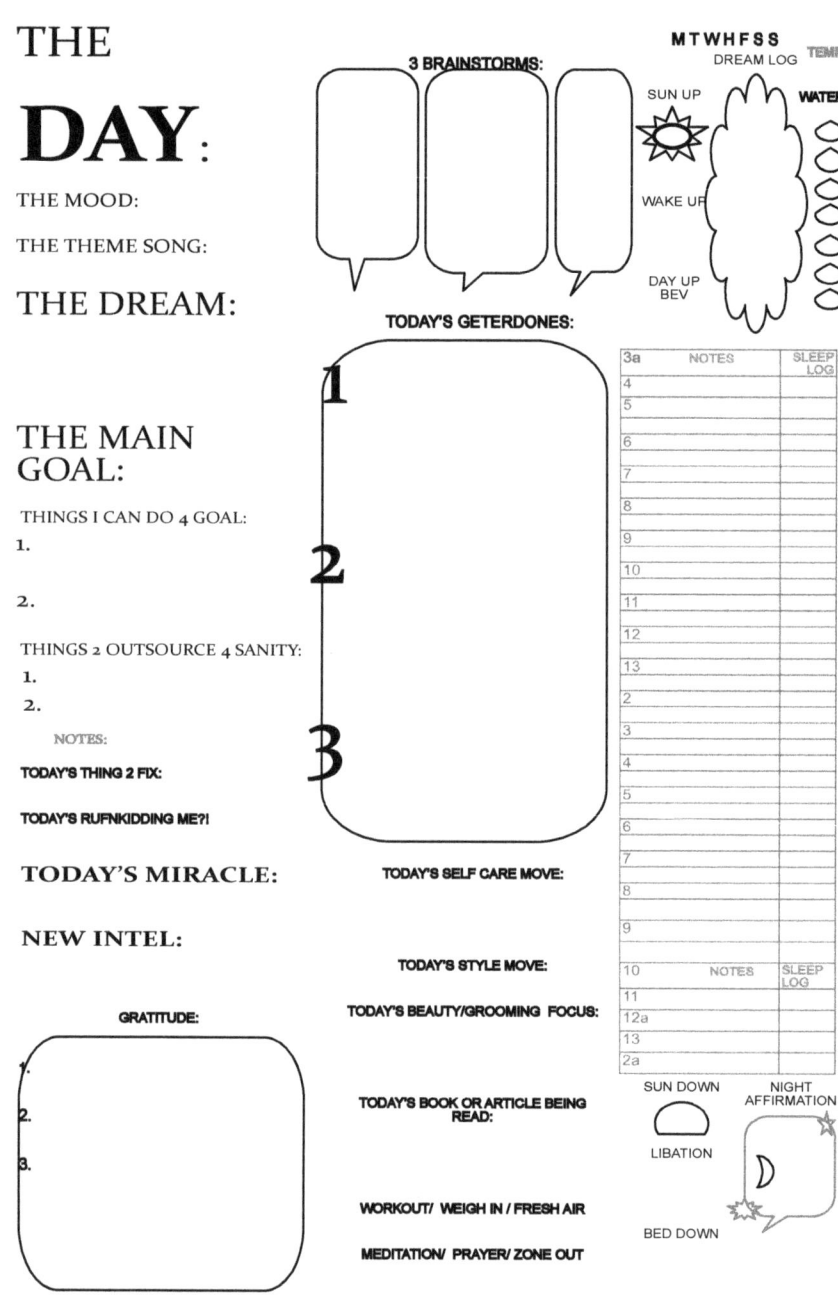

THE
pregaming:

THE recap:

THE
DAY:

THE MOOD:

THE THEME SONG:

THE DREAM:

THE MAIN GOAL:

THINGS I CAN DO 4 GOAL:
1.

2.

THINGS 2 OUTSOURCE 4 SANITY:
1.
2.

NOTES:

TODAY'S THING 2 FIX:

TODAY'S RUFNKIDDING ME?!

TODAY'S MIRACLE:

NEW INTEL:

GRATITUDE:

1.
2.
3.

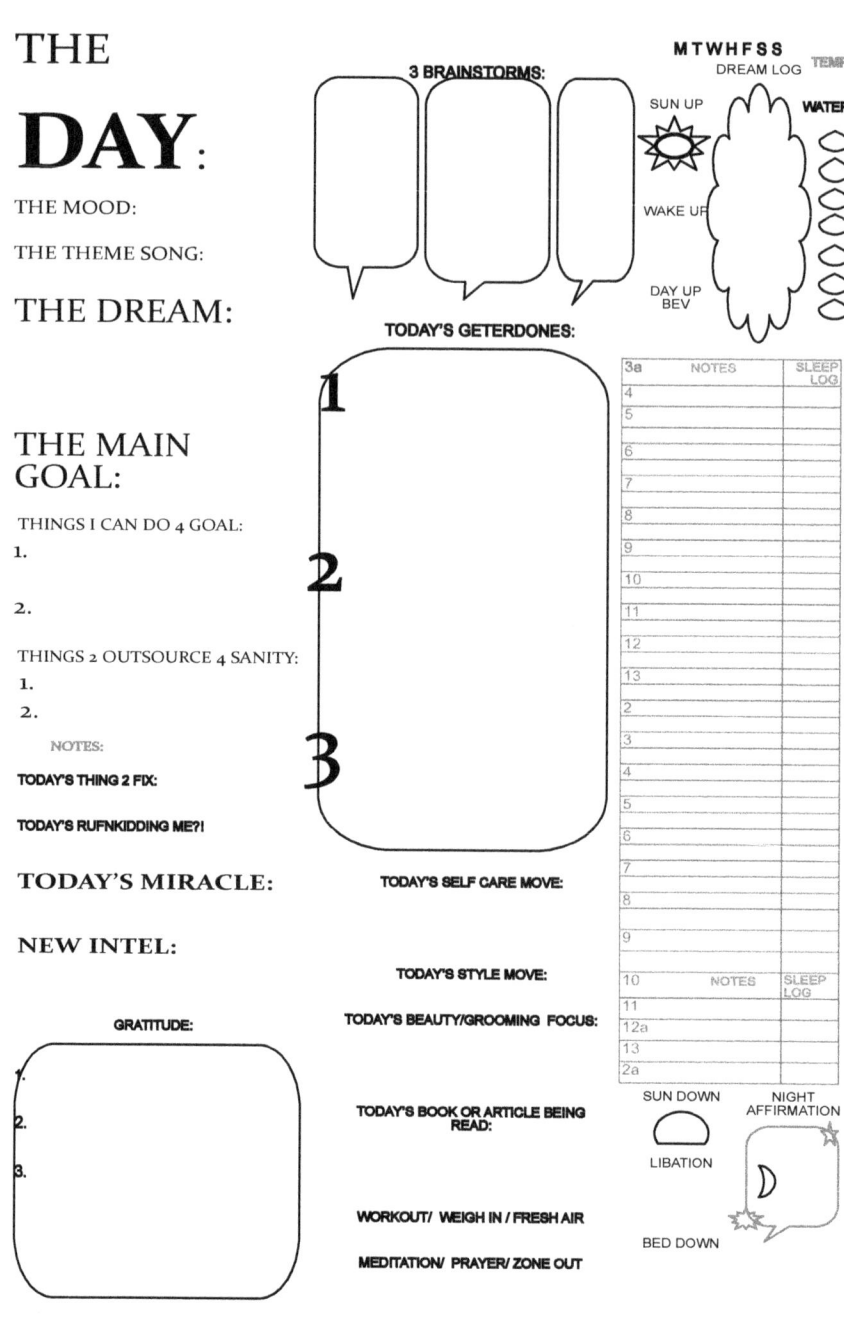

3 BRAINSTORMS:

TODAY'S GETERDONES:

1

2

3

TODAY'S SELF CARE MOVE:

TODAY'S STYLE MOVE:

TODAY'S BEAUTY/GROOMING FOCUS:

TODAY'S BOOK OR ARTICLE BEING READ:

WORKOUT/ WEIGH IN / FRESH AIR

MEDITATION/ PRAYER/ ZONE OUT

M T W H F S S
DREAM LOG   TEMP
SUN UP
WATER
WAKE UP
DAY UP BEV

3a	NOTES	SLEEP LOG
4		
5		
6		
7		
8		
9		
10		
11		
12		
13		
2		
3		
4		
5		
6		
7		
8		
9		
10	NOTES	SLEEP LOG
11		
12a		
13		
2a		

SUN DOWN   NIGHT AFFIRMATION

LIBATION

BED DOWN

THE
pregaming:

THE recap:

THE
DAY:

THE MOOD:

THE THEME SONG:

THE DREAM:

THE MAIN GOAL:

THINGS I CAN DO 4 GOAL:
1.

2.

THINGS 2 OUTSOURCE 4 SANITY:
1.
2.
   NOTES:

TODAY'S THING 2 FIX:

TODAY'S RUFNKIDDING ME?!

TODAY'S MIRACLE:

NEW INTEL:

GRATITUDE:

1.

2.

3.

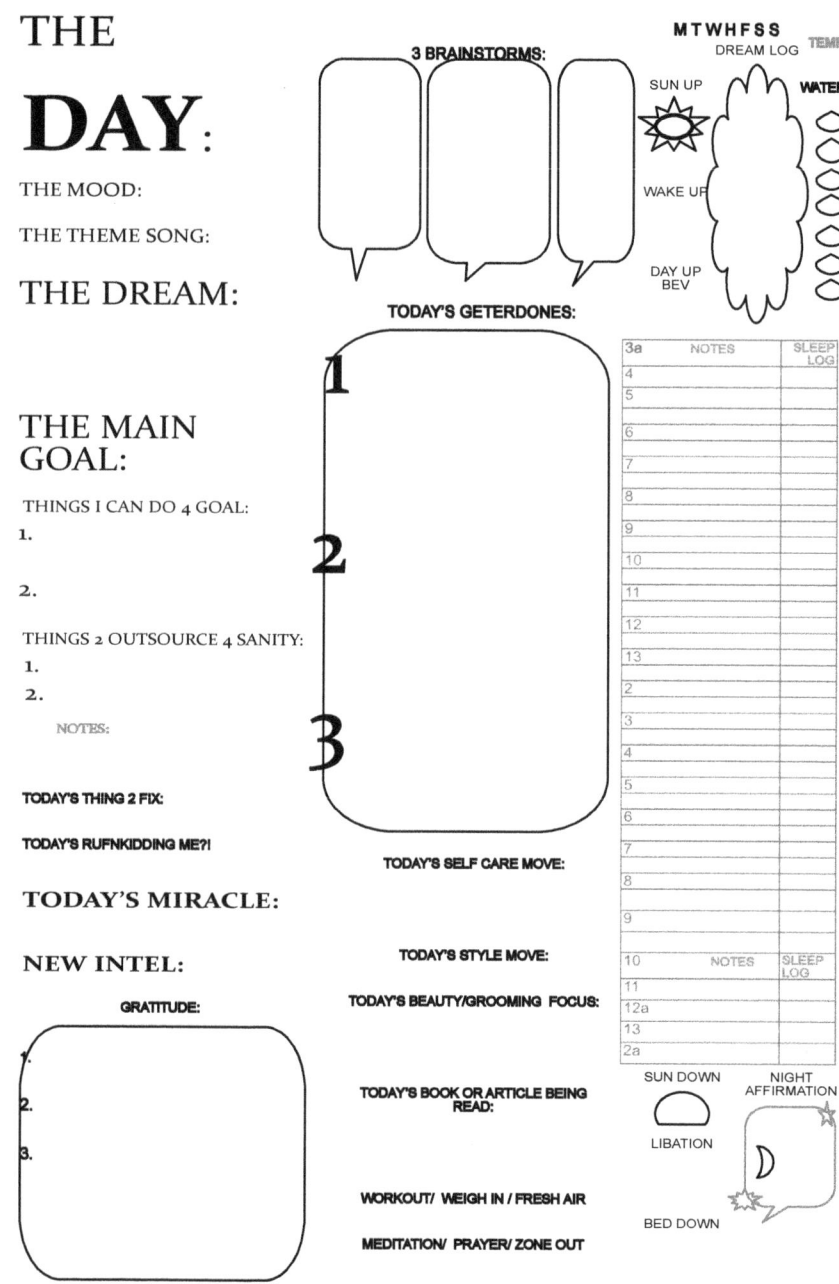

3 BRAINSTORMS:

TODAY'S GETERDONES:

1
2
3

TODAY'S SELF CARE MOVE:

TODAY'S STYLE MOVE:

TODAY'S BEAUTY/GROOMING FOCUS:

TODAY'S BOOK OR ARTICLE BEING READ:

WORKOUT/ WEIGH IN / FRESH AIR

MEDITATION/ PRAYER/ ZONE OUT

THE
pregaming:

THE recap:

THE DAY:

THE MOOD:

THE THEME SONG:

THE DREAM:

THE MAIN GOAL:

THINGS I CAN DO 4 GOAL:
1.
2.

THINGS 2 OUTSOURCE 4 SANITY:
1.
2.

NOTES:

TODAY'S THING 2 FIX:

TODAY'S RUFNKIDDING ME?!

TODAY'S MIRACLE:

NEW INTEL:

GRATITUDE:
1.
2.
3.

3 BRAINSTORMS:

TODAY'S GETERDONES:
1
2
3

TODAY'S SELF CARE MOVE:

TODAY'S STYLE MOVE:

TODAY'S BEAUTY/GROOMING FOCUS:

TODAY'S BOOK OR ARTICLE BEING READ:

WORKOUT/ WEIGH IN / FRESH AIR

MEDITATION/ PRAYER/ ZONE OUT

M T W H F S S
DREAM LOG   TEMP
SUN UP
WATER
WAKE UP
DAY UP BEV

3a	NOTES	SLEEP LOG
4		
5		
6		
7		
8		
9		
10		
11		
12		
13		
2		
3		
4		
5		
6		
7		
8		
9		
10	NOTES	SLEEP LOG
11		
12a		
13		
2a		

SUN DOWN

LIBATION

BED DOWN

NIGHT AFFIRMATION

THE
pregaming:

THE recap:

THE
DAY:

THE MOOD:

THE THEME SONG:

THE DREAM:

THE MAIN GOAL:

THINGS I CAN DO 4 GOAL:
1.

2.

THINGS 2 OUTSOURCE 4 SANITY:
1.
2.

NOTES:

TODAY'S THING 2 FIX:

TODAY'S RUFNKIDDING ME?!

TODAY'S MIRACLE:

NEW INTEL:

GRATITUDE:

1.
2.
3.

3 BRAINSTORMS:

TODAY'S GETERDONES:
1
2
3

TODAY'S SELF CARE MOVE:

TODAY'S STYLE MOVE:

TODAY'S BEAUTY/GROOMING FOCUS:

TODAY'S BOOK OR ARTICLE BEING READ:

WORKOUT/ WEIGH IN / FRESH AIR

MEDITATION/ PRAYER/ ZONE OUT

M T W H F S S
DREAM LOG   TEMP
SUN UP   WATER
WAKE UP
DAY UP BEV

3a	NOTES	SLEEP LOG
4		
5		
6		
7		
8		
9		
10		
11		
12		
13		
2		
3		
4		
5		
6		
7		
8		
9		
10	NOTES	SLEEP LOG
11		
12a		
13		
2a		

SUN DOWN   NIGHT AFFIRMATION

LIBATION

BED DOWN

THE
pregaming:

THE recap:

THE pregaming:

THE recap:

THE DAY:

THE MOOD:

THE THEME SONG:

THE DREAM:

THE MAIN GOAL:

THINGS I CAN DO 4 GOAL:
1.

2.

THINGS 2 OUTSOURCE 4 SANITY:
1.
2.

NOTES:

TODAY'S THING 2 FIX:

TODAY'S RUFNKIDDING ME?!

TODAY'S MIRACLE:

NEW INTEL:

GRATITUDE:

1.
2.
3.

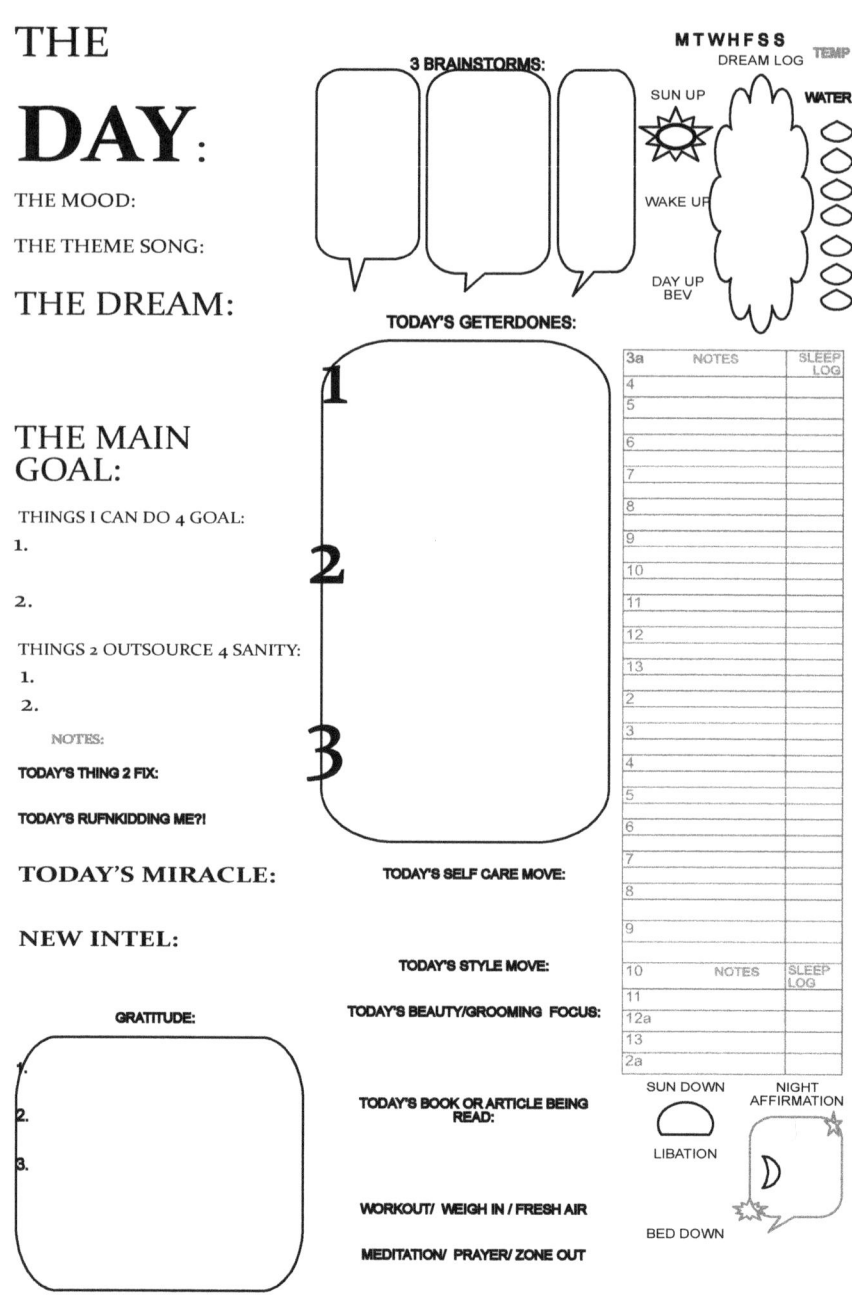

3 BRAINSTORMS:

TODAY'S GETERDONES:

1

2

3

TODAY'S SELF CARE MOVE:

TODAY'S STYLE MOVE:

TODAY'S BEAUTY/GROOMING FOCUS:

TODAY'S BOOK OR ARTICLE BEING READ:

WORKOUT/ WEIGH IN / FRESH AIR

MEDITATION/ PRAYER/ ZONE OUT

M T W H F S S
DREAM LOG   TEMP

SUN UP   WATER

WAKE UP

DAY UP
BEV

3a	NOTES	SLEEP LOG
4		
5		
6		
7		
8		
9		
10		
11		
12		
13		
2		
3		
4		
5		
6		
7		
8		
9		
10	NOTES	SLEEP LOG
11		
12a		
13		
2a		

SUN DOWN   NIGHT AFFIRMATION

LIBATION

BED DOWN

THE
pregaming:

THE recap:

381

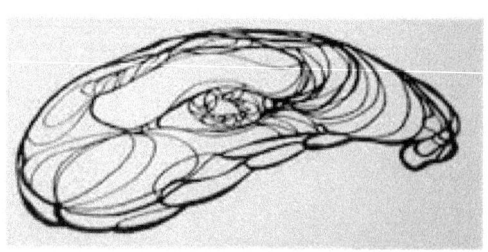

angel brynner.

KOKOPELLIMA PRESS

www.ingramcontent.com/pod-product-compliance
Lightning Source LLC
Chambersburg PA
CBHW050858240426
43673CB00009B/275

9781950077854